EXPLORE

EAST ANGLIA

ITS COAST, COUNTRYSIDE AND HERITAGE

ACKNOWLEDGEMENTS

The authors would like to express their gratitude to the following:

Mr. David Moyse and the Lowestoft and East Suffolk Maritime Museum for the photograph of herring drifters.

The Great Yarmouth Museums Service for permission to use the illustration of Nelson stepping ashore at Gt. Yarmouth, and for the photograph of the Nelson Monument.

The Trustees of the Burston Strike School for permission to reproduce the postcard of Tom and Annie Higdon.

The Director of the Norfolk Museums Service for permission to use interior photographs.

To all the East Anglians who have made this project possible we would like to offer our sincere thanks.

We are especially grateful to Mr. Donald Morrison for his invaluable help and advice; to our families for their patience and support, and especially to the well-travelled Peter, Sarah and Edward.

EXPLORE EAST ANGLIA
Its Coast, Countryside and Heritage
By Mark and Elizabeth Mitchels

First published 1989
Revised edition 1995
© Mark and Elizabeth Mitchels 1995

COUNTRYSIDE BOOKS
3 Catherine Road
Newbury, Berkshire

Produced through MRM Associates Ltd., Reading
Typeset by Acorn Bookwork, Salisbury
Printed in England

Front cover: Wivenhoe, Essex
Back cover: Lavenham, Suffolk

Map on page 88 reproduced by courtesy of the AA. Maps are based upon Ordnance Survey maps with the sanction of the controller of HM Stationery Office Crown Copyright reserved.

ISBN 1 85306 043 7

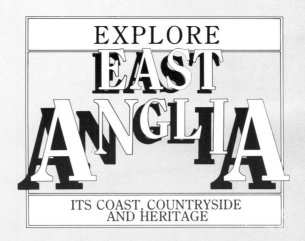

EXPLORE
EAST ANGLIA

ITS COAST, COUNTRYSIDE
AND HERITAGE

MARK & ELIZABETH MITCHELS

COUNTRYSIDE BOOKS

CONTENTS

To help you get the most out of your visits and travels round East Anglia, each attraction featured in the book is accompanied by a section giving opening times, approximate cost and other basic information.

The 'price guide' for each attraction should not be regarded as indicating value for money. It refers to the admission charge for one adult at the time of publication:

A: under £2.00
B: £2.00–£4.00
C: over £4.00

Prices will inevitably go up during the life of this book, but the guide letter will still indicate the relative cost.

The reductions for children are usually about half, with smaller concessions for pensioners. Party rates are often available too.

Many properties are owned by the National Trust and English Heritage, and members are allowed in free. If you intend to visit a lot of the attractions in this book, membership is strongly recommended!

INTRODUCTION

East Anglia is flat in the same way as Scotland is all mountains and kilts, Yorkshire is all moors and cricket and Cornwall is all quaint fishing villages and old sea dogs. That is to say, there is more than a grain of truth in it, but the explorer will soon realise that such visual cliches are more misleading than helpful.

Mountfitchet Castle, Essex

The counties which make up East Anglia are Essex, Suffolk, Norfolk and Cambridgeshire, the last of which includes the old county of Huntingdonshire. Understand-

St John's Abbey Gateway, Colchester, Essex

ably, people get rather hot under the collar about boundary changes, but for the purposes of this book we have used the current boundaries, and can only offer our commiserations to those who prefer to stay with the old county names.

Farming is still East Anglia's most obvious occupation, and the size of the fields and the complexity of the machines which traverse them bear witness to the continued importance of the region for the nation's food production. But it is tourism that is set to affect us all. The region is being discovered: castles, houses, villages and rivers are now available to all, and the apparently unstoppable passion for nostalgia has found in East Anglia a perfect centre.

The Old Coastguard Tower, Walton on the Naze, Essex

Brightlingsea, Essex

The Green at Long Melford in Suffolk, showing the Almshouse and Holy Trinity Church

Other regions have major roads which cut through their prettiest countryside and villages, exposing them to public view and the attendant pressures of population; East Anglia's perceived dullness and uniformity have kept it isolated. Only recently have the beauties of the eastern counties been discovered on a large scale.

It is quite unnecessary for anyone to apologise for the Fens being flat. That is precisely why they are interesting; these wetlands are home to rare flora and fauna. They have a beauty all of their own, and a wonderful power to enthrall visitors who were about to dismiss them as dull.

The Village Sign at Cavendish, Suffolk

Kersey, Suffolk

Their story is one of gradual and unremitting destruction, and the threat to the few remaining areas of genuine fen is only just being understood. It is so easy to transform our environment; often we need to learn how to preserve it. There are two places called East Anglia: the landscape as it was before Industrial Man changed it, and the thriving modern region. Both are attractive in their own way, but they stand in uneasy alliance.

Old Weavers' Cottages Bildeston, Suffolk

East Anglia is a tangle of rivers. Some have seen commercial activity in their time and caused towns to rise and fall; others are more tranquil, dividing the fields and flowing into the Broads and lakes. All have contributed to the history of the area. The first English sailed up them to settle and farm, and the Danes followed them, bringing

The former post office at Ipswich, Suffolk

The coast of East Anglia still has to be fully discovered. There are stretches of sand and shingle where you can walk for hours and see scarcely one other person. The beaches may not be washed by warm waters, but many of them are popular with families. Once the herring fleets dominated the coast; now they are a sight only to be seen

Bungay Castle, Waveney, Suffolk

more years of terror and destruction. All eventually embraced the land, and worked to make it yield plenty. Today the river traffic is no longer carrying grain, timber, and wool, but displaying the brightly coloured sails of pleasure boats. The rivers are becoming known to ever-increasing

Woodbridge Tide Mill and Quay, Suffolk

numbers of yachtsmen who regard them with proud affection, and to anglers who sit staring into the waters with eternal optimism.

on sepia postcards. The technology which brought efficient fishing also brought overfishing, and EU quotas have diminished the fleets.

Less than a hundred years ago the Norfolk Broads were virtually unknown, except to those who lived and worked there. Today pleasure boats swarm rather than

The Maltings at Snape, Suffolk

glide across their waters, packed with holiday makers who may be afloat for the first time. Where once the helmsmen used decades of experience to take them through the network, now the weekend skipper can buy a chart, learn the rudiments of navigation and tune into the local radio for weather reports. Here at least they have the advantage, for miles of the Broads are only revealed to those in boats.

Wool accounts for the splendid architecture of the region; the prosperity it brought enabled merchants to

West Stow Anglo-Saxon Village, Suffolk

Sightseeing by horse-drawn landau at Great Yarmouth, Norfolk

build for themselves fine timber houses, and for God they founded fabulous churches. These are the historic centres of each community, and each has its different treasure. Many timber houses have survived throughout the region, and every town and village can boast their glory.

The River Ant at Ludham Bridge on the Norfolk Broads

Market towns are spread throughout these counties, and some of them have changed very little over the centuries. Although they may not be grand or famous for

Pull's Ferry, Norwich, Norfolk

Looking into the Walled Garden at Felbrigg Hall, Norfolk

anything in particular, they are all worth exploring for the atmosphere they convey of East Anglia. Cities like Norwich and Cambridge are among the finest in the country, combining the best of the past and the present with skill and style.

Detail of the Wellerhaus Showman's Organ in the Thursford Collection, near Fakenham, Norfolk

Castle Rising, Norfolk

John Clare's Birthplace, Helpston, Cambridgeshire

Any part of Britain has a character of its own because it has a different history. That of East Anglia remains important today, for we live with the consequences – for good or ill. It is not enough to refer only to castles, houses, churches and towns; we need to know about the people who built them and lived in them. Warriors, artists, musicians, writers, all were influenced by their East Anglian experiences. The visitors who leave the highways and take to the minor roads will find their own lives enriched as well. They will return refreshed to their busy, noisy lives, but they will also have learned something about the people they have met and the country they inhabit. They will surely want to return.

Mark and Elizabeth Mitchels
Suffolk

A distant view across the fields towards Elton Hall, Cambridgeshire

ESSEX

TILBURY FORT

For most people the mention of Tilbury Fort summons up schoolroom pictures of Queen Elizabeth on a white horse proudly addressing her troops in 1588, for it was there she made her speech about having the body of a woman but the spirit of a king, and a king of England too. Alas, nothing of the Elizabethan fort survives, but there is still much worth visiting.

Tilbury is clearly signposted now if only because it is also a major port, handling container traffic. The brown English Heritage signs are well placed and direct the visitor to the spacious car park. The final yards of the approach include the aptly named public house 'The World's End', a weatherboarded inn dating from 1778.

It was Henry VIII who first appreciated the advantages of building a fort by the Thames 25 miles downstream from London to protect the capital's approaches. He began it in 1539, and at full strength it had a garrison of just nine soldiers, all on 6d per day.

This is not the place to tell the story of the Armada, but it is necessary to explain that the Spanish fleet intended to sail up the Channel to Flanders, where they would take on board the invasion army to subdue England. This force would attack London from the east. Hence the importance of Tilbury. Elizabeth had the fort strengthened, and a great camp was established outside it. Here, on August 8th 1588, she made her stirring speech to the troops.

In 1667 England was at war with Holland, and doing badly. The supreme insult to national pride occurred when the Dutch sailed up the Thames and towed away the English flagship. As a result Charles II ordered Sir Bernard de Gomme, his Chief Engineer, to rebuild the fortifications at Tilbury. It is the walls of this fort which confront the visitor, and it is the best-preserved fort of this period to be found in England.

By the 17th century military experts realised the power of cannon: gone were the days when thick stone walls were sufficient defence. Instead enormous earthworks supported by low brick walls cushioned the impact of enemy cannonballs. The double moat and its distinctive draw-bridges were designed to frustrate the attacking infantry.

Tilbury Drawbridge

The Water Gate

Elsewhere severe winters had occasionally allowed troops to cross frozen moats so at Tilbury sluice gates were fitted to drain the water. The original main entrance was the Water Gate on the river side.

The complicated shape of the fort is best appreciated from above; an aerial photograph shows how the enemy would always be in the sights of several gun batteries. The Thames was only 800 yards across at this point, so in theory no ship could pass Tilbury without being at risk from its guns. Defoe observed at the time: 'they must be bold fellows who will venture in the biggest ships the world has heard of to pass such a battery'.

In the 18th century the fort was used as a depot for recruits. The only excitement during this period happened in 1776 when, during a cricket match between Kent and Essex, a dispute broke out and the team from Kent rushed angrily into the fort: in the ensuing fight three men were killed.

The fort continued to be a military storehouse up to the First World War, when gunners firing from the parade ground shot down a German Zeppelin – the only occasion during the 300-year history of the fort that its guns were fired in anger.

English Heritage
Open: April to Sept: 1000–1800, Oct to Mar: 1000–1600
Price guide: A

SOUTHEND AND HADLEIGH CASTLE

Southend is one of those place names which conjure up an immediate image: like Blackpool or Skegness it means that holidays and seaside fun are here again. A glance at the actual place reveals all this to be true, but there is more besides, and the true explorer should try and find the other points of interest in this Thameside town.

The resort was already popular at the start of the 19th century, and it thrived after the introduction of the railway line in the middle of the century. Suddenly, London had its very own seaside beach within an hour's travel.

Southend is quite rightly proud of the pier, which dates from 1889 and reaches well over one mile out into the bay. A fire destroyed the facilities at the seaward end in 1976 but the intrepid walker still has a bracing hour's exercise in prospect. He will seldom be alone, for the pier is one of the most popular vantage points for the fishermen of Southend, who strive to land flounders, eel, bass or mullet.

Unlike many resorts the beach at Southend does not merely offer a view of the horizon, interrupted only by passing ships, because it looks across to the Isle of Grain.

View from the Esplanade

The arrivals and departures associated with England's greatest river ensure constant activity. The beach is a mixture of sand and shingle, and ideal for family fun and relaxation. The Esplanade extends the length of the beach and is lined with shops selling all manner of wonderful things. There are over a thousand acres of parks and gardens.

Entertainment is central to Southend's appeal, and all age groups are catered for. For children there are the pleasures of the beach and the excitements of Peter Pan's Playground, which includes a big wheel, slides and rounda-

bouts. Amusement arcades and more energetic rides look after adolescent visitors, and this same group is likely to be attracted towards the Horror Museum beside the pier. Here too is located the half scale replica of the *Golden Hinde*, which is well worth seeing. Those who prefer to watch others can do so from the comfortable depths of a hired deckchair. In August they will have the added interest of the annual barge races which take place between Greenwich and Southend.

The museum in the old Prittlewell Priory features the Crow Stone which originally stood on the beach at Chalkwell, and marked the eastern extent of London's jurisdiction.

Hadleigh Castle

There are now several different coastal towns running into each other alongside Southend, and their names confirm their salty origins: Leigh-on-Sea, Westcliffe and Thorpe Bay. These are graceful residential areas, and while no doubt many people do make a living from the tourists there are just as many who work in the business sector, which includes the headquarters of a major credit card company and an important regional airport.

Hadleigh Castle is about five miles from the centre of Southend, and offers wonderful views over the entire coastline and across to Kent. To get there, start from opposite the charming church of St. James the Less in Hadleigh and follow the road towards the coast. It soon becomes a track and finally reaches the castle field.

The first castle was built here in 1230, but the present ruins date from 1360. The walls and towers are labelled and it is quite easy to understand the castle's layout. But in all honesty the visitor should go there for the view – and take a picnic too.

Never Never Land
Open: April to Oct: Sat & Sun 1100–2200
All week during school holidays

Prittlewell Priory Museum
Open: All year: Mon 1300–1700, Tues to Sat 1000–1700

Hadleigh Castle
Open: Any reasonable time

THE CROUCH ESTUARY

South Woodham Ferrers takes its name from a Norman knight called de Ferrers who was rewarded with land following the conquest of England in 1066. For most of its history the people worked to produce salt, but recent times have seen great changes, for this is now a new town, created in 1973, and still growing. The Queen opened the square in 1981 and toured the interesting housing developments which comprise a mixture of 120 building styles all laid out along broad access roads, converging on a modern shopping centre in a pedestrian precinct. It is not to everyone's taste but it does have excellent amenities.

The Marsh Farm Country Park is only 20 minutes from the town centre and was created along with it in the 1970s. Here you can inspect a commercial farm which specialises in cattle, sheep and pigs, as well as keeping goats, ducks and chickens. Raised walkways through the traditional buildings allow the life of the farm to go on, although the stockmen will stop to answer questions. Children in particular will enjoy seeing the young animals which are born and raised here. A nature reserve links up with a river path giving a three-mile walk beside the Crouch saltmarshes, where there are waterfowl and waders to watch.

River Crouch at North Fambridge

The river is only kept in check by banks, and at North Fambridge a high tide can cover the road. In 1897 severe flooding devastated this area and some of the damage to the walls was never repaired. Even now it is a bleak place, although ideal for bird watchers, and the sailors who tie up their craft in the Marina. The 15th-century Ferry Boat Inn is said to be haunted by a former ferryman, and a glass of his favourite drink is always put out on the bar on Christmas Eve. Across the water is South Fambridge where you can buy fresh lobsters. It is also the start of a five-mile walk beside the river.

At Burnham-on-Crouch the river is almost ¾ mile wide, and there is a lot to see. At low tide the waders maintain a ceaseless chorus as they search for food, and someone will be painting or improving his boat. High tide brings scores of brightly coloured sails and spinnakers. Nearby Creeksea claims to be the place where Canute attempted to turn back the tide.

Burnham on Crouch waterfront

Burnham-on-Crouch is home to two of the five sailing clubs on the river (the Royal Burnham and Royal Corinthian), and they both have a national reputation. During Burnham Week in late August this bustling harbour is indeed 'the Cowes of the East Coast', and the races are of the very highest standard. Yacht design and boat building also go on here. A walk beside the river, along the quay which runs between the boatyards and the houses with their tiny, flower-filled gardens, is one of the most pleasant ways to discover Burnham's charms, while a visit to the museum will reveal much about its past.

The town has a great deal of genteel elegance, with small shops of traditional character and a wide main street lined with pretty Georgian-style buildings. Many are weatherboarded and sparkle from fresh paint. The Octagonal Clock Tower is most unusual and has no doubt beckoned many a tired sailor home.

The Crouch offers the enthusiast 15 miles of river sailing, and at its most easterly point concludes with Dengie Flats, a saltmarsh. Here the tide retreats by as much as two miles, leaving a vast area that is now a strictly protected bird sanctuary.

Weatherboarded houses in the main street

Marsh Farm Country Park
Open: Feb to Oct: Mon to Fri 1000–1630. Sat, Sun, bank holidays and summer school holidays 1000–1730
Price guide: A

Burnham Week
In late August, daily 1400–1630

Burnham-on-Crouch Museum
Open: April to Dec: Wed & Sat 1100–1600
Price guide: A

THE SAXON CHAPEL BRADWELL

The Saxon chapel at Bradwell is built on the site of a much older settlement: a Roman fortress. Elsewhere in East Anglia there is evidence of such forts established to guard the coast against attacks by Saxon raiders; here, between the rivers Blackwater and Crouch, there survives a fascinating reminder of the changes which occurred once the Romans departed. To reach the site from Maldon or Burnham-on-Crouch requires careful navigation, but the trip has its own interest since the houses along these winding roads are superb examples of the Essex skill in weatherboard construction.

After reaching the village of Bradwell-on-Sea, continue along the signposted road until you reach the car park by the farm. From this point you will need to walk the final quarter of a mile, and this is appropriate as the track beside the field is the Pilgrim Way, one of the oldest paths in Essex, and probably used by the Romans when they built their fort in 286. Today you may find yourself walking between fields of corn edged with mallow, and accompanied overhead by larks and swallows. The first view of the chapel, solitary against a vast horizon of coastal wetlands, is evocative and impressive. Time slips away and the site assumes some of the mystery it must have had centuries ago.

The Chapel of St Peter's-on-the-Wall, on The Pilgrim Way.

The Roman fort Othona became a victim of the changing coastline; two thirds of it are covered at high tide, and very little remains visible. There is a diagram inside the chapel showing what it may have looked like.

In 653 King Sigbert of the East Saxons (from whom Essex derives its name), called for missionaries from Northumbria. From Lindisfarne came St Cedd, and he chose the ruined fort at Bradwell as his base. The proper name of the chapel is St Peter's-on-the-Wall, because it sits across the landward wall of the fort, and it uses Roman masonry. It would have been bigger then, as the curved apse marked out in the grass shows. This was Cedd's cathedral, from which he converted the people of Essex. Then there would have been a busy settlement here; now it stands alone, overlooking marshes which are home only to flocks of wildfowl.

There are few details of its subsequent story; although in 1750 it was still described as a chapel, by 1774 it was listed as a barn. It continued as such into the present century, and this had the fortunate effect of preserving the building. In 1920 it was restored and reconsecrated by the Bishop of Chelmsford.

The Church at Tillingham

It is non-denominational and evensong is still heard on Sundays in July and August. The interior, with its high stone walls and wooden benches before a plain altar, is all the more touching for its simplicity. Our awareness of the part played by this chapel in church history makes a visit a memorable experience.

There are a number of interesting things to see in the area. The village of Tillingham is perfectly grouped round the 13th-century church, and its weatherboarded cottages which date from the 1880s are most attractive. In 616 King Ethelbert gave Tillingham to St Paul's Cathedral and it has remained their property ever since! The Bradwell nuclear power station offers a startling contrast to Roman forts and Saxon chapels, both in size and purpose. Close to this is an unusual memorial to the men who served at RAF Bradwell and who died in the last war. More cheerfully, at Waterside on the Blackwater estuary is a quiet creek and a marina for 500 sailing boats.

RAF Memorial at Bradwell

Saxon Chapel Bradwell
Open: All reasonable times
Price guide: Free

MALDON AND THE RIVER BLACKWATER

The town of Maldon occupies a ridge overlooking the River Blackwater. It began as a Saxon settlement, and by the time of Domesday Book it was the second most important borough in Essex. But now it is a more tranquil spot, and has had to endure a period of decline as a trading port. For the person who likes to ramble and explore this is ideal territory, as every street seems to lead down to the water's edge and the graceful barges which still dominate the quayside.

Hythe Quay recalls the town's Saxon origins – hythe means wharf in Anglo-Saxon. Maldon's prosperity depended on its ability to ship grain and fodder, particularly to London, and the town's ship-building yards ensured a constant demand for imported Scandinavian timber. In the last century the great barges with their enormous red sails thronged the river, trading all along the east coast. 2000 barges were said to operate from Maldon in 1900. One type of barge working out of the port was so successful it was known as a 'stackie', because it could carry an entire haystack! Even today it is possible to catch something of the flavour of the 19th-century port, for it is still the home of many magnificent barges. Some provide sailing experience for young people, while others are available for charter. They are both beautiful and fascinating, with their complex rigging and towering masts.

Thames barges anchored off the Hythe

The production of sea salt still continues here, and the salt works is the last in Britain. Maldon has a vivid maritime past and the flourishing boatyards confirm it has a bright future too.

Promenade Park is the best way to approach Hythe Quay as it gives you the view mariners would have seen of Maldon as they navigated the last few bends of the river. The tower of St Mary's Church first catches the eye; the white wooden steeple which crowns the stone tower was put up in 1740 and is known as the Mariners' Beacon.

All Saints' Church and the Blue Boar Inn

At the top of High Street stands All Saints Church with its unique triangular tower, dating from the 12th century. Perhaps the street plan of the time, now long forgotten, called for this unusual shape. Within this church is buried Edward Bright who died in 1750 weighing 42 stone! The burial register observed him to be 'comely in his person, affable in his temper, a tender father and valuable friend.'

The Moot Hall began as the home of Lord D'Arcy in 1440, and is really a tower. The brick staircase is one of its best features. In 1576 it was sold for the sum of £55 and became the Moot Hall and Court House to the Maldon borough. So it remained until 1974. It is still open to visitors and the Court is preserved. The balcony on formidable pillars was added during the 19th century and was used for occasions such as announcing the winner of an election.

St Peter's Tower is all that remains of a church which collapsed in 1665. A certain Doctor Plume, the Archdeacon of Rochester, who died in 1704, bequeathed to Maldon his outstanding collection of old books and left money to build a library to house them. The Plume Library was built against St Peter's tower. The upper floor is all panels and 17th century volumes.

The Blue Boar Inn on Silver Street is very old; its stables date to the 15th century. The interior is a wealth of panelling, and on warm days it is fun to sit in the old courtyard, surrounded by activity but not a part of it! The King's Head in High Street bears the image of Henry VIII and really does date from those turbulent times. Even older is the Swan Hotel.

The rivers Chelmer and Blackwater converge at the picturesque Beeleigh Falls, and here, too, is the old Chelmer and Blackwater Canal which was built in the late 18th century to avoid high road tolls. It ran for 14 miles and had 11 locks. It was in turn stifled by the railway – but only temporarily, for the railway has now gone, and the boats continue to ply their trade. The canal is particularly busy at Heybridge Basin where boats, lock gates and swans make for a picturesque scene beside the Old Ship Inn overlooking the river and Northey Island.

A half mile riverside walk from the town brings you to the site of the Battle of Maldon. In 991 Anlaf the Viking's fleet sacked Ipswich and then sailed up the Blackwater. He made camp on Northey Island only to discover that Earl Bryhtnoth and the men of Essex were gathered at the end of the 80 foot causeway which linked the island to the mainland. It was only passable at low tide. Anlaf was effectively trapped. But he knew his opponent to be honourable, and he appealed for leave to cross the causeway, and so make the battle fairer. Bryhtnoth agreed. The battle which followed was a disaster for the men of Essex: all their leaders, including Bryhtnoth, were killed. The causeway can still be seen, and the battlefield, marked only by a plaque on the sea wall, is a haunting place. Motorists may prefer to drive out along the B1018 to Latchingdon, and park near South House Farm from where it is a short walk to this evocative site. One of the earliest poems in the English language commemorates the Battle of Maldon, and to celebrate its anniversary, local craftswomen have created a 42 foot long embroidery which depicts the history of Maldon between 991 and 1991. It is well worth seeing. Northey Island itself is the property of the National Trust, and is a Bird Reserve. Permission to visit must be obtained beforehand from the Essex Naturalists' Trust.

The Causeway to Northey Island

O sea Island, in the middle of the river, is also approached by a causeway but the penalties of failure to judge the tide are more severe, as the rusting cars witness. It is owned by Cambridge University and has a resident population of 10. The island is not open to the general public. The 9000 Brent geese are free to drop in when they please, of course.

This is a river for recreation now, and innumerable slipways and creeks serve the sailors who delight in discovering the pleasures it has to offer. In common with many East Anglian rivers it reserves its greatest treasures for the waterborne explorer; the novelist Arnold Bennett sailed a barge here and described it as 'the incomparable Blackwater'. Ramsey Island and Bradwell Waterside (the latter overlooked by the twin blocks of the nuclear power station) are the last of the marinas on the south bank of the river. Bradwell Creek is sheltered by Pewit Island, and years ago wildfowlers used to shoot from punts on the river. Bradwell-on-Sea churchyard has a whipping post, and a cage which could hold up to six offenders.

Sailmaker's lofts at Tollesbury

At Tollesbury on the northern shore of the Blackwater there is now a yacht harbour where once over 70 fishing smacks moored. In 1907 the arrival of the railway from London led to London yachtsmen using the enhanced facilities of Tollesbury and large yachts were moored off the quay. One of them, *Merrymaid*, dating from 1904, is still there. The tall wooden sailmakers' lofts here have been carefully restored, and give an idea of what the waterfront looked like a century ago, while miles of lonely saltmarsh allow marvellous views across the river to Bradwell.

Maldon Museum
Open: Contact local tourist office

CHELMSFORD

Chelmsford is the county town of Essex, a cathedral city and the home of many famous industrial and commercial products. The first impression of the centre confirms all this, but can also suggest it is a modern creation. This is far from the truth: the Romans used the town as a staging post between London and the regional capital, Colchester. Just beneath the pavements of this 20th-century success story are the foundations of houses from that distant time. There is a lot to explore.

The Chelmsford and Essex Museum

The Chelmsford and Essex Museum at Oaklands Park is an excellent place to start. It is set amid beautiful grounds which prepare you for the pleasurable experience ahead, for this is a modern museum. It is quite likely that you will find children everywhere, tackling projects and work sheets. You may even find a notice on a door informing you that only under-sevens are admitted! The exhibits are clearly labelled, and this compensates for the lack of a guide book. The rooms contain displays on such topics as prehistory, Roman Essex, social history, natural sciences and local industry. They are well presented and it is fun to pass from one to the other. There are always exhibitions of painting, and the glass collection is outstanding. Included are items which make us all feel too old, such as a display of hi-fi equipment down the years, and a costume room which brings fashion up to the present.

The Essex Regiment Museum shares the Oaklands site. Here the story is told of the Regiment's foundation in the mid-18th century to its present incarnation as the Third Battalion of the Royal Anglian Regiment. A long and distinguished history is presented to the layman through a series of display cases and information boards.

In the city centre stands the Shire Hall, which was designed by the Surveyor to the County, John Johnson, and built between 1789 and 1791. Even in these days of buses, lorries and cars it retains its dignity above the fumes and noise. The late Sir Nikolaus Pevsner placed it high on his list of the best buildings in Britain, describing it as 'thoroughly civilised.' So indeed it is. Johnson was also responsible for the fine stone bridge over the river.

Some cities are dominated by their cathedrals, and like it that way. Chelmsford's cathedral is engaging, because it is on the same modest scale as the people and buildings which surround it. The diocese was created as late as 1914, and the old church of St Mary the Virgin, St Peter and St Cedd was enlarged to fulfil the new role. It dates from the early 15th century, but a great deal is more recent. In 1800 workmen preparing a vault for a burial brought the roof down, and the nave had to be virtually rebuilt. The blend of old and new is brilliantly achieved throughout, and while there are many touching signs of its antiquity (the Mildmay tomb dating from 1571 includes the charming sentiment '. . . they had fifteen pledges of their prosperous love: seven whereof were females, eight were males . . .'), the cathedral is light, modern and perfectly suited to its task. The south-east corner has a delightful sculpture of St Peter, wearing enormous sea boots and carrying a Yale key!

The city streets are constantly changing as old shops give way to new, although the street plan has been retained where possible. An impressive glass shopping centre welcomes the visitor to an arcade of tempting attractions.

Chelmsford Shopping Centre

Chelmsford Museum
Open: All year: Mon to Sat 1000–1700, Sun 1400–1700

THE WOODEN CHURCH, GREENSTED

Timber has always been in plentiful supply in East Anglia, so it has made good sense to use it as a building material. To the west of Chipping Ongar there is a survivor of a bygone age which is unique in Europe: a wooden church dating from Saxon times.

Greensted is a pretty village surrounded by woodland and fields, and the Church of St Andrew stands at the end of a hedge-lined cul-de-sac. Here is a religious site which may previously have been sacred to pagans; it was quite common for the Christian Church to superimpose its faith on places of pagan worship. St Cedd brought Christianity to Essex and caused a church to be built at Greensted in 654.

The glory of Greensted is the nave, which dates from 845 when the Saxons enlarged their church. It is possible to be so precise about the date because modern science has enabled us to formulate a chronology by studying tree growth rings. Even now it is clear how the walls were constructed. Tree trunks were split lengthwise into three. The two outer curved beams, with their bark retained, would form the walls, while the centre section went to support the thatched roof. The wall beams were set into a log which ran the length of the nave, and each log was held to its neighbours by a tongue-and-groove joint. These still survive, and at the north-west end you can also see one of the original corner posts formed from a complete tree trunk. The Saxons would have lit the interior by fire torches, and the scorches they made can still be seen.

The invasions of the pagan Danes inevitably led to Christian martyrs, and St Edmund is one of East Anglia's celebrated sufferers. He was tied to a tree, shot with arrows, and his severed head thrown into the forest, where it was later found to be guarded by a friendly wolf. His body is said to have lain at Greensted while on the way to interment at Bury St Edmunds in 1013, but this claim is as open to dispute as the site of his death. During the 19th century a carved beam was added to the roof commemorating the wolf's devotion, and a stained-glass window depicting St Edmund was inserted.

The cattle drover's cross

The north west corner of the church

The Normans pulled down the wooden chancel and built one of flint. This was in turn replaced by brick in the 16th century, and the interior benefited from the increase in light from the larger windows. The white weatherboard tower is believed to date from the 17th century although there is still some doubt about this.

In 1837 the church was greatly altered when the Rector, Philip Ray, undertook restoration work. He replaced the decayed wall sill with brick, renovated the present porch, inserted the stained glass and added six dormer windows into the Tudor tiled roof. He also wrote the first book about the church. He is buried in the graveyard close by.

Greensted is still a place of worship, and the visitor should try to pause inside and reflect on the extraordinary continuity of use which it has enjoyed. The interior is very dim and it is easy to overlook the more recent fittings and appreciate the church's Saxon character.

By the gate in the churchyard is a broken wooden cross which stands above the grave of a cattle drover, who got drunk and in this condition commenced cutting grass with a scythe. He cut himself badly, screamed in vain for assistance, and bled to death. Rather more noble, although just as anonymous, is the crusader who lies beneath the shield-shaped stone by the south wall of the nave.

Open: Any reasonable time
Price guide: Free

PAYCOCKE'S HOUSE, COGGESHALL

About 5½ miles east of Braintree on the A120 is the large village of Coggeshall, which has every reason to harbour a grudge against its most celebrated tourist attraction, Paycocke's House, if only because it distracts attention from the other treasures which line its streets.

John Paycocke (farmer, butcher, wool merchant and cloth maker) built Paycocke's House for his son Thomas's marriage. Thomas died in 1518 but the Paycockes continued to live there until the male line died out in 1584.

Paycocke's House

Before stepping inside the house, it is helpful to know its subsequent story because much of what we see today is the result of the rather sad history which befell it in the intervening centuries.

By the beginning of the 19th century Paycocke's had lost its splendour. It was divided into at least three tene-

ments and the fabric of the building suffered prolonged neglect. So much so, that in 1890 the cost of carrying out essential repairs led one prospective buyer to contemplate removing whatever fittings were worth salvaging, and then demolishing the house! By a stroke of good fortune this terrible fate was averted when the local historian G.F. Beaumont intervened and prevented the sale. Instead the

One of the carved figures flanking the carriageway doors

house was purchased by Edward Noel who carried out considerable restoration work, including a new roof and the insertion of new windows on the street side. The National Trust assumed responsibility for the property in 1925 and since that time it has been leased to tenants who open it to the public three afternoons a week.

The exterior of Paycocke's House as seen from West Street is magnificent, and it helps to know that at the time of its building a foreign visitor to London remarked that English merchants liked to show their wealth and status by the degree of close studding they could afford to incorporate in their houses. By this standard Paycocke's is among the very best. Close studding is the practice of placing the vertical wall beams as close together as possible, thereby stressing the quantity of timber you could afford. Here they are infilled in brick nogging in herring-bone pattern, another extravagant statement! It is just possible that the original house may have possessed three storeys. The long and finely-carved fascia board with its vine-leaf frieze conceals the joists of the only storey to survive. It is well worth stopping to examine the frontage because there are so many points of interest, including the carved figures which flank the carriageway doors and the complex timber patterns which give the house its appeal.

The interior is a delight: dark carved beams grace all the rooms, and the entrance hall is large and panelled, bathed in light from the elegant mullioned windows. The dining room is distinguished by its grand fireplace and linen-fold panel work, both of which date from 1520. Throughout the tour of the house the visitor is struck by its homely scale, and this is carried into the lovely garden, with its well kept flower beds and lawn. The rear buildings are older than

The dining room

the main house, and may have contained store rooms for wool and living accommodation for the servants.

This is a wonderful place to visit, and the fact that children still live and play within it should gladden the heart of John Paycocke and assure him that his gift is still giving pleasure.

Coggeshall Market Hill offers a view of unbroken attractions in all directions. In Stoneham Street is the hexagonal clock tower which commemorates the Silver Jubilee of Queen Victoria. Church Street takes the visitor past scores of timber-framed buildings, and concludes with the magnificent 15th-century Woolpack Inn which stands at the church gate.

The church of St Peter Ad Vincula dominates this part of Coggeshall. It stands in a beautiful sloping churchyard at the end of several pretty access lanes, all with delightful houses and gardens. The interior is light and cheerful and

Stoneham Street, Coggeshall

well restored following disaster in the Second World War when a German bomb destroyed the nave and tower. Fortunately the Paycocke brasses in St Katherine's aisle were spared. Of interest too is the memorial to Mary Honywood who died in 1620 leaving 367 descendants! She is shown kneeling before a Bible, while above two skulls remind us all of our mortality.

East Street follows the course of the old Roman road, Stane Street, and until recently was the busy traffic thoroughfare, but a bypass has come to the rescue. Long Bridge near Market Hill claims to have arches which use the oldest bricks made in England, but for an explanation of this we need to go to the Abbey ruins, south of the village.

In 1140 King Stephen founded an abbey at Coggeshall, and gave it to the Cistercian Order, who are said to have re-introduced brick-making to this country. The very small bricks in the Abbey Guesthouse are said to date from this time, and Long Bridge re-used the bricks after the abbey's dissolution. The Cistercians also introduced sheep farming to this area, and so directly contributed to Coggeshall's prosperity. The 14th-century Grange Barn was their store, and this great timber barn with its massive roof which slopes almost to the ground has only just been restored. The Gatehouse Chapel survives and is now the Chapel of St Nicholas. The old abbey watermill is still in full working order.

Coggeshall's greatest treasure is its unity of style. There are so many streets and houses here which provide a marvellous experience of a time long past. This is still a place to be explored on foot.

Paycocke's House
National Trust
Open: Mar to Oct: Tues, Thur, Sun and bank holiday Mondays
1400–1730
Price guide: A

ESSEX RAILWAYS

Nostalgia for the days of the steam railway owes quite a lot to the fictional world of *Brief Encounter* and *The Railway Children*, but that hardly explains why children should be as keen as their parents to savour the smells and sounds of old-fashioned locomotives. East Anglia has a number of railway preservation societies and they share the ability to involve the public in an experience enriched by their own infectious enthusiasm.

The Colne Valley Viaduct

The railway age was in its infancy when in 1846 The Colchester, Stour Valley, Sudbury and Halstead Railway Company was formed. It hoped to exploit the trade passing up the Stour and Colne valleys by constructing a branch line which began at Colchester. One of the stations built to serve this line was at Chappel and Wakes Colne. This is now the headquarters of the East Anglian Railway Museum. It is located approximately mid-way between Halstead and Colchester on the A604. The visitor cannot fail to be impressed by the magnificent viaduct which spans the Colne valley, with its 32 arches and 1000-foot length. Unfortunately the cost of building this marvel so crippled the fledgling railway company that it had to abandon plans to run the line to Halstead. Stung by the perceived affront the good burghers of Halstead formed their own company, raised the necessary £40,000 and built the six-mile track from Halstead to Chappel and Wakes Colne, which then continued on to Colchester – all at a cost to the passenger of 5p, or a shilling as it was then.

The East Anglian Railway Museum at Chappel and Wakes Colne

The Stour Valley Railway Preservation Society was formed in 1968 with the intention of saving at least a section of this branch line, and its headquarters were located at Chappel. It was successful, and a pay train continues to use this track, so do take extra care! The Railway Museum was opened here in 1986, and the visitor will find all the sights, smells, sounds and grease of the age of steam. There are three platforms, suitably furnished with enamel advertisement boards, milk churns and flower beds, and two of them are linked by a splendid bridge which gives excellent views of the restoration workshops, cranes, water towers and signal boxes. This is a place where you are encouraged to explore. The museum possesses a number of steam locomotives, and has Steam Days regularly throughout the season.

The Colne Valley Railway, meanwhile, was initially a great success, and by 1863 had reached Haverhill. Castle Hedingham Station was built in 1861 and served the needs of the local brickworks. But times changed, and by 1964 it was redundant. At this point the Colne Valley Railway Preservation Society came to the rescue, and moved the station, brick by brick, two miles along the track to its present location! Now it stands as a charming reminder of a vanished England. The staff are very helpful and enthusiastic. Several steam locomotives pull an interesting variety of carriages, and the 20-minute journey up and down the track is good value. The restaurant carriage at the station still operates, and has a fine reputation. For children there is a superb guide book, full of information and ideas. A picnic site beside the river marks the start of a nature trail which can include a trip to Hedingham Castle.

The Colne Valley Railway

Both these railway stations at Chappel and Castle Hedingham are full of things to see and do. They may be operated by separate preservation societies, but these share a common aim: to inform and entertain us with a glimpse into the world of steam railways.

East Anglian Railway Museum
Open: All year: Mon to Fri 0930–1700, Sat & Sun 1000–1730
Price guide: B
Colne Valley Railway
Open: Mar to Dec: 1000–1700
Price guide: B

HEDINGHAM CASTLE

It is always difficult to look at the ruins of a great castle with any true understanding of its purpose, because so much has changed. We have come to regard castle remains as pleasing and pretty; Hedingham Castle stands beside a picture-postcard village, surrounded by tranquil parkland. It has not always been so.

In 1140 Aubrey de Vere, King Stephen's Chamberlain, began to construct a great castle, designed for him by the Archbishop of Canterbury, no less. The keep stands to a height of 110 feet, with flint walls 12 feet thick in places, able to withstand the most determined siege. We know that de Vere must have been a wealthy man because he gave his castle a facing of Barnack stone, brought all the way from Northampton. Most castle builders could only afford to use this stone for the corners and windows. The original scaffolding required small holes to be made in the facing stones, and you can still see these holes running from top to bottom of the keep. There were two high curtain walls, and the drawbridge was sited where the Tudor bridge is today. The moat was probably dry. As part of the defensive preparations, all the trees and bushes for miles around would have been cleared, creating a bleak landscape.

The keep is entered by way of the outer stairway, which would have been covered. Close by is the dungeon where hapless prisoners would have suffered from the dark and damp conditions, even without the use of torture. The chevron design over the main doorway is a sure sign of Norman architecture. A portcullis would have offered some protection here, and the groove it occupied can be seen. The entrance room was used by the garrison as a barracks,

and connected with the other floors by a spiral staircase, consisting of 124 steps, all going upwards in a clockwise direction. This forced the attackers to hold their swords in their left hands as they tried to ascend the stairway, putting them at a distinct disadvantage. Was everyone right-handed? Today both left- and right-handed people are welcome to buy souvenirs and refreshments in this room.

The next floor is the Banqueting Hall, complete with minstrels' gallery. The arch is 28 feet across. Here would have taken place banquets of the sort beloved of film-makers, with rushes on the floor, trestle tables, proud knights, flowing wine and finger-eaten venison. Music and jugglers would have been there if the lord could afford them. Tradition says that Henry VII dined in this hall, his host sparing no expense, and then fined the poor man for being too extravagant.

Above this floor was the dormitory, where the lord and his family had their apartments – probably only curtained-off bed spaces. The view from the top of the castle is spectacular.

Visitors should go down into the cellars where barrels of wine and sacks of flour were stored. Legend says that there was a well in the cellar and that during a siege the Hedingham garrison taunted their attackers by throwing fresh fish from the walls! The doorways here were not part of the original castle but were added much later, in the 18th century.

Emerging into the sunlight, visitors should take advantage of the setting to relax, sparing a thought for all those over the centuries for whom this place was anything but peaceful.

Hedingham Castle
Open: April to Sept: Sat to Thur 1100–1700, Sept to Oct: Sat & Sun 1100–1700
Price guide: B

THREE ESSEX VILLAGES

Whatever excuses we make for our behaviour, one of the reasons we love visiting other people's towns and villages is our insatiable curiosity. We want to look through the windows and peer round the corner into the garden. What makes villages particularly suitable for this prying is that many cottages have no front gardens, affording an even clearer view inside. The owners seem to enter into the spirit of the game, too, doing their best to encourage visitors. Of course, if you are fortunate enough to own a lovely house, you like others to share your pleasure. Envy and curiosity; no wonder Agatha Christie's sleuth, Miss Marple, lived in a closely-knit community!

The ingredients of a beautiful village are hard to define, for they are seldom present in equal measure. For most of us they include such rustic features as church, pub, thatched cottages, village green with pond, and ducks a-plenty. Few villages are so perfect, but that does not prevent us from recognising a tranquil, idyllic scene when we come upon it. There are hundreds of villages in East Anglia which are deservedly celebrated for their beauty and sense of calm, but they are all different. As you travel through the region we hope you will discover many such places, although some of the loveliest houses and gardens are not in villages, but stand alone as farmhouses or solitary

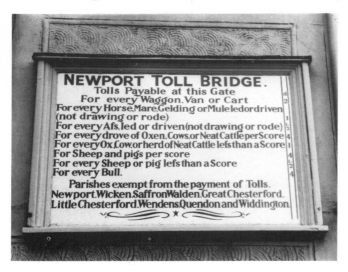

treasures. Beauty is indeed in the eye of the beholder, and while most people would accept that our choice of villages is reasonable, they need not agree that they are outstanding. Perhaps they prefer one a mile or two away, and wonder how we came to ignore it!

The villages of Essex were once remote and quiet, but now most of them are served by improved roads which bring them within reach of the capital. Newport today is cut in two by the B1383 from Saffron Walden to Bishop's Stortford, and is within sight of the M11 motorway. Just how different it once was is shown by the sign on the old Toll House, beside the bridge over the river. Here is a notice of fees to be charged for carrier's carts, farm waggons and even people on foot. The view through the village is delightful. Many of the houses are dazzlingly white; weatherboarded, brick or plaster. A profusion of flowers bursts from even the tiniest earth border, and roses do

Monk's Barn, Newport

indeed surround many windows. For those who like timber-frame construction there are several excellent examples of the carpenter's skill – not to say art.

Monk's Barn looks rather dull and out of place at first for it is of dark wood and rich worn red brick. A closer inspection brings rewards: the brick is arranged between the timbers in a herringbone pattern, which makes even the infill a source of interest. The first floor provides evidence that this is no yeoman's cottage, for the window sill is enormous, over a foot deep, and carved exquisitely to represent the Virgin in Heaven. After centuries of seasonal onslaught it has weathered remarkably well, and still conveys the status of the building it adorns. In fact, this was once the summer retreat for monks from London's church of St Martin le Grand. They probably fled the capital during the hot months to escape the plagues which thrived amid the squalor of the city streets.

Crown House, Newport

24

In a small close beside the church of St Mary is a row of whitewashed cottages representing many periods of building, but existing together without discord, some beneath generous thatch which rolls lazily over the eaves. Flowers bloom everywhere.

The Green is easily missed, as it is only found by passing under the railway bridge. Here is a line of white boarded and plastered houses facing a small enclosed garden. As a collection they are charming, but individually they have many fine points. The Crown House actually has a plaster crown over the front door, and the patterned plasterwork, known as pargetting, extends across the entire street walls. Further along a group of small weatherboarded fronts seem to resent the attention being given to their grander neighbour.

Finchingfield has all the attributes of the archetypal English village. A wide swathe of grass sweeps across the floor of a valley, and stops beside a large duck pond, crossed by a red-brick bridge. The road bends as it climbs a

Finchingfield

The Old Guildhall, Finchingfield

gentle hill, winds past a windmill and white timbered cottages, some with thatch, and goes over the crest beside the old church. It is a lovely scene and attracts thousands of visitors, some by the coachload, every summer.

The village stands up to the influx of tourists remarkably well. Of course there are restaurants and gift shops, but they are part of the attraction, and fit into the view. Finchingfield is photographed and painted to a quite remarkable degree but motorists seem to appreciate the problem and without direction gravitate to the parking places overlooking the village, while remaining out of picture!

The old Guildhall stands at the entrance to the churchyard. It offers a fine view of the commanding Norman tower of the Church of St John the Baptist. The Guildhall is used by a local pottery club, and examples of their work are on sale upstairs. The entrance is reached through the archway.

But Finchingfield is more than a pretty scene. It has that quality which money cannot buy, and builders cannot create: it has a story.

In 1621 William Kempe, a gentleman of the village, accused his wife of infidelity. In a closed community, and

living in a time of harsh punishments, he could hardly have accused her of a more serious offence. When he learnt of her innocence Kempe was appalled to think what he had done, and took a vow of silence for seven years. She died in 1623, and he maintained his self-imposed punishment until his penance was discharged. But by this time he was a broken man, and being taken suddenly with sickness he tried to call for help, only to discover the seven years of silence had taken their toll. He could not utter a word, even to save his life, and he died in 1628 a victim of his own tragic folly. His monument may still be seen in the Kempe Chapel.

Manuden is very close to the border of Essex with Hertfordshire, and is best approached from Stansted Mountfitchet, where it is signposted. The village is grouped around the stone church of St Mary the Virgin, and thatched cottages overlook the churchyard, shaded from the sun by tall trees. Timber and thatch are everywhere; even the farmyard in the village centre has a magnificent thatched timber barn. The main street is lined with white-painted houses which seem embarrassed by their graceful appearance, as if afraid they may become the object of envious attentions. This is Essex at its loveliest and best.

Manuden Village

Finchingfield Guildhall and Museum
Open: April to Sept: Sun & bank holidays 1400–1730
Price guide: Free

THAXTED

Nothing can convey the sheer delight of the first glimpse of Thaxted main street, for whichever way you enter the town you have a view of timber and whitewashed walls which is hardly rivalled anywhere in England. The town retains the street plan it had in 1500. Even better, it is much more than just a satisfying general view; all the buildings repay careful attention for while they contribute to the general effect, each is a self-contained gem. Nor are they museums and government offices. These are houses, shops and places of work, as they have been since they were first constructed.

Thaxted has a very long history, which certainly goes back to Saxon times. During the Middle Ages the wealth of this part of England was based on the wool trade, and the prosperity it brought enabled merchants and farmers to build large and magnificent houses, and to make generous bequests to the church. Dominating the main street is the church of St John the Baptist, with its spire reaching up to 180 feet. Once inside, the visitor is struck by its simplicity and brightness. There are few stained glass windows, no pews, and no dusty monuments lining the walls. The nave is bathed with clear light from the large clerestory windows which also illuminate the splendid beams and carved bosses of the 16th-century roof. The size of the church also gives a clue as to the population of the town in the 1340s when the building was started.

Interior of St John the Baptist Church

The main street of the town is a collection of many styles of architecture, but they harmonise together most beautifully. Clustered around the church are some of the most distinguished buildings and chief of these is the Guildhall, with its open ground floor and elaborately timbered upper storeys. This is what the England of Dick Whittington should look like! In addition to wool, Thaxted also had a busy trade in cutlery manufacture and the Guildhall began as the meeting place of the Guild of Cutlers. It was completed long before the church and so is very ancient, and has subsequently seen service as council chamber, school, gaol and now a museum.

John Webb's Windmill and the spire of St John the Baptist Church

Stoney Lane is a cobbled alleyway which runs beside the Guildhall up towards the church. The splendid timber-framed buildings survived the fire of 1881 which destroyed 29 houses. In 1728 one of these houses became the home of a young butcher and his wife. He did not stay here long, for soon his debts forced him to turn to robbery – highway robbery. His name was Dick Turpin.

To the other side of the Guildhall is Fishmarket Lane, and this leads up to the Almshouses and cottages beside the churchyard, and on out of the town to John Webb's Mill, named after the man who built it in 1804. This lane makes a lovely walk, and although the mill ceased working in 1907 it is open to visitors as a museum of bygones.

Fine buildings are everywhere: just beside the church is the former King's Head pub, with its lovely dark timbers; next door is Clarance House, in serious red brick, dating from 1715 and showing that medieval and Queen Anne can complement each other nicely. The composer Gustav Holst (*The Planets* Suite) lived in Thaxted from 1914 until 1925 and a plaque on the wall of The Manse in the main street marks his music room. Make time to explore the town, and take one of the excellent guide books as your companion. The harmony to be found here is an inspiration to us all.

The Guildhall

Guildhall
Open: April to end Oct: Sat, Sun & bank holidays 1400–1800
Price guide: A

John Webb's Windmill
Open: May to Sept: Sat, Sun & bank holidays 1400–1800
Price guide: A

PRIORS HALL BARN, WIDDINGTON

There is something quite magnificent about a timber building. There was a time when all of southern England was covered by dense forest, and so it is hardly surprising that our medieval forefathers used wood in their construction work before they went to the trouble of using stone. Fire, storm and decay have deprived us of many thousands of old wooden buildings, so those which survive are to be treasured.

Priors Hall Barn stands in a farmyard close to the village of Widdington, in a loop of unclassified road off the B1383 south of Saffron Walden. The comparative inaccessibility of the farm probably contributed to its endurance. In many ways it is an ordinary farmyard, with a duck pond, buildings around a courtyard, tractors of all ages and in the background the humming of a generator. The largest building of all is also the best, for beneath the long tiled roof is a medieval barn of outstanding quality, little altered since the 14th century.

Nothing can prepare you adequately for the moment when the door is opened and your eyes grow accustomed to the light within. The only suitable analogy is that of entering a cathedral, for both exude a sense of calm through longevity, and both draw your eyes heavenwards, following the columns and beams into the uppermost gloom.

The barn stands 124 feet long, 38 feet wide and 33 feet high. There are two entrances on the south side. As in a church it is wise to stand at one end and take time to

appreciate the beauty of the design, and how it works. At Priors Hall Barn most of the main timbers are original, making the study even more exciting.

The barn is divided into eight bays. Each is braced with timbers chosen for their curve, and then split to give pairs. The modern replacements were sawn to shape. More than anything else one is struck by the perfect symmetry of it all, the warm colour of seasoned oak, and the extraordinary skill and hard work which must have been involved. The huge aisle posts had to be propped in position, and they still show the notches made for this purpose by the carpenter. Several half-size timber joints are exhibited, showing the complexity of construction which is hidden from view, as well as a marvellous model of the building. For reasons of economy, the barn used green timber which was then allowed to season in situ, producing the distortions which are such a feature of these old buildings. The roof then, as now, was tiles.

The name originates from the time of William the Conqueror, who gave the estate at Widdington to a French priory in gratitude for their support. The French sent over a religious community to supervise the work of the estate, but they were most unpopular, and in 1379 ownership passed to William of Wykeham. He founded New College, Oxford, and gave it the income of the Widdington estate. Improvements on the farm are thought to have included the building of the great barn to store the entire year's crop. It was customary to store the corn in sheaves and thresh it on the barn floor as required – hence the need for space. In 1920 New College sold the farm and a subsequent owner presented the barn to the Department of the Environment in 1976 following the collapse of the roof. Extensive repairs were put in hand, which were completed in 1983. It is a tribute to the barn's design and to the craftsmen who built and restored it that the great storm of 1987 only dislodged a few tiles!

English Heritage
Open: April to Sept: Sat & Sun only: any reasonable time
Price guide: Free

SAFFRON WALDEN

Saffron Walden is set in lovely countryside, and its old timbered buildings convey to the visitor a sense of wellbeing that makes exploring on foot a delight.

After the Norman Conquest Geoffrey de Manderville was given the manor, and around 1100 he built a castle on the low ridge overlooking the Cam. Now only the remains of the keep still stand.

The Middle Ages brought prosperity with the flourishing cloth industry. There was an additional source of wealth in the form of the saffron flower *Crocus sativus*, which thrived on the local chalk soil. The dried orange stigmas of the flowers were used in foodstuffs, as medicine and as a dye. For 400 years the town was the centre of saffron production in England – hence the prefix to the name, and its adoption as the symbol of the town, shown in the carvings in the church roof and in the municipal coat of

The Sun Inn

arms. But production was costly: many thousands of crocuses were needed, so when an artificial alternative was introduced in the 19th century demand fell sharply and

Saffron Walden was left with only its beautiful buildings as witnesses to its former prosperity.

The old Corn Exchange in the Market Square is now the Tourist Information Centre. Tours leave here every Thursday and Sunday afternoon in season. The Market Square itself is largely Victorian (the drinking fountain, for

Detail of plasterwork showing Tom Hickathrift defeating the Wisbech giant

instance, was exhibited at the Great Exhibition of 1851). But the street names betray the old trades of the town: Butcher Row and Mercer Row were medieval merchants' streets lined with stalls. From here Market Hill runs up to Church Street, and at the junction stands the Sun Inn (now a secondhand booksellers'). This is a splendid group of 14th-century buildings later decorated with plasterwork depicting a local hero, the carter Tom Hickathrift, defeating the Wisbech Giant with an axle for a club and a wheel as his shield!

The Church of St Mary the Virgin dominates the town with its 193-foot spire. This, however, is quite modern, having been added in 1832 to replace the previous wooden lantern. The church itself was rebuilt in the 15th century and is very fine. The interior is long, high and light with many interesting memorials and tombs. In the north aisle is a window to the memory of John Frye, organist here for more than 60 years, who won the post after a competitive examination at the tender age of eight! Between the church and castle, in the castle grounds, is the museum which has a collection covering natural and local history. At the far end of the common, once the castle green, is the extraordinary turf maze. First recorded in 1699 but thought to be much older, this strange circular pattern cut into the grass may only be 100 feet across, but if you follow it to the centre you will have walked a good mile!

A more conventional hedge maze is to be found at Bridge End Gardens at the top of Bridge Street. Here, too, are a rose garden, a formal Dutch garden and a grotto. There is

The Museum

Church of St Mary the Virgin

even a mystery trail involving a complicated crossword which can only be solved by keeping your eyes open as you walk around the gardens.

Further down Bridge Street on the Cambridge road are some of the best buildings, such as the Eight Bells Inn, and the Youth Hostel which has fine carvings and oriel windows. The Close is an old house with an unusual oval window. These are only a few of the many fascinating houses, inns and shops which crowd the streets of Saffron Walden.

The turf maze

Saffron Walden Museum
Open: April to Oct: Mon to Sat 1000–1700, Sun & bank holidays 1430–1700
Price guide: A

Bridge End Gardens
Open: All year, daily
Price guide: Free

AUDLEY END

At the foot of the south staircase in Audley End is an engraving made in 1676. The inscription reads: 'The General Prospect of the Royal Palace of Audlyene'. Our first view is indeed of a great Jacobean palace rather than a house, and what we see today is less than half the original building!

Henry VIII gave the estate of Walden Abbey to Sir Thomas Audley in 1538 but it was his grandson Thomas Howard, Earl of Suffolk, who created Audley End. He was Lord Treasurer to King James I, and set out to express his wealth and importance in stone. Audley End was built to a grand scale, with staterooms and apartments built around two courtyards. The main work was completed by 1614. When James I visited his minister's new address he is said to have drily remarked that it was 'too large for a king, but it might do for a Lord Treasurer'. Soon aferwards Howard was convicted of embezzlement and sent to the Tower. Nine days later, having paid a fine of £30,000, he was back,

The House from the east

poor and in disgrace, and he stayed at Audley End until he died. His successors were unable to maintain the huge property and it soon became a massive financial liability.

But it was the sheer size of the building which attracted King Charles II, who took it over in 1669: 'Many ancient houses of the Crown having been demolished [during the Civil War] we have taken a liking to Audley End.' Three kings were to hold court there and at last its magnificence was being appreciated. But not for long: architectural fashion changed and the buildings fell into a sorry state of decay. In 1701 the fifth Earl of Suffolk regained possession of Audley End for his family. Its condition was so bad that storms rendered it unsafe to cross the courtyard for fear of being struck by a falling chimney.

During the 18th century the wings were demolished, floors were added and rooms assumed new uses. On the directions of Sir John Vanbrugh the outer courtyard buildings were pulled down. Sir John Griffin Griffin became the owner in 1762 and he employed the talents of Robert Adam and 'Capability' Brown. The former preserved the integrity of the Jacobean house front while adding many classical touches both inside and out. The Tea House and Palladian Bridges over the River Cam exemplify his technique of placing ornamental works in a natural landscape. On high ground overlooking the east side of the house the Temple of Concord commemorates George III's recovery from insanity in 1792. The next century saw even more changes dictated by fashion or circumstances.

The Tea House Bridge

The Great Hall contains a Jacobean oak screen which is beautiful and awe-inspiring. It is quite impossible to understand how it could have been painted white during the 18th century, but it was! Vanbrugh added the white stone screen which stands at the opposite end, and he also built the grand stairways.

During the 1939–45 war Audley End housed the Polish section of Special Operations Executive, preparing those brave men for their parachute missions into occupied Europe. In 1948 the house was purchased by the nation but many of the items within it remain private property. Audley End has a great deal to offer the visitor, besides a wonderful stately home. The grounds are beautifully laid out and full of pleasant surprises. The park is enormous; there is even a miniature railway. Throughout the season there is a full programme of special events, including battle reconstructions, car rallies and music festivals.

English Heritage
Open: April to Sept: Wed to Sun: Grounds: 1200–1800,
House: 1300–1700
Price guide: C

MOUNTFITCHET CASTLE

Some of the best ideas are also the simplest. All over the country castle remains poke out of grass-covered mounds, made comprehensible only by a profusion of notice boards and our imagination. If only we could experience the reality of life in that era! At Mountfitchet Castle, Stansted, there is a Norman Castle as it would have been following the Conquest in 1066. This is 'The Castle Time Forgot'; it is as if some mysterious force has taken us back through the centuries and we are looking not at ruins, but at a fortress in use. Normans are frozen at their tasks, like victims of an East Anglian Pompeii.

But the castle is no fraud: Robert Gernon, Duke of Boulogne, was granted this estate by King William and built a wooden castle for his protection. Later the timber walls were replaced by flint. King John had reason to curse the family of Mountfitchet when they forced him to honour Magna Carta in 1215. When John's fortunes revived he lost no time in levelling the castle; nevertheless the foundations still remain, and in reconstructing the castle the present owners were obliged to leave them undisturbed. The oak palisade fence looks as though it goes deep into the ground, but in fact it rests on concrete sleepers!

The Castle Gallows

The visitor's first encounter with the castle is with a stockade of oak timbers, following a line of ramparts and ditches. Outside these walls are cattle pens, and farm implements looking like nothing seen today. Everywhere sheep, goats, ducks and geese create authentic bedlam.

Sentry tower

The gateway to the castle lies over a drawbridge, and is crowned with severed heads, while beyond we see a gallows with a corpse swinging gently in the breeze. Once inside the great grass-covered bailey we are never able to escape the stare of the soldiers high up in the guard tower. It is quite impossible to distinguish between education and entertainment at Mountfitchet, because the join is seamless. While you are looking in the brewhouse or smithy, and smiling at the meticulous attention to detail, you are learning about life almost a thousand years ago. The surgeon (or torturer – there seems to be little difference) is shown at work, while from his patient issue screams which carry across the open space of the bailey courtyard, as indeed they once did. The tiny churchyard contains hastily dug graves for victims of marauders, and even one killed by a wild boar. Military matters take pride of place, of course, and there is a fascinating array of weapons and defences, including a full-size siege tower and catapult.

As you would expect, the lord and his family had the best accommodation, but that is not saying much. Within the inner bailey, approached by yet another wall and drawbridge, stands a small timber building which was the Great Hall. From its battlemented tower a sentry maintains vigilant scrutiny of a poor Saxon who tends the herb garden. Within, the family are shown at their meal, and the tableau is truly outstanding – we expect them to ask us to leave, and if they did we probably would because we do seem out of place.

Mountfitchet Castle is an unusual combination of experiences, because even while you are enjoying the recreations, like the drunk snoring in the pig sty, you are constantly being provoked into thinking about the more serious aspects of life then and now. Perhaps the most unsettling thought of all is that this place existed to subjugate the English and that 'we' would never have got within a bowshot of it!

Open: Mar to Nov: daily 1000–1700
Price guide: B

COLCHESTER

Colchester is proud of its status as Britain's oldest recorded town. It dates back to AD10 when the powerful Cunobelin, king of the Trinovantes tribe, established his capital in the area of Lexden, now a suburb of Colchester. The Roman invasion of AD43 was directed towards this town, and the Emperor Claudius gave strict instructions that before it was taken, he should be summoned from Rome to take his place at the head of the victorious legions. He brought over a few elephants, too, which suitably terrified the tribesmen. Once the conquerors turned west to subdue the rest of southern Britain, Colchester became the colonia of Camulodunum – a settlement for retired soldiers.

In AD60 Boudicca, queen of the Iceni tribe, led a revolt against the Romans and swept through East Anglia in an orgy of hatred, revenge and violence. Colchester was feebly defended, and held out for a mere two days. What followed was destruction on a grand scale: the inhabitants were slaughtered, their bodies mutilated, and those who took refuge in the Temple were burnt alive. The entire settlement was devastated by fire – archaeologists have found thick layers of ash and blackened wattle-and-daub. The Romans won the last battle, of course, and even behaved better towards the natives afterwards. They also belatedly constructed a wall round the rebuilt city. Originally it was over 3,000 yards long and 18 feet high, with bastions and gateways at intervals. Even now almost a mile of it can be seen, and one of the best ways of exploring this

The Hole in the Wall pub on the Roman Wall

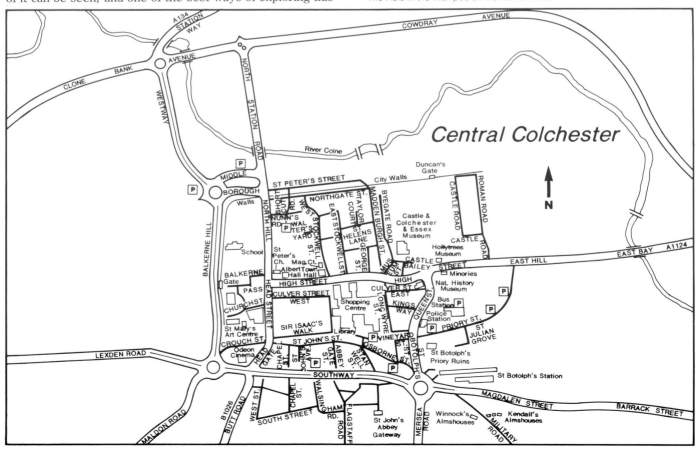

fascinating city is to trace the course of the remains, which include gateways such as the Balkerne Gate, with its neighbouring public house, The Hole in the Wall.

The Normans built their castle on the Roman temple platform. The keep was constructed in 1076 and is the largest ever built. From the beginning Colchester was a royal fortress, able to withstand assaults by ambitious barons. It was three storeys high then; the top floor was removed in 1680. For much of its life it doubled as a prison, receiving its first inmate in 1226, its last in 1835.

Throughout the Middle Ages Colchester grew wealthy on the cloth trade, and part of the city is called the Dutch Quarter, evidence of the Flemish weavers who brought their skill to England in the 16th century.

The English Civil War found East Anglia to be staunchly on the side of Cromwell and the Parliamentary forces. By 1648 the campaign was over, the King was a prisoner, yet Cromwell's army showed no signs of disbanding. Throughout eastern England this was a matter of concern and rebellions broke out, which for the most part were swiftly dealt with. But the royalists of Colchester held out against General Fairfax for twelve weeks, from June until August 1648, and the traces of their battle can be seen today: in East Street, beside the river Colne, stands The Siege House (now a restaurant), which bears the scars of musket fire, obligingly circled in red.

The Castle Museum makes an exellent starting point for a tour of Colchester. The central courtyard has been roofed, and within are imaginatively presented displays of items from the city's long history. There is a wealth of Roman material: the memorial in stone to Marcus Favonius Facilis shows him as a centurion of the Second Legion, holding his vine-staff of office, and the detail is so good a modern armourer could recreate his tunic and weapons. Of the same date, before AD60, is the tombstone to Longinus, a cavalryman from what is now Bulgaria. He is shown riding over a barbarian, and subsequently Boudicca's followers disfigured his features, leaving the trampled victim intact. There is a well-preserved Roman mosaic, the Beryfield pavement, and a model of the Claudian temple. Outside, the Norman gateway tower is crowned with a tree said to have been planted in 1815, the year of Waterloo. In the park behind the castle is the Avignon Garden, with its perfect flower beds.

The Siege House

Close by stands Hollytrees, an 18th-century house with a collection of domestic objects from the last two centuries. The pretty gardens make the ideal place to rest. Opposite is The Minories Art Gallery with its extensive art and craft collections.

Colchester Castle

Churches are not all they seem in this city, and two of them, All Saints (opposite the castle) and Holy Trinity (near the library) have been transformed into museums of natural history and social history respectively. St Botolph's Priory was the first house for Augustinian canons established in England, and was built by the Normans using Roman stone and tile. It was bombarded by the roundheads during the 1648 siege, but the west end with its Norman arch and gigantic pillars gives some idea of its magnificence. Eudo Dapifer, a Norman conqueror, founded St John's Abbey in 1096, and was buried there. Only the 15th-century gateway remains, scarred by cannonballs fired during the siege, but now surrounded by lawns and pretty cottages.

Colchester has largely kept its medieval, not to say Roman, street plan and the effect is most pleasing, particularly in the Lion Shopping Precinct area where old and new merge together without discord. Close by is Tymperley's Clock Museum, exhibiting Colchester-made timepieces. Here lived William Gilberd, physician to Elizabeth I, and said to be the first man to study electricity. Both Gilberd and the Elizabethan composer William Wilbye are buried in Holy Trinity Church a few yards away.

Since the time of the Napoleonic war Colchester was a garrison town for many famous regiments and corps of the British army. The Searchlight Military Tattoo was the

St Botolph's Priory

fame: Dane Skin door means just that, because for centuries the south door was adorned with a small piece of what was said to be the skin of a Viking raider. It seems that the men of Essex had little sympathy to spare for those who desecrated their churches, and the flayed skin was intended to deter others. It seems likely it would! The exhibit is now on show inside. There are also 12th-century wall paintings which are among the best in the county.

The history of Layer Marney Tower, seven miles south-west of Colchester, off the B1022, is a cautionary tale because it shows how even the grandest plans can be upset by considerations of mortality. Sir Henry, first Lord Marney, was a trusted adviser to both Henry VII and Henry VIII, and he embarked on a great project to build a noble house. He began with the gateway, making use of the latest ideas from Italy, and gradually a tribute to the Renaissance began to soar above the trees. Unfortunately Sir Henry died in 1523, and the workmen must have been directed to adorn his monument in the church of St Mary the Virgin nearby, where he rests in a tomb of black marble under an elaborate canopy. His son and sole heir, Sir John, died only two years later. Thus only the gatehouse tower survives to hint at the splendour he planned. It is built of brick, and its eight floors have many windows which are among its most striking features. It is open to the public and offers excellent views over the countryside.

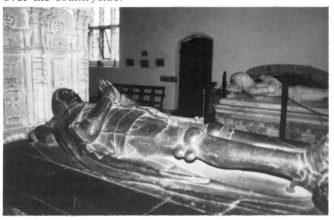
The Layer Marney Tombs

largest in Great Britain. More recently, the town has held Classical Music Spectaculars, with fireworks and festivities during the summer months. These not only entertain the many visitors to the town, but also raise money for charity.

Colchester Zoo is situated to the south-west of the town in 40 acres of parkland, and contains over 150 species, from rhinos to otters, crocodiles to emus. Feeding time offers the best opportunity to see animals, but there are also entertaining events at other times which include displays of birds of prey, sea lions and snakes – and the elephants' bath time. The excellent programme given to every visitor contains a cheerful map so no one needs to miss anything. There are also noticeboards allowing you to judge the relative heights, weights and skills of all sorts of animals – including humans, who come out rather badly!

Outside Colchester there are several places of interest, two of them in the region of Lexden, which is likely to have been the site of Cunobelin's capital. Lexden Triple Dyke was excavated in 1961 and is thought to mark the defences. Even more evocative is the Lexden Tumulus, excavated in 1924. Legend told of King Cunobelin being buried in gold armour, so there was considerable excitement when pieces of gold and chain mail were found in a grave here. We will probably never know for sure, but it is nice to think we know the whereabouts of Shakespeare's Cymbeline, the nursery rhyme's Old King Cole and the last of the Ancient Britons all rolled into one! The site is in a field down Fitzwalter Road, off the old A12, but the finds are on show in the Castle Museum.

Five miles west of Colchester is the village of Copford Green where the church has a particularly grisly claim to

Colchester Castle and Museum
Open: All year: Mon to Sat 1000–1700, Mar to Nov, also Sun 1400–1700
Price guide: B

Minories Art Gallery
Open: All year: Mon to Sat 1000–1700
Price guide: Free

Timperleys Museum
Open: April to Oct: Tues to Sat 1000–1700
Price guide: Free

Natural History Museum
Open: All year: Tues to Sat 1000–1700
Price guide: Free

Colchester Zoo
Open: April to July daily 0930–1800, Aug: daily 0930–1830, Sept: daily 0930–1800, Oct to April: 0930 to an hour before dusk
Price guide: C

Layer Marney Tower
Open: April to Oct: Sun to Fri 1400–1800, bank holidays 1100–1800
Price guide: B

BOURNE MILL, COLCHESTER

There can be few places that are more agreeable to live in than a water-mill. It represents the power of a bygone age, when each building was truly independent, and not connected to the others by the modern umbilical cords supplying electricity, gas, communications – and even water. The tenant of Bourne Mill can walk to the centre of the living room, look down through a glass panel in the floorboards and see a full-size overshot water-wheel waiting the command to turn. A nearby lever opens the sluice gate and the main drive shaft is soon revolving at the bottom of the stairs! Across the ceiling more wheels and canvas straps rumble into life and the work of the day can begin. All in a charming cottage room.

Bourne Mill is in Colchester. The B1025 to West Mersea passes two army barracks and a fork to the left leads between a row of suburban houses and a lake. Parking is at the roadside, and it is quite likely that before the ignition is switched off the ducks will be waiting to be fed.

The Bourne Brook runs into the River Colne, and once supported three mills. In addition to the obvious income from milling, the owner could always count on rent from fishermen, a tradition which survives today as the bank is still lined with permit holders who stare into the depths, each seeing the catch of a lifetime.

The present building is of stone construction, with an impressive weather-board lucomb or locum in the roof from which the sack hoist operated. It has ornate pinnacled gables which suggest the Dutch influence which was prevalent at the time of its construction. The materials used to construct the mill include Roman brick, Abbey stone and Walton mud. The main doorway support combines all three. The walls are 27 inches thick.

The mill was built in 1591 for Sir Thomas Lucas, an Essex gentleman, who used it to spin yarn for the manufacture of bay, a light woollen fabric. In the 19th century the mill was adapted to grind corn. The changes this entailed took up much more room and it was at this time that the main floor of the mill was invaded by the machinery seen today. Previously it had only occupied the lower room beside the water-wheel. At one point in its history the fishing parties who surrounded the pond were as important as the milling activity. A particularly large pike was sent to Queen Victoria, and we must hope it arrived in a decent condition, although her reaction to the gift is not on record. Other things brought to the bank were less triumphant. The large expanse of unguarded water proved too great a temptation for the desperate and deranged of Colchester and it soon had the reputation of being a suicide's final port of call. Mrs Legerton, the daughter of a tenant of Bourne Mill, recalled helping her father bring two bodies to land in a single night.

By the turn of the century advances in flour milling had bypassed small water-mills. Yet for a few more years it survived by producing animal feed. Some time after the First World War Bourne Mill ceased working, and was presented to the National Trust in 1936. Today it provides an oasis in the city. Fishermen and ducks occupy themselves with the pond, and the garden is a delightful feast of colour with waterside plants, herbs, flowers and weeping willow.

National Trust
Open: All bank holidays, Sun & Mon. Jul & Aug: Sun & Tues 1400–1730
Price guide: A

THE RIVER COLNE

The waterfront at Wivenhoe

Since Roman times the Colne estuary has been farmed for oysters. In the 19th century over a hundred oyster boats worked the creeks for what were described as 'West Mersea Natives'. Since then this stretch of coast has witnessed enormous changes in the local way of life: once it was smuggling, then sea fishing, next building ocean racers and most recently yachting and tourism. But the faithful oyster has kept going through it all, and to this day Colchester shows its gratitude by holding the great oyster feast in October, to which the Mayor, Corporation and invited guests sit down. The oyster beds are hardly available for inspection, but the shoreline is pock-marked with man-made pools in which the oysters are stored.

Mersea Island is linked to the mainland by The Strood, a causeway created by the Romans. To see from this vantage point the sun set across the glistening mud flats of Ray Creek is a truly memorable experience. The Mersea shoreline is a wonderful mixture of boat-building yards, attractive chandleries, the Lifeboat station and of course, shops with oysters for sale. The museum in the High Street tells the history of the island, and includes a gun punt, a reminder that in days gone by wildfowling was another source of income for the riverman.

Brightlingsea was a port in the Middle Ages and continues so to this day. It has the distinction of being one of the Cinque Ports, which made an agreement with medieval kings that in return for tax advantages they would supply ships of war when requested to do so. Brightlingsea retains the air of a busy boatbuilding and trading centre, while the more recent arrival of the pleasure yacht has not been neglected. There is a fine open hard by the Custom House, and those with unsteady sea legs can watch the holiday sailor go about his inexplicable pursuits. It is odd that Brightlingsea church should be so far out of the town, but one explanation lies in its proximity to Alresford Creek, once a bustling waterfront but now the haunt of herons.

St Osyth Priory Gateway

St Osyth Priory gateway is spoken of as being one of the finest in the land. The delicate flint flushwork is carried across two enormous towers and over the great gateway. St George and the Dragon are depicted in stone, too, but the dragon has a handicap: his tail has a knot in it! The property is owned by the de Chair family, who have res-

tored the house and gardens. There is a fine collection of paintings, including 'Whistlejacket' by Stubbs, who made a career out of painting horses. Part of the priory is now a convalescent home. St Osyth was a nun beheaded by Vikings in 653. Apparently she picked up her head and walked with it to a nearby church. Because the locked door swung open to receive her she is also the patron saint of those who lose keys!

Further up along the Colne's tree-lined length is Wivenhoe, an attractive quayside village. At the top of Rose Lane is a fine example of pargetting (ornamental plaster-work), and many of the narrow lanes contain pretty gardens and restored cottages. The Rose and Crown on the river-front is the perfect place from which to watch the world go by.

Higher up still, and on the east bank, there is the University of Essex, while opposite there is the un-likely combination of uses described as Fingringhoe Wick Ranges and Nature Reserve. In fact the military are safe and conscientious neighbours, and the reserve, which covers 125 acres, is a sanctuary for many species of birds.

Mersea Island Museum
Open: May to Oct: Wed to Sun 1400–1700
Price guide: A

St Osyth's Priory
Open: May to Sept: Garden & Monument: daily 1000–1700, Art collection: daily except Sat 1030–1230, 1430–1630
Price guide: B

Fingringhoe Nature Reserve
Open: Daily, except Mon 0900–1800
Price guide: Free

THE ESSEX SUNSHINE COAST

It is easy to believe that in summer the whole of the British population makes the exodus to the resorts of the Mediterranean. So it comes as a surprise to know that a fair proportion of us stay in Britain and enjoy a fortnight of gentle fun in such resorts as we find on the Essex Sunshine Coast.

Clacton-on-Sea is the southernmost of the trio of holiday spots and also the largest. It has amusement arcades, ice cream kiosks and a giant pier; but it also has an air of gentility. Perhaps it is the line of elegant hotels fronting the Marine Parade, or the beautifully maintained gardens at the top of the steep slope to the sea; perhaps also the predominance of deckchairs betokening the less frantic kind of holiday which may be had here. The beach is seven miles long and south facing, and the soft sand shelves gently. Once down the hill, you may take a long, level walk by the shore. No dogs are allowed here. For the young and energetic, the pier is the centre of activity. Opened in 1872, it covers a staggering five acres and it has many attractions, including thrilling fairground rides. Fishermen may also try their hand here, or you may just take an interesting walk.

Horses exercising on Frinton beach

Just to the north-east lies Frinton-on-Sea, separated from Clacton by green fields. There is a vast difference between these two resorts. In contrast to Clacton's busy atmosphere, Frinton is quiet and calm – there are no pubs – and its low blocks of private flats look out on to the open expanse of the Greensward and down to the sea. Here is a leisurely town offering an antidote to the fun of the fair.

Further up the coast again is Walton-on-the-Naze which is above all a family resort. The beach at low tide is a child's dream – perfect for sandcastles, beach cricket and paddling, for the sand shelves so gently that you can wade out for a hundred yards and the sea will still only reach your knees! The pier is almost half a mile long and although it has its share of amusements it is popular with anglers. The town is most pleasant, with many green areas and flower beds, and even the shops have an appealing village individuality. Towards the northern side are facilities

Walton-on-the Naze sands

such as a children's playground, clock golf and tennis courts, and the former lifeboat station is now a Heritage Centre. North-east of Walton is the Naze, an open area topping the cliffs, with a conspicuous brick tower built as a navigational aid in the 18th century. From here there is a superb panorama back towards the beach on one hand, and inland towards the Walton Backwaters on the other. Part of the Naze is a nature reserve and it is a good place for spotting migrating birds in spring and autumn. There is also a short nature trail to follow and you may be lucky enough to see rare butterflies.

The Walton Backwaters are an area of saltmarsh and creeks, another favourite spot for birdwatchers and a haven for yachtsmen planning to explore the estuaries of the Stour, Orwell or Deben. From Hamford Water (Arthur Ransome's *Secret Water*) a shallow boat may reach Beaumont Quay, built with stones brought from the old London Bridge. This is a place of picturesque names as well as of unspoilt scenery: the Twizzle, Skipper's Island, and, just north of Kirby-le-Soken, the saltmarsh called the Wade. One of Ransome's characters, crossing the Wade on the way back from Walton, says 'I don't suppose the people in the town ever dream they're so near the Secret Water', and the calm of the Backwaters remains unruffled by the proximity of those busy resorts.

Kirby-le-Soken Quay

Clacton Pier
Open: Daily all year: from 0900
Price guide: Rides vary

Walton Heritage Centre
Open: July to Aug: daily 1400–1700
Price guide: A

HARWICH

Thousands of tourists pass through Harwich to and from the Continent, but it is sad that so few linger in this old port.

The *Mayflower* was a Harwich vessel, and its captain Christopher Jones lived in a house in King Street. From here in 1620 began the voyage which led to the colonisation of Massachusetts. It is only fair to point out the ship leaked like a sieve, and subsequently had to put into the more famously associated ports of Dartmouth and Plymouth.

The 17th Century treadmill crane

Samuel Pepys was associated with Harwich. Much more than just a diarist, he was Secretary to the Navy during the reign of Charles II, and during the Dutch Wars he maintained the Royal Navy as a fighting fleet. He made many visits to Harwich because he was not only keen to inspect the dockyard, but was also the Member of Parliament for the borough. From this time dates the unique treadmill crane, which used to be employed in the dockyard, but now stands on the Green, south of the harbour.

Dovercourt Lighthouse

There may seem to be an abundance of lighthouses, but they were not all in use at the same time. In 1818 two were built, called High and Low for obvious reasons. The High dominates the town, and its brick tower is now a private residence. The Low lighthouse is sited on the seaward side of Harwich. It is made of metal and looks rather squat, as though it feels it should be taller! It now houses the Maritime Museum. Of later vintage is Dovercourt, the creation of another MP for the town, John Bagshaw, who in 1854 exploited the coming of the railway by turning this part of the coast into a fashionable resort. Just a short distance to the south are two black-and-white octagonal metal towers on stilts; these were built in 1863 to replace the earlier lighthouses. They are now redundant, too. The Green and the seashore offer wonderful views across this busy estuary. Do bring a pair of binoculars.

During the wars against Napoleon Harwich was a naval base, indeed The Three Cups hotel is proud to remind visitors that Nelson stayed there before sailing out to do battle. To protect the anchorage a great redoubt was built in 1810. This massive circular fortification was designed to withstand a siege, and its cannon had a clear field of fire in all directions. It is surrounded by a dry moat 20 feet deep. Within there is a parade ground and accommodation for 300 soldiers. It last saw service in the 1939–45 war. Now its solitary cannon glares down at the encircling allotments whose lines of advancing French beans stir uneasy memories. In 1969 work began on restoring the fort, and it is now open to the public. The entrance is opposite 43, Main Street.

Harwich looks like a Dutch painting when seen from Shotley, with the spire of St Nicholas' Church rising above the waterfront. There are many listed buildings, among them several old pubs, such as the Angel, Alma and Globe. The passenger terminal at Parkeston Quay dates from 1883 and is not so interesting as some of the older wharves. From Halfpenny Pier a passenger ferry used to cross to Felixstowe; nowadays the *Brightlingsea* will take you for a lovely trip around the bay, but the fare has gone up a bit! Trinity House has its Headquarters here, hence the red lightships anchored in the bay, and also the yard full of brightly painted buoys, as though at a reunion.

Wholly unexpected, but no less welcome, is the Harwich Electric Palace built in 1911. This 'silver screen' cinema ended its active commercial life in 1953. It has been restored to its original condition and now gives screenings of old films in authentic surroundings.

The Redoubt
Open: All year: daily 1000–1700
Price guide: A

Low Lighthouse Maritime Museum
Open: Easter to Sept: 1400–1700
Price guide: A

THE STOUR ESTUARY

The Stour estuary is beautiful throughout its eight-mile length, and its higher reaches have become our common heritage through the works of John Constable. Rivers are more than just sights: they combine sounds, scents and emotions in an almost tangible form, and any attempt to experience their subtle magic must involve waterborne travel. These brief notes, unfortunately, address themselves only to the landlubber!

Mistley Towers

Mistley is exactly what a river port should be. It lies at the mouth of the Stour, and looks out over a vast expanse of water, across to gentle hills and rich farmland. At low tide, which leaves only the barest of channels, the mudflats teem with waterbirds and the wrecks which poke through the ooze speak volumes of how little the business of the town has changed. From Furze Hill there are magnificent views, and the imagination needs little prompting to appreciate the meaning of Mistley: the 'wood where mistletoe grew'. At Baltic Wharf coastal craft still tie up, unload

The swan fountain

timber and take on grain, while the mute swans glide silently past. Mistley has the simple lines of a Georgian town, which is hardly surprising, because it was for a time intended as a spa. Richard Rigby inherited the estate in 1732, enlisting the help of Robert Adam who rebuilt the church in 1776, giving it two tall towers in the classical style. The church was pulled down in 1870 but the towers were permitted to remain, if only because they had become navigational marks! Rigby's hopes for Mistley were dashed when he was dismissed from government office and bankrupted in 1782, and the unusual (and lifelike) Swan fountain is all that remains of his spa.

The tree-lined banks are as much as a mile apart at Holbrook, but the distance is unimportant because sound travels with exquisite clarity and the anchored craft are dwarfed by the scale of the landscape. The Royal Hospital School here was originally established at Greenwich in 1715 for the sons of sailors. The present grand buildings bear a striking resemblance to the Naval College at Dartmouth, complete with a lofty clock tower, parade ground and figurehead overlooking the river. From Lower Holbrook to the water's edge is a pleasant quarter-mile walk.

Barge moored at Shotley

Erwarton Hall has a fine, ornate brick gatehouse, which dates from 1549, while the present house was built in 1575. Local legend says Anne Boleyn stayed at an earlier house on the site, and met Henry VIII there. Before her execution she is reputed to have said 'Let my heart be taken to Erwarton where I spent so many happy days'. In the 19th century a small heart-shaped casket was discovered sealed in a wall in the church, and shame on you if you doubt the story! The local pub is appropriately called The Queen's Head. For many years the Hall was the official residence of the Captain of HMS *Ganges*, the naval training establishment at Shotley. Up until 1905 there really was a wooden warship of that name anchored there, but then a land base was created which served the Royal Navy until the 1970s. A marina was opened in June 1988 on the Orwell side of the Shotley peninsula. The views are spectacular, looking across the rivers Orwell and Stour to Felixstowe with its giant cranes and Harwich with its picturesque skyline. Off Shotley in 884 King Alfred defeated the Danes in a great naval encounter, taking 16 ships, and drowning all his prisoners. To this day it is known as Bloody Point.

Mistley Towers
Open: All reasonable times
Price guide: Free

SUFFOLK

CONSTABLE COUNTRY

The Haywain

In 1832, as John Constable was travelling to London from his family's home in East Bergholt, he passed through Dedham Vale on the Suffolk–Essex border and remarked on how beautiful it was. 'Yes, sir', one of his fellow-passengers answered, 'This is Constable's country'. And so it has been ever since. This valley of the river Stour has been immortalised by Constable and in the minds of English people everywhere remains the image of all that is best in the English countryside.

John Constable was born in East Bergholt in 1776, the fourth of six children of a prosperous corn merchant. Golding Constable had inherited Flatford Mill on the Stour and he later acquired the mill at Dedham and a windmill at East Bergholt. He also had a ship moored at Mistley, which was used to transport the grain to London. John attended Dedham Grammar School, and after an unsuccessful spell as an apprentice miller he left his younger brother to continue the family business and set off to study at the Royal Academy. He was homesick in London and constantly harked back to his boyhood in East Bergholt: 'I love every stile and stump, and every lane in the village, so deep-rooted are early impressions'; and so he would return to Suffolk to spend the summer. As he walked from his parents' home to visit relatives in Dedham and Nayland, he filled notebooks with detailed sketches of the landscape. These he later used to compose his masterpieces: 'willows, old rotten banks, slimy posts and brick work . . . I love such things . . . As long as I do paint I shall never cease to paint such places . . . Painting is but another word for feeling'. It is said that he sat so still to observe and paint that one day a field mouse was found in his pocket! On one visit home he met Maria Bicknell, the grand-daughter of the Rector of East Bergholt and 12 years Constable's junior. There was much opposition to their match, since Constable was, and seemed likely to remain, an impecunious artist. But after a courtship lasting 16 years they were finally married, and spent 12 happy years together before Maria died of consumption. Constable was devastated: 'I shall never feel again as I have felt, the face of the world is totally changed to me'. Despite professional success (he was elected to the Royal Academy in 1829), Constable lived the rest of his life quietly, caring for his seven children and surrounded by his devoted friends. He died in 1837 and was buried beside his beloved Maria in Hampstead Parish Church.

'Constable Country' is an area within about ten miles of East Bergholt, from where the artist would set off on his sketching expeditions, on foot or on horseback. The landscape here is familiar to us all through Constable's depiction of it: rich farmland, gentle hills, tall trees shading peaceful lanes, and running through the valley, the River Stour itself.

St Mary's churchyard at East Bergholt showing Golding Constable's grave and the bell house

Any lover of Constable's art will wish to begin by seeing his home village of East Bergholt. Constable described it as being 'pleasantly situated in the most cultivated part of Suffolk, on a spot which overlooks the fertile valley of the Stour'. The village has changed somewhat since Constable's time, and unfortunately the place of his birth was pulled down in the last century. But a small studio used by the artist still stands next to the garage – it is now a private house. Perhaps the most interesting building is the Church of St Mary. Constable sketched and painted it many times; his great friend Dunthorne, Willy Lott and Constable's parents are all buried in the churchyard. Here, too, is the unique 16th-century bell house. Because the church tower was never built due to lack of funds, the bells had to be housed in a specially constructed cage, where they are counterweighted and rung by hand.

Just south of East Bergholt lies Flatford. Here in the Stour valley is the mill owned by Golding Constable and painted many times by his son. Built in 1733, the mill itself is now a Field Studies Centre, offering courses in such topics as geography, natural history and photography; there are short summer courses, too, in calligraphy, cycling and nature studies, to name but a few. The building, therefore, is not open to the general public, though it may still be viewed from outside. The best time to visit is in the late afternoon, when the warm red bricks exude a marvellous glow reflected in the mill pond.

Willy Lott's cottage forms part of what must be Constable's most famous painting, *The Haywain* of 1821. This huge canvas took five months to complete. Constable painted it in London, based on a full scale study of the scene – a typical Suffolk waggon crossing the ford in front of Willy Lott's cottage on a summer's day. Willy Lott was a semi-invalid whose delicate health prevented him from ever straying from his home – though it did not stop him living to the grand old age of 88! The cottage is much as it was and may still be seen across the ford, now calm and green, encroached upon by willowherb, reeds and bindweed. There is something magical in being able to take up the artist's standpoint and consider this scene which is so

Countryside near Boxted

familiar and yet whose beauty is ever renewed.

From this point you may walk on to East Bergholt, or return back up the lane towards the bridge. This leads past the Granary Barn Museum which has a collection of rural bygones including bicycles, agricultural implements and craftwork. Bridge House, now owned by the National

Willy Lott's cottage as it looks today. It formed part of Constable's *The Haywain*

Flatford Mill

husband lived in Dedham, so Constable was a frequent visitor. The mill has been greatly modernised, but the river here is still shady and pleasant. In the main street the eye is drawn to the magnificent church which Constable featured in many of his paintings. There is another connection with art here. Sir Alfred Munnings, the 20th-century artist who specialised in painting horses, lived in Castle House; it is now open to the public.

Cottages at Stoke-by-Nayland

Just to the north is Stratford St Mary. Unfortunately, the main A12 divides the church from the village, but it is a beautiful building. The village is rather long and has lost some of the beauty it had when Constable sketched it in the 1820s.

To the west lie the villages of Stoke-by-Nayland and Nayland. The former has a splendid church tower, 120 feet high and visible from a great distance. This was another of Constable's favourites. Opposite the church is a group of timbered cottages, and the village has many pretty buildings. So it is with Nayland. The church has a painting by Constable over the altar, but the village is worth visiting for Fen Street alone, where the cottages have individual bridges across the stream.

Trust, is a low thatched cottage with cream-washed walls. Here you may buy postcards or refreshments. On the opposite side of the bridge you may hire a rowing boat, or walk along the mill pond's edge and admire the view of swans and reflected sunlight.

The village of Dedham lies on the south bank of the Stour. It is a delightful place whose main street retains much of the charm it must have had in Constable's day. The mill was owned by his father, and later his sister and her

Dedham village

View towards Stoke-by-Nayland church

Sir Alfred Munnings Art Museum
Open: April to Oct: Sun & Wed 1400–1700, Aug: Sun, bank holiday
Mon, Thur & Sat 1400–1700
Price guide: B

GAINSBOROUGH'S HOUSE, SUDBURY

The name of Thomas Gainsborough conjures up his portraits of elegant ladies and proud gentlemen set serenely in classical landscapes. Gainsborough is one of our best portraitists and the nature of his work obliged him to spend much of his life in the busy society of Bath and London; but his keen perception and attention to detail were first practised on the landscapes of his native county, and he always acknowledged the debt he owed to those early years of observing the scenery: 'Suffolk made me a painter'.

The house where Gainsborough was born in 1727 stands in the street which now bears his name, just off the Market Square in the town of Sudbury. His father was a wool merchant, and Thomas was the youngest of nine children. He showed talent from an early age and loved sketching the beautiful scenery of the Stour valley. On one occasion he played truant after successfully forging a note to his headmaster which asked 'Give Tom a holiday'. When his father found out the ruse, he was furious. But on seeing the lovely sketches his son had made on his day off, he prophesied that 'One day Tom will astonish the world'. So impressed was he that he sent the 13-year-old Thomas to London to study art. Here the boy made a modest living by selling drawings and painting backgrounds for eminent artists. Here, too, he later met and married the beautiful Margaret Burr, and together they returned to Sudbury, to a house in Friar's Street, just a few hundred yards from

Gainsborough's House seen from the garden

Front view of Gainsborough's House

restored and is maintained as a memorial to Gainsborough as well as an art centre: there is a craft gallery, a research library and a print workshop, so the creative process is continued from the past into the present. The façade of the house is early Georgian, and the interior is simply furnished in the same style. There are information boards giving an illustrated biography of the artist, and mementos and contemporary paintings. Most importantly, there are letters, sketches and paintings by Gainsborough. Each room deals with a different period of his life in Suffolk, Bath and London, and the excellent portraits are accompanied by detailed notes. The overall impression is of a spacious and genteel dwelling which perfectly conveys the atmosphere of the 18th century.

On the ground floor is a large gallery which is used for temporary exhibitions, and this leads to a lovely sunny garden. In the summer this is the setting for displays of modern sculpture – in strange contrast to the old-fashioned shrubs and trees of this walled haven.

Gainsborough's statue on Market Hill with St Peter's Church in the background

where Thomas was born. They had two daughters who appear in several charming and graceful portraits. Gainsborough had a number of commissions at this time, and one notable portrait is of Robert Andrews and his wife, seen relaxing with their dog on their estate, while to the horizon stretches the Suffolk landscape with its golden cornfields and wooded valleys. So began Gainsborough's life as a portraitist; soon he moved to Ipswich where his reputation quickly grew. He progressed to Bath in 1759 and thence to London, where he died of cancer at the age of 61.

Gainsborough portrait of Mr & Mrs Andrews

Gainsborough's house was run down and about to become a bicycle store when it was bought by the Gainsborough's House Society in the 1950s. Now it has been fully

The town is understandably proud of its links with the artist and a statue of Gainsborough, palette in hand, stands on the Market Hill as a permanent reminder of this most famous of Sudbury's sons.

Open: All year: Sun & bank holidays 1400–1700, Jan to April: Tues to Sat 1000–1600, April to Oct: Tues to Sat 1000–1700, Nov to Dec: Tues to Sat 1000–1600
Price guide: B

LONG MELFORD

Long Melford presents a picture of the English village as we all imagine it should be. A cluster of pretty cottages, with roses and ivy clinging to their pastel walls, stand opposite a red-brick Tudor almshouse, while in the background rises a fine old flint church. Add to this 13 acres of village green and you have a scene of rare beauty. Once gypsies used to hold a horse fair here, beside the brick conduit which stands at the junction with the road to Cavendish. Now the trade is more often in ice-cream, and picnickers enjoy the views.

Trinity Hospital, the almshouse, was built by Sir William Cordell of Melford Hall in 1573. It was designed for 12 old men and two servants, so they must have lived in some comfort, for it is very large. The expanse of brick is prevented from seeming too austere by the white cupola which rises from the centre of the roof.

Lane leading to Holy Trinity Church

Holy Trinity Church can certainly claim to be the finest church in Suffolk. It was built in the late 15th century by the clothiers of Long Melford, including John Clopton of nearby Kentwell Hall, and is a spectacular monument to the Perpendicular style. Around the battlements are the names of the benefactors. The tower was struck by lightning in 1709, and was rebuilt in brick soon afterwards; only in 1903 was it faced with flint. There are almost 100 windows, many of them containing very old stained glass, so the interior is bathed in sunlight and colour. The window in the north aisle showing the Duchess of Norfolk is believed to have been used by the illustrator Tenniel as the model for the Duchess in *Alice in Wonderland*! In his will dated 1494 John Clopton provided for a chapel to be established, and it has a striking lily window. The chantry chapel next to it has a fireplace for the priest whose job it was to offer prayers for his soul. The Lady Chapel is unusual in that it is almost detached from the church, and has an interior cloister. It has a very fine carved roof. For centuries this was the 'Publicke school for Melford', and there is still a multiplication table on the east wall.

The best tomb in the church shows an armoured figure asleep upon a rug. This is Sir William Cordell, the builder of Melford Hall which overlooks the green on the eastern side. He was a wily lawyer who rose to become

Melford Hall

Speaker of the Commons. Melford Hall was built in 1560 on the site of a hunting lodge used by the Abbot of Bury St Edmunds. The bricks were probably made with clay from the present village pond. When Queen Elizabeth visited in 1578 she was greeted by 2000 men, and treated to lavish entertainment and 'sumptuous feastinges'. The house today reflects the changes carried out in later centuries, but the Long Gallery survives. The most notable features are the six towers, each with a lead cupola, which stand out against the sky. An elegant octagonal summer house peeps above the high perimeter wall. Topiary hedges, an ornamental pond and a sunken garden make this a lovely place to visit. The east front shades a large courtyard with a central fountain and beyond is wooded parkland grazed by sheep. In 1786 Melford Hall became the property of the Hyde-Parker family, who included several distinguished admirals. It is now in the care of the National Trust.

The village is about a mile long and Tudor rubs shoulders with Georgian and Victorian throughout. The tree-lined street has many delightful inns and shops and is worth exploring at length!

The octagonal summer house at Melford Hall

Melford Hall
National Trust
Open: April: Sat, Sun & bank holiday Mon 1400–1730, May to Sept: Wed, Thur, Sat & Sun 1400–1730, Oct: Sat & Sun 1400–1730
Price guide: B

KENTWELL HALL

'Have ye news of the Spaniards?' asks a child, fear and excitement in her face. The year is 1588 and while the Armada is expected daily in the Channel, a great country house in Long Melford makes frantic preparations to defend England and her Queen.

A historical re-creation at Kentwell Hall is an experience of the highest order: the owners, Mr and Mrs Patrick Phillips, lead us through a time tunnel to reveal their Hall as it was 400 years ago when it belonged to William Clopton and his family. The house, which stands just north of Long Melford at the end of a long drive across sweet smelling meadowland, was built in the mid-16th century and is surrounded by the prettiest of moats. A narrow brick bridge leads to the courtyard, with its unusual brick-paved mosaic maze, and bursts of colour signal flower beds, waterlilies and trailing plants. The setting is perfect.

At the far end of the meadow a group of soldiers from the Trained Band are attempting to teach very raw recruits the basics of soldiering: archery, quarterstaff combat and the use of artillery. Their leader does not take kindly to being observed by outlandishly-clad strangers, and may even accuse us of being spies in the pay of Spain. We shall move on, towards the workers in the estate fields; they are simple friendly folk, more interested in learning from us the latest rumours from London, and in noticing that 'thou hast a strange turn of speech'. Against the background of Kentwell's warm brick, they seem to live a life of idyllic contentment, leaning on their pitchforks and drinking ale from leather bottles. Everywhere there is activity: sawyers tackle a giant tree trunk, smiths hurry to produce weapons for the soldiers as the labourers slowly gather in the harvest.

Inside the Hall the servants bustle to and fro, politely elbowing the visitors aside with the command: 'Make passage!' In the kitchen, cook, maids, bakers and assorted wenches struggle to cope with the mountains of vegetables brought in by the gardeners. Light filters through the slats of the high windows and casts stripes across the walls. Mistress Bett puts the finishing touches to her elderflower fritters and rede rose dessert. In the Great Hall 'persons of qualitie' heed the words of their dancing master, singing teacher or lutenist, and look forward to their meal. A company of travelling players is rehearsing a work by young Christopher Marlowe.

Outside the children are playing, enjoying a respite from the strictures of their master. Around them the work of the house goes on: in the dairy, cheese is being made; the spinners and weavers ply their craft in the Great Hall, while the dyers plunge cloth into vats of richly-coloured liquid. Beyond, in the walled garden, the herbs are tended, and a tramp lurks suspiciously in the long grass beside the moat, where fish elude the rod of Will the basketmaker. Bee-keepers, ostlers, shepherds – all these and more live and work here, frequently huddling together to gossip, or simply to offer a bite to eat: 'Master Weaver, wilt thou partake of some victuals, 'tis but humble fare.'

A day at Kentwell is not humble fare; it is an indelible experience and as near as we shall ever get to stepping back in time. And don't tell them the Armada was defeated – you'll break the spell.

Overlooking the moat

House and gardens
Open: April to June: Sun 1200–1700, July to Sept: daily, Oct: Sun
Price guide: C

Historical Re-creation
Open: June to July. Check for dates
Price guide: C

THE UPPER STOUR VALLEY

Cavendish has the sort of beauty which makes it a favoured choice for chocolate boxes or jigsaw puzzles: a broad and pleasant green rising to a group of pink-washed and thatched cottages beside a 14th-century church. But the village has much more than this one famous view: the whole of the main street is lined with picturesque old houses and inns. Cavendish became prosperous in the heyday of the wool trade; now it no longer has such wealth, but the pride of the inhabitants in its old world charm is evident in the care lavished on its homes and gardens.

The cottages on the green are almshouses which have the collective and rather surprising name of Hyde Park Corner. They were restored from ruin in the 1950s, but later burned down and have now been rebuilt. Behind them is the fine church of St Mary. The chancel was built by the will of Sir John Cavendish who died in 1381 and left the handsome sum of £40 for the purpose. He had been Chief Justice under Richard II, and it was his younger son who killed the insurrectionist Wat Tyler, for which the King awarded to him and his heirs for ever a £40 pension. But the rebels of Suffolk, hearing the news of Tyler's death, turned on Sir John who had time only to hide his valuables in the belfry before he was caught by the mob, dragged off to Bury St Edmunds and killed.

Cavendish is the proud possessor of one of England's few vineyards. This has been established at Nether Hall, a Tudor house to the north of the church. In 1972 the vintner Basil Ambrose planted the first vines and soon was producing prize-winning wines. Now the Hall, grounds and vineyard are open daily to the public. Visitors may take a complimentary glass of wine or buy themselves a larger quantity to enjoy!

Tucked away on the south side of the main street, close to the duck pond, is the Sue Ryder Foundation Headquarters and Museum. At the end of a leafy drive is the Old Rectory, now a Sue Ryder Home in which 40 sick and disabled people live and are cared for. Here, too, lives Sue Ryder – Lady Ryder of Warsaw, to give her proper title. The museum building is to the right, and for a small charge the visitor can learn not so much about Sue Ryder herself, but about the Foundation which bears her name. True, the first display of the museum shows a re–creation of Sue Ryder's childhood home, which illustrates the forces which shaped her personality, but after the security of family life we are plunged into the sorrow of war.

Sue Ryder served with the S.O.E., mainly in Eastern Europe, and she was touched by the suffering of its people; she became determined to help them positively and directly – not for her the delegation of duties! She visited Polish prisoners held after the war in German prisons, bringing them comfort and news of their families, and succeeded in having the vast majority of her 'boys' repatriated; she set up the Foundation in the early 1950s and

Cottages and St Mary's church on the Green at Cavendish

established the network of Homes. Originally these were simple prefabricated buildings shipped out to Poland and Yugoslavia and erected by British and Commonwealth volunteers. Now the work has spread all over the world; there are more than 20 Homes in Britain, and their aim is to alleviate the suffering of all kinds of people.

The Priest's House at Clare

This museum acts as an exhibition hall for the fine craft work carried out by those who live in the Homes. There are carved wooden figures, beautiful rugs, intricate embroidery and crochet work, and soft toys, all created by leprosy patients, paraplegics, the mentally handicapped and others. Details are sometimes given of the patient and skilful men and women who in their suffering created such works of art. There is, for instance, a rosary made from scraps of bread saved from their meagre ration by two women prisoners in a concentration camp, or the lattice-work bag woven by a young paraplegic. The museum makes us aware of the continuing problems of the world, and encourages us to resolve them. One of the inspiring thoughts quoted here is Donne's famous reminder of our common humanity: 'No man is an island'. In considering the work of the Foundation, you cannot doubt it.

The town of Clare is a very ancient settlement, called 'Clara' in Domesday Book, and Richard de Bienfait, the Norman knight to whom the manor was given after the Conquest, adopted the surname 'de Clare' which he passed to his descendants. The family has left its mark in many spheres: Clare College, County Clare, The Dukes of Clarence and even claret. Once the castle built by de Clare dominated the town; now only a stump of wall remains on the summit of the 100 foot mound. In 1865 a youngster, Walter Lorking, was digging in the bailey yard and found a gold crucifix studded with pearls – a reliquary made, perhaps, during the reign of Edward III. Queen Victoria expressed a desire to own it, and in return gave Walter three gold sovereigns.

Today the grounds of the castle resound to the cries of children and the calls of their parents, for the area has been made into a country park. The old railway station is now an exhibition centre, with a clear and interesting account of life in a medieval castle, and there are nature trails to follow. Climbing the castle mound should afford a glorious view of Clare, but unfortunately the view is often obscured by undergrowth.

At the centre of the town is the church of St Peter and St Paul. This large and beautiful building dates from the 14th century. Inside it is spacious and light, with many points of interest, like the 16th-century brass lectern with its proud eagle.

Overlooking the churchyard is the Priest's House of 1473, now a museum, which is clad in pargetting of a lavish and splendid style. As well as panels of intricate flowers, the west wall shows the arms of the Clares. Of particular note is the carved windowsill on the first floor.

There are scores of lovely houses in Clare, and they are best explored on foot. Many remain as their first owners intended, while others bear witness to enormous changes. The Grove, for example, possesses all the characteristics of a 15th-century timber house, but it has a 19th-century doorway with Greek Doric columns. Despite this the effect is harmonious. The Swan Inn, too, is worth looking at with its magnificent 10-foot-long carved beam showing a white swan chained between two trees. These pretty buildings, the wide leafy roads and abundance of flowers make this town one of the loveliest in the area.

Detail of the windowsill of the Priest's House

Close to the river is the priory. There was a religious community here from 1248 to the Dissolution in the 16th century. In 1953 the Augustinians returned, and now live and work in the prior's lodging.

Stoke-by-Clare is charming, but its claim to fame rests on the mean shoulders of Sir Hervey Elwes, who lived at Stoke College. This 18th-century gentleman was once described as being 'without a friend on Earth', and it is not surprising. He was the archetypal miser – he repaired windows with brown paper, he wore only old clothes which his predecessors had left in their wardrobes, and he really did count his fortune each night before going to his bleak bed. 'The ringing of his guineas was his greatest joy' said a contemporary. As you pass through this pretty village, think of the miser who always went to bed early to spare himself the unnecessary extravagance of a candle!

Sue Ryder Foundation Museum, Cavendish
Open: All year: daily 1000–1730
Price guide: Free

Ancient House, Clare
Open: April to Sept: Wed to Sat 1430–1630, Sun 1100–1630
Price guide: A

HADLEIGH

Hadleigh is a historic town lying in the pretty valley of the River Brett. For many years it suffered the perils of through traffic; now the by-pass means that visitors can explore the town and its surroundings in a more leisurely and tranquil fashion.

Parking is free and the large car park off Magdalene Road is a good place to start a walking tour. The High Street, which runs parallel with the river for almost a mile, is crowded with houses and shops of different periods and architectural styles. These bring gaiety and interest to any shopping trip. Colourwashes of yellow, cream and Suffolk pink contrast with red brick and timber, and Georgian stands next to Tudor with apparent unconcern. Some of the houses are decorated with pargetting; this is a design on plasterwork formed by indenting or raising patterns, sometimes with a sort of comb or grooved trowel, and sometimes, as in Hadleigh, more freely drawn. Each craftsman developed his own style which became his trademark, and Hadleigh shows some brilliant examples of the art. They are brightly painted, and their intricacy merits more than a passing glance.

Detail of pargetting

Most of the best houses date from the town's most flourishing period when the wool trade was at its height. Hadleigh was ideally placed, with the River Brett providing power to drive two mills as well as clean water for washing the wool and fulling the cloth. A fine illustration of the town's glorious past is provided in the 15th-century Guildhall. This was the meeting place of five major guilds and the centre of the town's commercial life. The central portion, the former Market Hall, is unusual in having three overhanging storeys; its timber frame is infilled with plasterwork of an ochre colour and it overlooks the churchyard – a peaceful setting for what must have been a bustling quarter.

Near the church is another 15th-century building: the red-brick Deanery Tower. This is a gatehouse built for the new rectory of Archdeacon Pykenham, who died before the building could be completed. The Church of St Mary has an Angelus bell which, at 600 years, is supposed to be the oldest in England. Inside is a tomb purporting to be that of the Viking King Guthrum, who ruled over East Anglia and

The 15th century Guildhall

the Midlands in the 9th century. His capital was at Hadleigh where he established a church and was buried in 889. But 'Guthrum's tomb' dates from the 14th century!

Hadleigh was known as a centre of Protestantism, and one of its rectors has earned a place in the history of martyrdom. Dr Rowland Taylor was appointed in 1544 and his bluff good humour made him a popular figure; church congregations grew and the townsfolk became renowned for their grasp of Biblical texts. When in 1553 the Catholic Queen Mary was crowned, the Bishop sent a priest to ring the bells of Hadleigh Church and to say Mass in celebration. Dr Taylor angrily threw out the priest; he was soon arrested, taken to London and put on trial before the notorious Bishop Bonner. He refused to recant his Protestant faith and was brought back to Hadleigh to be burned at the stake. He was met by the townspeople who cheered him with their support, and he even had time enough to joke with his captors, saying that the worms in Hadleigh churchyard would be sorry to have been cheated of such a feast as his body would have afforded. The spot where he died, on Aldham Common, off the Ipswich road, was marked by a stone: 'Dr Taylor in defending that was good / At this place left his blood'. The place is still marked.

Monument to Rowland Taylor of Hadleigh at Aldham Common

HIGH SUFFOLK VILLAGES

The first sight of Kersey, just north-west of Hadleigh, is likely to be of its church standing against the skyline above the rolling fields. This is High Suffolk – not high by national standards, certainly, but higher than the rest of the county – and the landscapes are less exposed. Here are fertile hills divided by pretty streams and rivers, and the roads are narrow and winding. So it is that, whichever way you approach Kersey, your first view of the main street will come as a surprise. The road turns a sharp corner, and suddenly the beautiful vista is before you: down the hill lined by timbered cottages to where the ducks paddle in the Splash – a tributary of the River Brett which runs across the

The Crown Inn, Bildeston

The Splash at Kersey

road – and up the other side, past more haphazard cottages. Kersey is full of colour, from the washes of the houses to the flowers in the magnificent gardens or hanging outside 'The Bell'.

The Church of St Mary has a square flint tower and a splendid panelled south porch, discovered in 1927 hidden under a lath and plaster ceiling. It dates in part from the 14th century, and originally it was faced by a priory on the opposite hill. Very little now remains, but it gives some idea of the former prosperity of Kersey whose weavers produced a strong woollen cloth named after the village. Lindsey, a few miles away, produced a lighter cloth called Lindsey-Woolsey. Lindsey is a scattered community; its simple thatched Chapel of St James dates from the 13th century but for some time its sanctity was overlooked and it was used as a stable.

Bildeston, too, has some lovely old weavers' cottages close to the market place. It was known for its blue cloth and blankets; later the villagers had to turn their hand to making coconut matting. One wealthy wool merchant's house is now 'The Crown' – one of the most haunted pubs in England.

Chelsworth is nothing short of idyllic. The river runs parallel with the main street and is crossed by a red brick bridge. The banks of the Brett are dotted in spring with daffodils, and the many trees cast dappled shadows. The old cottages are flower-bedecked; even the public telephone box is swept clean and polished, for the villagers take a real pride in the beauty of their surroundings.

Monk's Eleigh is on the Lavenham road, and tourists making for that most famous of wool towns may well pass the village by. But a glance up the slope of the village green (complete with Victorian pump) takes in pretty cottages on either side, and St Peter's Church on the rise.

Chelsworth Village

Polstead is picturesque, but many will come here because of a rather grisly murder in the last century. Maria Marten lived in what is now called Marten Lane; she was seduced by William Corder, the son of a wealthy farmer, and lured to the Red Barn, in the belief that they were going to run away to be married. Corder wrote to her parents later to assure them that the marriage had taken place. But Maria's mother kept dreaming of the Red Barn, and eventually her husband dug there and found Maria's body. Corder was tracked down, tried and hanged in Bury St Edmunds in 1828. It is said that 10,000 spectators attended his execution, and the hangman sold off the rope at a guinea an inch. The Red Barn was burned down in 1842, but more gruesome reminders of this celebrated case may be seen in Moyses Hall Museum in Bury St Edmunds.

LAVENHAM

Lavenham has been called our finest medieval village, and no tour of East Anglia should miss this glorious wool town, frozen, as it were, in its prime. There are more than three hundred listed buildings, most of them connected with the weaving trade, most saved from ruin and sympathetically restored. Here are no modern shop fronts or brash supermarkets; all is in harmony with the restrained cottages of natural timber and pretty colourwash.

Why has so much remained here? The answer lies in the shifting fortunes of the wool industry. At Lavenham's peak in the 15th and 16th centuries, weavers worked on

Carved figure of John de Vere on the Guildhall

individual looms in their cottages, and the cloth was taken by clothiers to be finished by fulling, stretching and brushing. But by 1700, wars on the Continent and the centralisation of markets in cities such as Norwich led to the decline of independent weavers. Soon the focus turned to the west and north of England, where water power was used in the developing industry, and later the Industrial Revolution demanded plenty of coal for its steam-driven machines;

Lavenham, having neither water nor coal, was passed by. So it has been fossilised for our delight, and even modern day intrusions like electricity wires have been buried so as not to spoil the effect.

The town stands on a hill, so that each turn gives us fresh vistas along streets of lovely shops and houses

Tudor shops in Lady Street

and to the green countryside beyond. The Market Place was long the centre of everyday life with its market and fairs. The cross dates from 1501, and the long building beside it is the Guildhall, built in 1529, with its fine carving around the porch and at the corner the figure of John de Vere, 15th Earl of Oxford, who gave Lavenham its charter. The town had three guilds to control hours of work and rates of pay, the quality of the finished product and to support members and their families in times of need. The guilds ended at the time of the Reformation and the Guildhall saw various use as a jail, workhouse, almshouse, wool store and finally the 'Welcome Club' for the American airmen based nearby! Now owned by the National Trust, it has on the first floor an exhibition dealing with the wool

The Priory

industry – including a loom – and local history up to and including the last war. Behind the building is a delightful garden where you can sit and digest all the information.

At the bottom of Lady Street is Water Street. Here stands de Vere House, which came near to ruin and was partly demolished by vandals; it has been beautifully restored and has brick nogging between the timbers, and carved doorposts. The Priory tells a similar story of near ruin and the public may now inspect the restored building. The house derives its name from the fact that it once belonged to the monks of the Benedictine priory at Earls Colne in Essex. The central hall dates from the 13th century and the rest was largely completed in the 16th. You may wander around, admiring the huge inglenook fireplace in the Great Hall (with its mummified rat to ward off evil spirits) and the Jacobean staircase. The garden overlooks open fields and conveys the atmosphere of the farm it was until recently. In the house, craftwork is on show and on sale, and the refectory on the first floor serves meals.

Church Street

At the junction of Water Street and Church Street stands the Swan Inn, with pargetting showing the Tudor Rose and the fleur de lys – Lavenham's trade mark which was stamped on the finished blue cloth. Incorporated in The Swan is another Guild centre, the Wool Hall, at the bottom of Lady Street. This was about to be demolished and

Church of St Peter and St Paul

shipped to America before its timely rescue. From The Swan there is a lovely view of crooked cottages leading up to the magnificent Church of St Peter and St Paul. It stands in an open position, dominating the flat lands beyond with its 141-foot high tower – which, it is said, would have been higher, except that the master mason unfortunately fell off the top. The Church was built at the turn of the 16th century when Lavenham's prosperity was at its peak. Funds were provided by the de Veres who were Lords of the Manor, and two clothiers, Simon Branch and the Thomas Springs – grandfather, father and son. It is a mark of the acceptance which the Spring family found that, not only was Thomas III, 'The Rich Clothier', awarded a coat of arms which he used liberally to decorate the tower, but that the Spring family became united to the de Veres in marriage. Many emblems are to be seen around the church, including the Springs' merchant mark and the de Veres' Star. The Puritan Dowsing destroyed all the stained glass, so that the inside of the Church is bright; the Oxford and Spring Chantries survive (the latter has a figure of St Blaise, patron saint of woolcombers), and the Branch chapel. The bells are renowned for their sweet tone. The memorial to those killed in the First World War, with their short biographies written by the vicar, makes interesting reading.

Many other buildings merit attention to their detailed carvings and clever timber construction as well as their integral beauty. Do not miss Woolstaplers, Shilling Old Grange or the Flemish Weavers' cottages in Water Street, Lavenham offers a rare chance to wander in a world apart.

Lavenham Guildhall
Open: Mar to Nov: daily 1100–1700
Price guide: B

Lavenham Priory
Open: Mar to Oct: daily 1030–1730
Price guide: B

Helmingham Hall Gardens

'An Englishman's home is his castle' runs the adage, and for many, Helmingham Hall is the epitome of security and tradition: a moat 60 feet wide surrounds a beautifully proportioned Tudor house, whose drawbridges are raised each night and let down each morning as they have been for almost 500 years.

But in spite of appearances, the history of Helmingham Hall has not always been serene. Indeed, this place has seen many changes. The house was begun in 1510 on the site of an earlier hall; it was originally a half-timbered building, foursquare around an open courtyard. Later the outer walls were faced with brick on the ground floor and tiled with false bricks above, giving a harmonious warm colour to the whole. Crenellations were added in the Regency period by the architect John Nash, who also gave the whole building a coating of grey cement! Fortunately, this covering was allowed to remain only some twenty years.

The house fell into disrepair and had to be restored in Victorian times. A few generations passed, and Helmingham Hall had not kept pace with progress: in the 1950s it still had no electricity or running water – drinking water was drawn from the moat! Since then the Hall has been sustained by the enthusiasm of the Tollemache family whose seat it has been since it was built.

Helmingham is nine miles north of Ipswich. The Hall is almost completely screened from the road by trees and is set on gently rising ground in magnificent open parkland. Some of the oaks are said to be almost a thousand years old. Others are obviously more recent, such as the one given to Lord Tollemache by his wife as a Christmas present. To the east, the visitor can take the path between the lakes known as the Leys up to St Mary's Church. But your gaze is inevitably drawn up the slope to the Hall; it is not open to the public, but you can walk right around it and admire the elegant façades, the decorated Tudor chimneys and the stateliness of this home secure against all intruders.

The gardens are formally laid. To reach them you cross a second, shallower moat covered in pink and white waterlilies, and walk on manicured lawns through a French parterre to the Walled Garden. Beyond the wrought-iron gates, you are dazzled by the summery colours of the flowers: yellow, orange and purple. The other seasons are not neglected: there is the Spring Border planted with bulbs, and the Meadow Garden, also resplendent earlier in the year. In late summer it is delightful to saunter down the Apple Walk, between trees laden with fruit.

The Hall is surrounded by 400 acres of land. There are herds of red and fallow deer, Highland cattle, and some 40 Soay sheep, a very primitive breed. This has been a deer park for centuries, but happily the deer are no longer hunted for their meat. You can watch them from the garden, but the best way to see them is to take a 'Safari Ride' in a trailer drawn by a Land Rover. This 30-minute trip takes in some of the rest of the park.

There are homemade jams, plants and flowers for sale in the stable shop, and a spacious tea room for refreshment. You may admire the horses, but a notice assures the unwary that they do bite!

Helmingham Hall Gardens
Open: April to Sept: Sun 1400–1800
Price guide: B

IPSWICH

The Anglo-Saxons created Ipswich in the 7th century, which makes it one of the oldest towns in England, and although worshippers of the god Progress have seen to it that nothing of this period remains above ground, the street plan of those far-off days remains. It is a reassuring thought that a building like the Willis Faber and Dumas headquarters, with its walls of smoked glass, still follows the curve of a road known to the Norman conquerors. The street names recall the past – Westgate, Northgate, Greyfriars – and a dozen churches stand witness to the prosperity enjoyed by the town throughout the medieval period.

Wool was the key to the town's importance. At first the port exported bales to Flanders where it was made into superior cloth, but later weaving skills were taught to the folk of Lavenham, Hadleigh and Kersey, so Ipswich grew richer by exporting finished cloth. The port beside the Orwell exported cheese and corn, too, and unloaded in return vast quantities of timber, wine and fish. Along the quayside merchants lived in fine houses which were also their shops and warehouses and accommodated their apprentices. Some of these timber buildings are now pubs, and the 'Neptune' is a good example. During the Tudor period the town grew and prospered. Henry VIII's great Lord Chancellor, Thomas Wolsey, was the son of a humble Ipswich trader and he began to build a college in the town; but his fall from grace was sudden and complete, and in 1529 his king halted the work. Only a sad brick gateway in College Street marks his final ambition. Near the site of his birth in Silent Street is a quite marvellous tablet to his memory.

Plaque to Thomas Wolsey in Silent Street

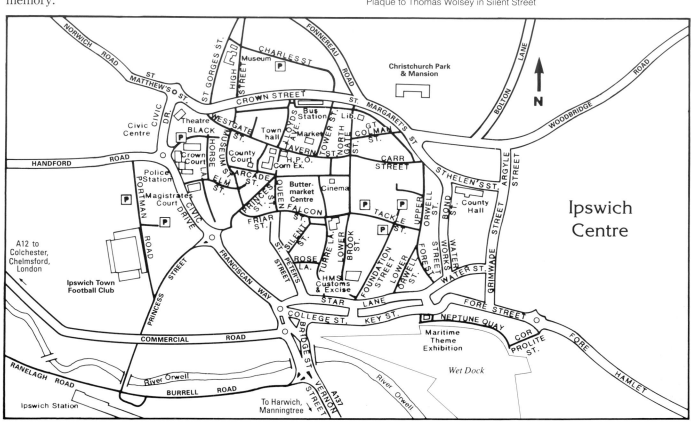

Detail of plasterwork on the Ancient House in Buttermarket

The Ancient House is one of the finest buildings of its type in Britain. Added to the original 15th century core of the structure is a magnificent exterior dating from the 1670s. The decorated plasterwork, or pargetting, covers every part of the surface. Most prominent is the great royal crest, in red, blue and gold leaf, which may commemorate the visit to the town of Charles II in 1668. Beneath the oriel windows are panels depicting the four continents (Australia had yet to be discovered).

Cornhill is the centre of the town, and it has been paved and so restored to pedestrians, as it was in the time when it was the site of St Mildred's Church, and a place of

Cornhill and Town Hall

Tower Ramparts Shopping Centre

pilgrimage. Corn was indeed traded there, and butter was sold in Buttermarket. Less obviously, fish were sold in St Lawrence Street, hens in Tower Lane and apples off Princess Street! In Tavern Street stands the Great White Horse Inn, famous because Dickens stayed there and gave it a sort of immortality in his first great success, 'The Pickwick Papers'. He described the white horse over the doorway as 'distantly resembling an insane cart horse'. Pickwick, returning at night, mistakenly enters the room of a middle-aged lady, has to hide behind the curtains of her bed, is discovered and . . . You can sit in the old courtyard and read the rest!

The days of Ipswich as a coach halt were numbered, for the railway arrived in 1846, bringing a wind of change which shows no sign of abating. The glass and metal shopping area, Tower Ramparts Centre in Tavern Street, was opened in 1988. The name harks back to the earthworks constructed there to keep out the Danes in the 9th century. A second shopping precinct, the Buttermarket, stands just to the south. The unique interior of the Wolsey Theatre on Civic Drive is another sample of Ipswich's venture into modern architecture.

Christchurch Mansion stands at the southern end of a huge park a few minutes' walk from Ipwsich town centre. Its beautiful warm red brick looks out over wide tree-lined lawns. It is amazing to think that at the end of the last century there were plans to demolish this fine Tudor house in favour of a housing estate! But fortunately the banker Felix Cobbold had foresight enough to purchase the property and to hand it over to the town corporation for the benefit of future generations.

Christchurch Mansion

The mansion was begun by Edmund Withipoll in 1548 on the site of an Augustinian priory. A century later it passed through marriage to the Devereux family, who remodelled the interior, embellishing it with painted panelling, and added Dutch gables and classical pillars to the exterior. Another hundred years passed, and the mansion was sold to the Fonnereaus, London merchants of Huguenot descent, who made their mark with decorative plasterwork and intricate flocked wallpaper. Finally, in 1896 it was opened as the town's museum and art gallery.

The changing tastes of the succeeding families mean that the building is fascinating in its own right. Few of the exhibits belong to the house itself, but they well convey the varying styles from Tudor times to the Victorian era. There is a great deal of exquisite wooden furniture and porcelain;

'The Walk'

the kitchen is equipped with intriguing old utensils, and the State Bedroom is elegant with its mahogany bed hung in blue and yellow, and its hand-blocked wallpaper.

The Wingfield Room was built in 1931 to display the fine carved panelling from the Wingfield family home in Ipswich's Tacket Street, and it is an impressive sight. The Wolsey Art Gallery was opened to the public in the same year and exhibits part of the Ipswich Museums' extensive collection of paintings. There are over a dozen works by Gainsborough, including portraits dating from his time as an Ipswich resident, and almost as many by Constable, including *The Mill Stream*, a sketch for what later became *The Haywain*. There are works by Wilson Steer and Munnings, as well as others by local artists or of local views. Contemporary works are not neglected, and there are often exhibitions of modern sculpture in the grounds in front of the mansion.

The circular pond in Christchurch Park

The park is enormous; there are avenues of great trees, especially lovely in spring or autumn, and two arboreta where you will find something colourful and interesting in any season. The flowerbeds are immaculate, and winding paths lead past ponds where ducks swim placidly. The wide-open fields at the northern end are ideal for dog walking and games, and the gently undulating terrain brings a feeling of the countryside to the heart of this busy town.

The Ipswich Museum has occupied its High Street site since 1881, and its origins as a Victorian showcase for static exhibits is evident in the central gallery, where the visitor is greeted by Rosie, the Indian rhinoceros. Mammals, birds, insects and shells fill the cases, and youngsters will be particularly fascinated by the skeleton of a boa constrictor and the evidence that once upon a time, mammoths and porcupines roamed the valley which the town now occupies. On the first floor an interesting exhibition examines the costume and artefacts of nations of the world. There is also a section on local history, including replicas of the Sutton Hoo and Mildenhall treasures, and a reconstruction of rooms in a Roman villa which was excavated in Ipswich.

Christchurch Mansion
Open: All year: Tues to Sat 1000–1700, Sun 1430–1630
Price guide: Free

Ipswich Museum
Open: All year: Tues to Sat 1000–1700
Price guide: Free

THE RIVER ORWELL

Orwell Bridge

Throughout its history Ipswich was a centre for trade and shipbuilding, but in the early 19th century this eminence was threatened by the silting up of the Orwell. Accordingly, action was taken; the process of dredging a main channel was begun, and continues to this day. Although it met with local opposition at the time, the New Cut which was opened in 1842 was a bold step and a wise one. A giant wet dock covering more than 33 acres was created, whose lock gates gave it independence from the rise and fall of the tides. Confident of the future the authorities built beside their new harbour a grand Custom House, opened in 1845. Now it is the headquarters of the Ipswich Port Authority. With its double stairway and imposing façade it resembles a stately mansion, and following recent restoration we can see it in its full glory. Ipswich is still a major commercial port, specialising in container traffic, and ships of 9000 tons may be seen slicing through the lines of delicate pleasure craft, en route to our EEC partners.

The graceful Orwell Bridge dwarfs most of the river traffic, but there are still a few large ships which justify the height of its centre spans. The Ipswich Marina is close by, one of three centres for boat enthusiasts. There are said to be over 3000 boats on the Orwell at the height of the

Ipswich Custom House

58

summer. Close by, too, is the Ostrich Inn – an odd name until you learn that it is a corruption of Oyster Ridge Inn!

From the Orwell Bridge you can see Freston Tower. This red-brick tower, six storeys high, dates from the mid-16th century. The prosaic explanation that it was a navigational aid is far less interesting than the story that its builder had a daughter, Ellen, who was educated here. She started on Monday on the ground floor with lessons in good

River Orwell

Freston Tower

works, and daily passed through weaving, music, the Classics, English novels and painting, reaching the roof in time to do a little astronomy!

At Woolverstone is another marina, and a reminder of a local heroine, Margaret Catchpole. She loved adventure and with her sweetheart, William Laud, became involved in the risky business of smuggling. Cat House here allegedly showed a china (or perhaps stuffed) cat in the lamplit window when the Preventive Men were about. The young couple were eventually captured in 1797; he was shot and she was transported to Australia where she died.

The Butt and Oyster Inn at Pin Mill is described by some as the best-known pub on the East Coast. Pin Mill is famous for its barge races in July and a Regatta in September, but it is worth a visit at any time. The Orwell is truly beautiful here, and to sit outside the pub with good beer, food and company, listening to the lapping water,

watching someone at work on a sailing barge, and with the occasional excitement of a ship bound for Ipswich is to rediscover true relaxation. The woods to the east are owned by the National Trust and offer lovely walks.

Across the river from Pin Mill is Orwell Park, now a private school, but in the 18th century the home of Admiral Vernon, nicknamed 'Old Grog' by his sailors. He it

The Butt and Oyster Inn at Pin Mill

was who won for them the daily ration of rum and water which was called grog. At Levington is the Suffolk Yacht Harbour basin. This is the final stretch of unspoilt river, with Trimley marshes attracting wildfowl and waders. The ever-growing and eternally illuminated sprawl of Felixstowe Dock seems set to conquer even those quiet reaches before long.

FELIXSTOWE

There are two distinct sides to the town of Felixstowe, and many visitors leave without ever having experienced the whole. The first, and more important facet from an economic point of view, is the dock. On its western side Felixstowe overlooks the wide estuary at Harwich Harbour, so it is readily accessible, particularly to the Continent. The dock was built on reclaimed marshland at the end of the 19th century, but it suffered bomb damage in the war, and the massive storms of 1953 silted up the channel. By the mid-1950s there were only nine dockers. Now the port covers many hundreds of acres with warehouses and cranes, and it is still expanding into the hinterland. Thousands of containers are handled here, and increasing numbers of travellers sail to and from Belgium and Scandinavia. This explains why many of the road signs on the town's approaches are in French and German!

The Docks

Felixstowe cannot boast a distinguished history; until Victorian times it was an insignificant fishing village with 500 inhabitants, and ancient monuments have left no trace. Nothing remains of the priory and the ruins of Walton Castle, built on a Roman site, have crumbled into the sea. One survivor is Landguard Fort, built on the shingle peninsula dividing port from town, and ideally placed to protect Harwich Harbour. The present fort dates from the 18th

Landguard fort and 20th Century defence tower

century, but the first dated from the 1540s, and saw active service against the Dutch who landed an army of 3000 men on the beach in 1667. In 1763 there was a scandal when the acting governor held a dance in the fort's chapel and used the altar as a bar! Another eccentric governor was Philip Thicknesse, a friend and the first biographer of Gainsborough, who stipulated in his will that his right hand should be cut off and sent to his son, to 'remind him of his duty to God, after having so long abandoned the duty he owed to a father who once affectionately loved him'.

The Promenade

The resort of Felixstowe is a relatively modern creation, promoted, like so many other seaside places, by the coming of the railway. It offers the holidaymaker two miles of fine shingle beach along the bay, safe bathing and a dry and sunny climate. Visitors will enjoy the long walk along the seafront, pausing perhaps at one of the many benches or deckchairs to admire the view. The old-fashioned beach huts have picturesque names such as Sunnyholme, Sea Shanty, Calme – and, more fancifully, Capri! The steep cliffs mean that the houses pile up in terraces. So, too, do the gardens, Felixstowe's pride and joy. 'The garden resort of Suffolk' provides a garden for the blind, planted with aromatic shrubs such as lavender and rosemary, and graced with a trickling fountain – but blind visitors should beware the unexpected steps! The seafront has a mass of bright geraniums, petunias, busy lizzies and marigolds, and the Spa Gardens are rightly renowned for their brilliant patterns and colours.

Entertainment takes many forms to suit all tastes. There is Charles Manning's Amusement Park, and on the pier is a giant slide and fun and games. A theatre provides cabaret, classical music, organ recitals, tea dances and band concerts. The sporting will appreciate the modern leisure centre beside the pier and the golf course on the cliffs. Children can enjoy the boating lake, yacht pond, electric cars and roller skating. The town centre has a variety of shops, many of them still privately owned and having the reassuring appeal of former days.

Landguard Fort
English Heritage
Open: May to Oct: Wed & Sun 1430–1700
Price guide: A

Charles Mannings Amusement Park
Open: April to Sept: Sat, Sun & school holidays 1100–2100, weekdays 1300–2100
Price guide: free with ride tokens from 20p

WOODBRIDGE TIDE MILL

In these energy-conscious times Woodbridge tide mill has a lot to teach us. While the sails of a windmill are idle until a breeze stirs them, and a watermill requires a fast-flowing river, the tides eternally rise and fall. Beside the Deben is the first recorded tide mill in England, mentioned in 1170, and it is now the last still working in the age-old manner. As the tide flowed up the river it forced open the gates of the mill pond. At the turn, the gates gently closed, trapping the water, which the miller then used to drive the machinery – twice a day, and without fail. The only difficulty was that the wheel could only be turned at low tide, so the miller would have to work at all hours of the day and night! The original pond probably held enough water for about four hours' work, but the present one, being much smaller, drives the mill for about half an hour.

For centuries Woodbridge tide mill was the property of the town's Augustinian priory, but at the Dissolution it reverted to the Crown, and was sold for £764 to the town's benefactor, Thomas Seckford. In Tudor times the miller would have ground corn for local farmers and merchants, and made a little extra money for himself by netting eels in the pond.

The present white weatherboarded mill was built by the Cutting family in 1793. Its appearance is so pleasing to the eye it is easy to forget it is an industrial building. The attractive red-tiled roof is of the mansard type which gives more space in the loft. Here the grain was stored, after being hauled up from carts by a hoist located in the lucomb, which has a trapdoor for the purpose. The hoist was also driven by the waterwheel. Once in the loft's storage bins the grain was fed down wooden chutes to the stones on the second floor. Although there are four, it is unlikely that they all turned at once. A metal agitator guided the grain to the stone's centre, and the chattering noise it made all day led to it being christened the damsel! If a working stone ran out of grain the risk of fire was high, so a bell rang to warn the miller in good time. The mill works during the holiday season, and comes alive as the water drives the three-ton wheel and the heavy machinery.

In the 19th century the mill was so successful that a granary had to be built alongside. Old photographs show barges with lovely names like *Prosperous Mary*, *Sylph* and *Friendship* tied up alongside, skippered by men with names like John Bull and Jeremiah Read. The photographs do not convey the backbreaking work entailed in unloading a barge. It took nine men a couple of days to do so, and then they had to load up with ballast for the return trip. The coming of the railway to Woodbridge in 1859 was a blow to the river traffic from which it never recovered.

In 1957 the main shaft of the mill broke. It was replaced by a diesel engine, and the great pool was sold, to become a yachting marina. Milling ceased with the retirement of Sid Desborough; weather, tides and rats soon reduced the timbers to a sorry state. By 1968 there were even fears that it would be blown down. It was put up for sale by auction. Many thought that the dangerous structure would have to be demolished, but in the nick of time it was rescued, a charitable trust was established, and fund-raising began. After extensive restoration the mill was opened to the public in 1973. When in 1981 the construction of a new pool enabled the machinery to turn again, it was clear that Woodbridge had saved an essential part of its heritage.

Open: May to Sept: daily 1100–1700, Oct: Sat & Sun 1100–1700
Price guide: A

WOODBRIDGE

Only the visitor who sees Woodbridge from the deck of a boat sailing up the Deben can fully appreciate its charm. The tall tower of St Mary's Church rises above a cluster of roofs, presenting a picture of harmony and continuity. Old and new exist side by side; fine houses, often with unexpectedly large gardens, stand beside estate agents and antique shops. Shopping in the Thoroughfare is still a pleasure, and although familiar names are to be found, there are also scores of local businesses, including a baker's of real distinction.

In many ways it is still possible to sense Tudor Woodbridge, and this is largely due to Thomas Seckford, lawyer, and Master of the Court of Requests to Elizabeth I, whose name dominates the town map. His family home,

The Shire Hall

Seckford Hall, is to the west of the town, and is now a first class hotel. Seckford purchased the land which had belonged to the Augustinian priory and built himself a fine town house in 1564. It is now a private school within the Seckford Foundation. Before his death in 1587 Seckford had bequeathed money to establish almshouses. In a much

enlarged form these continue to exist, and the imposing 19th-century buildings occupy the original site in Seckford Street.

The Market Hill still conveys the charm of a century ago, but many of its buildings are much older. The 15th-century King's Head is supposed to be the oldest building in

Buttram's Mill

Woodbridge, and along its side are carved faces, said to be of the first landlord and his family. In front of the King's Head a market is still held on Thursdays, continuing a tradition begun when the priory flourished. From here it is a short walk down a cobbled passageway to St Mary's Church with its magnificent porch decorated with flint flushwork lettering. On the other side of the square a plaque high on a shop wall recalls that here lived the poet Edward Fitzgerald, translator of *The Rubáiyát of Omar Khayyám*. On the river he kept a boat which he called *Scandal* – the chief product, so he said, of Woodbridge!

At the bottom of the square is The Bull Hotel. An ostler, George Carlow, directed that he should be buried there instead of in the churchyard, and you can see his tombstone in the yard. In keeping with his bequest bread is still distributed to the poor. Thomas Seckford was responsible for building the red brick and Dutch-gabled Shire Hall which dominates Market Hill – it bears his crest over the door at the head of the double stairway. Originally the open ground floor was used as the corn market, while the chamber above housed the Sessions Court; beneath the stairs were two lock-ups. The court moved from the building in 1985 after 400 years of continuous use, and it is now occupied by the Town Council and the Shire Horse Museum. Close to the Shire Hall is the Town Museum, which has excellent displays on the Sutton Hoo Ship Burial and other local themes. Woodbridge was once dotted with windmills, but now only Buttram's Mill, named after its last miller in 1928, remains intact. It is six storeys high and is open to the public.

Down beside the Bull Hotel runs New Street (well, it was new in 1600!) and here stands the Bell and Steelyard, with its extraordinary projecting wooden apparatus. This is

The port of Woodbridge was once very busy, and famous for salt, cheese and timber. This last ensured a thriving shipbuilding industry in the 17th century, with several frigates launched from slipways where now there are roads and houses. The quayside is still a great joy. It is no anchorage for floating gin palaces, but a berth for humbler craft, owned by people who love and respect the river. Even at low tide this is a delightful spot. From the railway bridge it is possible to overlook the Deben and feel how fortunate it is that the opposite bank remains totally unspoilt.

The Mariner

The Bell and Steelyard in New Street

The Riverside Theatre is a bold venture incorporating a modern theatre and cinema with an excellent restaurant. It has an ice cream parlour – an ideal place for reading the Town Guide which is an invaluable companion for any visit to the town.

On the end wall of a pretty quayside cottage is a painting of a mariner holding a sextant. This is believed to date from the 18th century; the lovely thing about Woodbridge is that, were he to return, he would still feel at home, and among friends.

Woodbridge Museum
Open: April to Oct: Thur to Sat 1000–1600, Sun 1430–1630
Price guide: A

Shire Horse Museum
Open: April to Oct: daily 1400–1700
Price guide: A

the steelyard: a weighing machine. Grain-filled waggons en route to Market Hill would be hoisted off the ground and weighed – it could cope with 2½ tons. Returning empty after market, they were weighed again; a simple calculation showed how much grain had been bought, and the bill could be settled – over a drink.

THE RIVER DEBEN

The River Deben is perhaps the most perfect of all East Anglia's rivers: for much of its length it remains unspoilt and idyllic. It begins north of Debenham, a village of colour-washed timber houses surrounded by rich rolling farmland,

Debenham cottages

and flows through the quiet gentility of villages such as Cretingham and Kettleburgh. It achieves tidal maturity in the luxuriant water meadows around Ufford, which takes its name from the Wuffingas who invaded in the 6th century, rose to dominate East Anglia and had their royal palace somewhere in the area of Rendlesham Forest. In 1939 excavations at Sutton Hoo, on the river bank opposite Woodbridge, revealed a ship burial of unprecedented splendour and importance; this is thought to have been the grave of Raedwald, the greatest of all the early rulers, who died in AD 625. The treasures are now displayed in the British Museum. More recent excavations have taken place and Woodbridge Museum has information about site tours.

Wilford Bridge at Melton marks the lowest crossing point of the Deben by road, and is nine miles from the sea. Formerly a gallows stood on the hill which overlooks it.

The *Maybush* at Waldringfield

Once there were six mills beside the river; now only Woodbridge Tide Mill stands as a working reminder of the past. The first known ferry from Woodbridge to the Sutton side began in Tudor times, and during the 19th century it was kept busy on warm summer days because men were only allowed to swim on the Sutton side. The river wall offers a wonderful walk from Woodbridge to Kyson Hill, a vantage point giving splendid views upriver and now owned by the National Trust. Once there were small docks distributed along the river and schooners, brigantines and barges would be seen tied alongside, or waiting for a favourable wind.

Below Kyson the river has a magic quality, only discovered by those afloat, for access by road is limited. One unclassified road leads down to Waldringfield, the site of a cement works until 1914, but now blessed with moorings which do not dry out, a narrow beach and the Maybush, a pub for those who like to mess about in boats. From here the MV Jahan sets out on trips on the river.

The River Deben at Ramsholt

Ramsholt on the east bank is one of the prettiest landing stages on the Deben. The church with its round flint tower is a landmark. Below it is the Ramsholt Arms, a solitary building overlooking lines of moored craft, and a place to visit on a summer evening when the colours of the sunset and the calls of the wildfowl are unforgettable.

Long before Woodbridge became a port, the creeks and inlets of Kirton, Falkenham and Kingsfleet formed an important anchorage called Gosford. It was eclipsed by the rise of Woodbridge and nothing remains.

The village of Felixstowe Ferry at the mouth of the Deben is a motley collection of bungalows and wooden huts, where you can buy fresh fish daily. The Martello towers lining this coast were defence batteries built during the Napoleonic wars. Some are derelict while others are private houses. The ferry across the Deben to Bawdsey continues the Suffolk Coastal Path which runs 50 miles from Felixstowe to Lowestoft.

Bawdsey Manor was created by Sir Cuthbert Quilter in 1882. He had made his fortune in the City and is said to have built a turret for every million he earned: there are 9! In 1936 the house passed to the Government and research on the invention of radar took place there. It is now occupied by a language school.

River Deben
Cruises on the *MV Jahan* start from Waldringfield at 1100, 1430 and 1830

ORFORD

Once upon a time some fishermen from the town of Orford found entangled in their nets a strange creature, 'naked and like a man in all his members', with a long ragged beard and a bald head. They brought him ashore and handed him over to the governor of Orford Castle, who tried by many means to discover more about the merman, as he was called. But the creature remained silent, 'although oft times hung up by his feet and harshly tortured'. At last his persecutors took him out to sea to study his behaviour there, taking care that nets surrounded their boat. He nimbly evaded them, and swam off – later returning of his own free will, however, to live at Orford on a diet of raw fish. Eventually he became unhappy and returned to the sea, and has never been seen again.

The Orford Merman is supposed to have appeared some time in the 1160s, which coincides with the building of the great castle in the town, the keep of which survives. King Henry II began the castle in 1166, to a daring new design which rejected the familiar square block in favour of an 18-sided keep within three buttress towers. Not only was it more difficult to undermine, but it was easier to defend. There was an encircling bailey wall but now only earthworks indicate its position. The total cost was about £1,400, and the garrison arrived for duty in 1171. It was captured by the French for a short time in 1217, and ceased to have a military function after the 13th century. It is worth

visiting if only to see what living in a castle was really like: dank, cold, enclosed and unhealthy. The best place to be is on the battlements where the views in all directions are worth all the effort of the 90-foot climb.

Stone for the castle was brought in by sea, and the port soon grew. During Tudor and Stuart times wool was the main export, and with prosperity came status: the town acquired a Mayor and a very fine set of regalia. But the shingle spit we know as Orfordness was inexorably moving south to cut off the larger ships from the North Sea, and trade was strangled. Defoe observed in 1722: 'the sea daily throws up more land to it, as if it were resolved to disown the place and that it should be a sea port no longer.'

Cottages at Orford

Market Place, with Pump Street and the oyster restaurant, is deservedly praised. St Bartholomew's Church was built in the 14th century, but the remains of the earlier Norman chancel may be seen. Fishermen and river folk no longer occupy the pretty cottages in Quay Street but they can still be found in the bar of the Jolly Sailor which has a reputation for good beer and company. There are fine views from the river walk which runs south from the quay to Chantry Point.

Orfordness is now 10 miles long, and is of interest to naturalists for plants like the yellow horned poppy, purple flowering sea pea and sea kale. There are also wildfowl and waders in profusion, attracted by the sea lavender and sea purslane. Five miles of the Ness have been acquired by the National Trust. In the river channel is Havergate Island, now an RSPB reserve for which permits are required. Boats leave Orford Quay for the bird sanctuary, and also for four-hour river trips. On the Ness are the remains of a Government Radio Research station, tall masts which transmit BBC World Service, and some pagoda-like structures which were used in the last war for ballistic experiments. The Ore entrance is at Shingle Street: a line of old Coastguard cottages and a Martello Tower on a very exposed shingle beach.

Orford Castle
English Heritage
Open: Jan to Mar: Wed to Sun 1000–1600, April to Dec: daily 1000–1800
Price guide: A

Havergate Island RSPB Reserve
Permits must be obtained in advance from: The Warden, RSPB Orford
Price guide: B

The Castle

ALDEBURGH AND SNAPE

The town of Aldeburgh must be one of the pleasantest places for shopping. The High Street is lined with individual, mainly old-fashioned shops, all of them conscious of the gentility which pervades the atmosphere. On summer mornings there are always plenty of visitors out to buy fresh bread or fish, or browsing among the excellent souvenir shops; on a cold winter afternoon when the town is bright with Christmas lights there can be few places to match it for colour and elegance. The High Street is, of course, the centre of activity and interest. The Town Steps lead off up a steep hill to where the grander houses have an unrivalled view of the town and sea; the terraced gardens of Adair Lodge offer a wide flower-filled space to sit and contemplate. The climate here is always fresh – some would call it cool – and holidaymakers enjoy Aldeburgh as much for the charm of its streets and the dignified style it conveys as for its attractions as a seaside town.

Thorpeness Meare

Much the same may be said of Aldeburgh's neighbour, Thorpeness. Two miles to the north, and separated from Aldeburgh by the flat land which once was a shallow harbour, Thorpeness is a purely artificial resort. Until 1910 it was a collection of poor fishermen's cottages; then the local landowner transformed it by first digging The Meare (a vast expanse of water, but with a depth of only three feet throughout), then building houses in a variety of styles, mainly mock Tudor. The result is a collection of eye-catching and realistic follies. This impression is confirmed by two other interesting landmarks: The House in the Clouds, a former water tower ingeniously disguised as the house it has now become, complete with weatherboarding and tiled roof; and the windmill, which looks authentic, but was in fact brought here from nearby Aldringham to enhance the view.

This elegant seaside air belies the erstwhile importance of the area: Aldeburgh was a fishing port, a shipbuilding town and a smuggling centre – an 18th century visitor remarked that all Aldeburgh men were smugglers save the parson! But the town's fortunes were washed away with the best part of the town, and the haven silted up. Evidence of

The Moot Hall, Aldeburgh

the decline may be seen in the 16th-century Moot Hall. This lovely red-brick and timbered building with its wooden staircase and decorated chimneys once stood in the middle of the town; now it stands, rather forlornly, by the sea front, separated from the shingle only by a modern concrete sea wall. The Moot Hall has a small display of local history which charts the changing coastline.

Fishing is still a daily occupation, and fresh fish, lobster and crab may be bought direct from the fishermen on the beach by the Moot Hall. Further to the south, and standing proudly in a brand new shed is the Aldeburgh lifeboat, ready for the signal which brings its crew running to the shore where they launch the boat from the shingle banks into the crashing waves. But Slaughden Quay, once a bustling waterfront, is now crowded with simple pleasure boats. The river Alde flows here to within 100 yards of the sea; but its exit is barred by the spit which stretches south for a distance of almost ten miles. On the spit stands a Martello tower, the northernmost of the line of defences built against the threat of a Napoleonic invasion. Slaughden Quay was once the inappropriate workplace for the poet

The beach at Aldeburgh

George Crabbe. He was born in Aldeburgh in 1754, in a house long since devoured by the waves, and he returned to the town for a brief spell as curate at the parish church. He described the harshness of life in his native town in 'The Borough', and it was this verse which inspired another Suffolk man, Benjamin Britten, to write his famous opera, *Peter Grimes*. Britten's connection with Aldeburgh was long and fond. He lived here for many years and composed *Billy Budd* and *The Turn of the Screw* in a pink-washed house on the seafront. He is buried here, too, in the churchyard off Victoria Street. A memorial window designed by John Piper shows representations of Britten's music in vivid colours. Other memorials in this fine 16th-century church are to Crabbe, and a touching recollection of the 1899 lifeboat disaster, when the boat overturned just after launching and many men were drowned.

Britten made Aldeburgh famous in international circles when in 1948 he established the Aldeburgh Festival of Music and the Arts to promote contemporary music and act as a showcase for his own work. At first, performances were held in Aldeburgh's Jubilee Hall, but this proved to be too small to cope with the ever-growing audiences, so other venues were found, including the churches at Orford and Blythburgh. In 1967 the Festival moved to the splendid new Concert Hall in the former maltings at Snape. The Aldeburgh Festival office, however, remains in Aldeburgh High Street, and here you can obtain tickets and programmes.

Snape is a village at the head of the Alde estuary, and the Maltings are set a short distance apart from Snape Street, on the south side of Snape Bridge. The view from

Snape Quay

the bridge is as beautiful as it ever was when the maltings quay was busy with barges loading barley for the brewery trade. The mellow brick buildings were built in the mid-19th century by Newson Garrett (father of Elizabeth Garrett Anderson, first woman doctor and first lady mayor – of Aldeburgh), and they make the ideal place for a concert hall which has the reputation of being the finest in Europe. Britten composed *Peter Grimes* while living at Snape in a converted windmill; he saw the Queen open the first Aldeburgh Festival in June 1967. Two years later the hall was destroyed by a disastrous fire, but it was rebuilt within the year; today its unadorned brick and simple wooden seats give it a superb acoustic quality. Performances are held for most of the year and include all forms of music from opera to jazz. The Britten–Pears School for Advanced Musical

The Maltings at Snape

Studies is also housed in one of the Maltings buildings. Around the hall are craft shops and exhibition rooms, and 'The Plough and Sail' recalls the dual interests of Snape's past and present. River trips by motor launch leave from Snape Quay and wind their sinuous course between the mudflats of the estuary. The landscape is quiet and isolated, and when you look back at the Maltings over the rustling reeds it seems the ideal place for music.

Inside the Maltings Concert Hall

Snape was the site of an important archaeological discovery: a Saxon ship burial was excavated in 1862, half a mile east of the church. Further excavations have recently taken place and there have been some interesting finds.

'Sailor's Walk' runs along the north bank of the Alde. On the south bank, three miles from Snape, is the tiny community of Iken. There is a large field car park for picnickers and walkers at a picturesque and secluded site near Iken Cliff. On the rise stands the flint tower and thatched nave of St Botolph's church.

Thorpeness Windmill
Open: May, June, Sept: Sat & Sun 1400–1700, July, Aug: daily 1400–1700
Price guide: A

Aldeburgh Moot Hall
Open: April to May: Sat & Sun 1430–1700, June & Sept: daily 1430–1700, July to Aug: daily 1030–1730
Price guide: A

FRAMLINGHAM

Framlingham Castle today presents a very clear picture of what it must have looked like in its heyday. From across the sparkling blue waters of the Mere it rises like Camelot, without a hint of the 20th century to spoil the impression. Water meadows, sometimes spotted with a profusion of yellow marsh marigolds, extend westwards and harbour wildfowl which feed and glide, or take to the air in a flurry of splashes and cries.

Queen of England before going to Mass in St Michael's Church. Years later she returned on a visit with her husband, King Philip II of Spain.

After 1555 Arundel Castle became the family seat of the Norfolks, and so Framlingham entered upon a long period of decline and neglect. In the 17th century it was presented to Pembroke College, Cambridge, and they pulled down all the inner buildings and replaced them with a Poor House, which is now the custodian's residence and a museum. Today the lawns of the courtyard, surrounded by the high walls, make an ideal setting for medieval tournaments and theatre productions.

Roger Bigod began building this castle in 1190, to a design which was heavily influenced by the returning crusaders: the keep was redundant; instead, a curtain wall with towers encircled the hall, stables, workshops and living quarters within the yard. There is an evocative drawing of how it might have looked by the artist Alan Sorrell, and he shows the courtyard surrounded by wooden buildings – all of which have long since disappeared. There are 13 towers, all lacking a back wall, and having a gangway across them. This was to complicate the task of any attacker who might have reached a particular section of the battlements. Today's visitor, by contrast, is welcome to traverse the entire circuit and admire the countryside from 40 feet up. The elaborate chimneys are of the 16th century and most of them are merely for show!

King John was a guest of Bigod in 1213, and must have spotted the castle's weaknesses, for when he besieged the castle two years later it fell after only two days of fighting. In Tudor times Framlingham became the seat of the Howard family, Dukes of Norfolk, whose crest is still displayed over the gateway. But the greatest moment in the castle's history occurred in July 1553 when Princess Mary defied the Protestants who championed the cause of Lady Jane Grey, and from the battlements proclaimed herself

The town of Framlingham is picturesque, particularly on market day when the stalls cover Market Place, as they have done since 1276. Many of the houses are older than their graceful 18th-century fronts suggest. The Crown Hotel is the oldest, dating from the mid-16th century, and within it preserves the charm of its coaching inn days.

The Church of St Michael contains many memorials to the Howard family, some of whom were reinterred here following the Dissolution of Thetford Priory. The finest is to Thomas, the third Duke, who was sentenced to death by Henry VIII but was spared because the King died during the night. Not so fortunate was his son, the Earl of Surrey, famous as a poet, who had been beheaded the day before. With them now is Henry Duke of Richmond, an illegitimate son of Henry VIII who died at the age of 18, and Sir Robert Hitcham who bought the castle and gave it to Pembroke College – who in turn donated the outstanding organ of 1674. Between them, the castle and church contain Framlingham's story.

Framlingham Castle
English Heritage
Open: Jan to April: Tues to Sun 1000–1600, April to Sept: daily 1000–1800, Oct to Dec: Tues to Sun 1000–1600
Price guide: A

SAXTEAD GREEN MILL

Anyone travelling along the A1120 from Stowmarket to Yoxford cannot fail to notice Saxtead Mill, which stands beside a pretty village green just west of Framlingham. In summer the cottage gardens are alive with colour, children play on the grass among the buttercups and all around stretch miles of farmland. It is about as far from an industrial scene as could be imagined; but until the 18th century a windmill was the most complex industrial machine known, and Saxtead Mill can lay claim to being one of the most advanced designs of windmill ever.

Even from a distance this great mill, with its glistening white weatherboarding, is seen to have two distinct parts. First is the brick round house, which takes the weight of all the rest. Above it is the main body of the mill – or buck as it is technically called. This is approached by a flight of stairs from the ground, and visitors who worry about such things should take care, for the treads are rather narrow, and the height is only truly appreciated when it is too late! The sails of this mill have a span of 55 feet, and are bewilderingly complex. They consist of features called whips, stocks, clamps and vanes, but only the last need concern us, for these are the venetian-blind-like shutters which control the speed at which the sails turn. At 46 feet high the mill stands like a beacon.

The great storm of 1987 caused a lot of damage in East Anglia. Considerable renovation work was carried out at the mill

The earliest reference to a mill on the site is in 1287, and we know something of the cost from local records. The carpenters were paid 73s 4d and the millstones gobbled up a further 33s, while the lock on the door cost a mere 2½d! The late 13th century was a period of agricultural prosperity, and the land for miles around must have produced more than enough grain to keep the miller busy. Good times and bad followed, and many mills were built and pulled down before the present one was erected in 1796 and Amos Webber got to work. During the 1850s it was renovated and in its final form embodied the state of the art in windmill technology. It continued to produce flour until the First World War, after which it went over to animal foodstuffs. The last miller, Mr Aldred, died in 1947, and the mill subsequently passed into national ownership.

Of course, the wind drives the sails, but the vanes decide whether it is to be harnessed. The actual on-off 'switch' is to be seen directly above the door at the head of the stairs, where a chain over a wheel opens or closes the vanes. Saxtead is a post mill, which means that the entire structure is built around a central post which can be turned to keep the sails into the wind, and so ensure maximum use. The buck does the turning, and the round house carries its weight. The sails are kept into the wind by a fantail (or fly) which is on the fan carriage at the base of the stairs. The blades of the fantail operate a gearing mechanism which moves the entire upper part of the mill (including the stairs!) around a small rail set into the ground. And it is all done by wind power.

Inside the mill the great post can be seen passing through three floors to the top of the mill, where the drive is taken from the sails via the spindle wheel. There are two pairs of millstones, and they were fed from grain bins in the roof. A wind-powered sack hoist took the strain out of the lifting, but conditions must have been cramped, dusty and dangerous. The ladders and trap doors are not easy to negotiate, and even today some visitors may find difficulty. But it is worth it to see one of the finest windmills in the land: a monument to 18th-century ingenuity.

English Heritage
Open: April to Sept: Mon to Sat 1000–1800
Price guide: A

EASTON FARM PARK

What better way to escape the bustle of workaday life than to relax in the tranquil air of the countryside? Here at Easton the visitor can enjoy the atmosphere of a Victorian farm beside the gentle River Deben. The Farm Park is tucked away from the noisy world, but it is easy enough to find by following the signposts from the A12 near Wickham Market.

The 35-acre farm was originally the model farm of the Duke of Hamilton, who owned the huge Easton estate and had the red-brick buildings erected in 1870. There was no farmhouse on this site, because the Duke lived at Easton Hall, whose serpentine or crinkle-crankle wall may be seen in the village. When the Duke died in 1919 the estate was sold, but many of the original buildings were retained, and other new structures have been made to fit in with the concept.

There are many static exhibitions to tempt the nostalgic or the agriculturally curious, including farm machinery, carts and barrows, tools, a forge where the blacksmith repaired the machines as well as shod the Suffolk Punches which worked the land, and – from a later date – veteran motorbikes! But undoubtedly the visitor will be drawn to the real life of the farm, which continues around him. On certain days there are craft demonstrations, but always there are animals. In Pets' Corner children can make friends with an assortment of smaller animals such as rabbits and lambs; in the paddock they can see and touch ponies, goats or donkeys, and feed them with the special mixture available at the shop. You may be lucky enough to see a sow with her litter of squirming piglets, and there are ducks and ornamental wildfowl everywhere, especially outside the Stable Tea Rooms where you can sit on the terrace looking over the moat.

Feeding the goats

Further afield, the livestock paddocks have various breeds of sheep including the Suffolk and the coloured Jacob, munching contentedly at the grass, and Suffolk Punches may be there with their foals. These are always fascinating to watch because of their beautiful chestnut colour and their stocky, powerful frames. The breed was developed in Suffolk and lacks the typical ankle 'feathers' of the cart horse which are a drawback on heavy clay soils. Before the last war almost 20,000 new foals were registered; later, with increasing mechanisation, the numbers dwindled almost to extinction, but they are now seeing a revival.

Suffolk Punches

In the paddocks are interesting breeds of cattle, like the Longhorn; but the visitor also has the chance to see more familiar breeds in the Dairycentre. This building, completed in 1976, allows you to watch the afternoon's milking from a specially constructed viewing gallery. Here, modern design and automation combine to allow one man to milk 130 cows.

The showpiece of the Farm Park is certainly the Victorian Dairy. The walls are beautifully tiled; the windows show the Royal Oak, part of the Hamilton crest, in stained glass, and in the centre of the floor is a little fountain: decorative but also functional, since it helped to keep the dairy cool. Here cheese and butter were made and milk kept before being taken to the Hall, and the equipment used is on show.

The visitor should allow time to take a stroll around the park, beside the river and through pasture and woodland. A nature trail examining the plant and animal life has been devised, and anglers may care to get a permit from the kiosk and spend the day waiting for the bite of roach, perch or pike – a tranquil occupation indeed.

Easton Farm Park
Open: Mar to Oct: daily 1030–1800
Price guide: B

MINSMERE NATURE RESERVE

Minsmere is one of the prime nature reserves in the country. These 1500 acres at the mouth of the little river Minsmere include shingle beach, sand dunes, reedbeds and marsh, heath and woodland. The variety of landscape is a paradise for many different species of birds and for those who like watching them. You do not have to be an expert ornithologist to enjoy a day here – there is plenty of help on hand in the form of books and leaflets in the reception centre – and the enthusiastic amateur will simply take satisfaction in the peace of this reserve, where man's regard for nature makes him instinctively lower his voice and tread carefully.

Many species of birds nest and feed at the Scrape

The area was deliberately flooded in the last war as a counter-invasion measure, and became a nature reserve when, in 1947, four pairs of avocets were found to have nested here. These long-legged, elegant waders with their black and white plumage had disappeared from Britain over a century before, driven out by the draining of their favoured habitat and the stealing of their eggs for food, so it was important to encourage their return. The RSPB – who took the avocet as its emblem – leased the site and eventually bought it, and although avocets did not nest at Minsmere again until 1963, they have now established a colony second in size only to its near neighbour at Havergate Island (a Reserve accessible only by ferry boat from Orford Quay).

The reserve is approached along narrow roads from the tiny village of Eastbridge, or from Westleton, further to the north. Watch out for the sharp turn on Westleton Heath. Visitors must have a permit, available from the reception centre, and here also the essential binoculars may be hired. You may buy a checklist of all the species the observant birdwatcher may count on a day's visit, and then you are free to wander as you will. There are way-marked trails to follow, each covering two miles or so. These are well trodden, so waterproof footwear is advisable except in the driest season.

The Scrape

Eight hides are strategically placed around the reserve, and in these simple wooden huts you may raise the narrow shutters and enjoy the splendid view without disturbing the wildlife. The Tree Hide overlooks woodland which attracts species such as the sparrowhawk, the nightjar and the nightingale. Most of the hides overlook the Scrape, a 55-acre artificial lagoon of brackish water ideally suited to waders who nest and feed here on their migrations in spring and autumn. You should spot the common tern, redshank and ringed plover, as well as the avocet. The marshland and reedbeds are popular with all kinds of wildfowl, as well as the less easily seen marsh harrier, bittern and bearded reedling, and the beach area is sometimes cordoned off to allow little terns to nest in peace. Birds are not the only inhabitants of this watery landscape; there are small rodents and deer, otters and butterflies, including the silver-studded blue. Watch out for adders basking on the paths in the summer!

There is also a public hide on the shore overlooking the Scrape, and access is from Dunwich Heath. This is an area of bracken, gorse and heather with a few sparse trees, and car parking on the headland allows marvellous views north to the conspicuous white lighthouse at Southwold, and south across Minsmere Reserve to the futuristic dome of the nuclear power station at Sizewell.

Minsmere Reserve looking towards Sizewell nuclear power station

Minsmere RSPB Reserve
Open: All year daily, except Tues, 0900–2100 (or sunset)
Price guide: B

THE LOST TOWN OF DUNWICH

It is a profoundly unnerving experience to stand on the sandy cliffs of Dunwich and look out to sea. While aware of our own mortality, we take consolation from the assurance that life goes on, and that the places we know and love will be shared by those who come after us. This lonely, windswept beach of shingle destroys that comfort. Where once a great city stood, its numerous houses dominated by beautiful churches, and its activities focused on the harbour wharves and warehouses which ensured its wealth and pre-eminence, now the sea has dominion. The entire city lies beneath the waves, visited only by fish, crabs and the

Ruins of Greyfriars Refectory

was consecrated as Bishop of Dunwich. As the centuries rolled on, Dunwich lost its ecclesiastical supremacy, but it still claims a Suffragan Bishop. At the time of the Norman Conquest the city was the envy of its less successful neighbours and defensive ditches with ramparts were dug;

The Ship Inn sign depicting Dunwich's seal

occasional intrepid underwater archaeologist. The Dunwich known to the Romans is now over a mile from the shore. And still the sea takes its toll.

Long ago Dunwich ranked as one of England's greatest ports; kings called on its fleet in times of war, and Dunwich mariners sailed the seas, trading in furs, timber, wine, wool and fish. When East Anglia accepted Christianity, it was to Dunwich that St Felix came, and in 636 he

The spit which destroyed the port; the harbour was off to the left.

the most westerly of these can still be traced.

The golden age for Dunwich came in the 12th century, when it covered almost a square mile, and up to one hundred ships rode at anchor in its enormous harbour. The

Fishing from the beach

shifting coastline of Suffolk had produced a shingle spit which moved south, creating an inland harbour whose access to the sea was controlled by the burghers of Dunwich. The annual fair held on the Feast of St James has recently been revived, and it was (and is) an occasion of great enjoyment and pride. Fierce rivalry with neighbouring Southwold and Walberswick sometimes led to fighting because the River Blyth which sustained them flowed into Dunwich harbour, and so they had to pay harsh dues.

But the sea would end the city's power: in 1286 a great storm rose up and swept away three parish churches, and almost blocked the harbour entrance. 'The sea then overtook a third part of the town, and so enfeebled the

The beach and cliffs

haven by storm and tempest that it closes up once or twice every year.' Throughout the century which followed Dunwich fought a losing battle against the sea. In 1342 a total of 400 houses were lost, and the Black Death caused a writer to lament that the city was 'wasted and diminished'. Attempts to cut a channel through the shingle spit were futile, and the neighbouring towns could only rub their hands with pleasure at their rival's downfall. The story of these years is told in the excellent museum in the village street; it has a splendid model of old Dunwich and lots of interesting exhibits.

Dunwich endured, but not as a port. Gradually the people realised it was all over, gathered up their possessions and moved away. With each year's storms another street, another church and more history crumbled into the waves.

The West Gate of Greyfriars

All Saints, the last church, held its final service in 1755, but only in the present century did it slide beneath the waters. Greyfriars was built across the town ramparts in the 13th century, and today its gateway and refectory ruins are all that remain, waiting patiently for the sea's call.

Dunwich Museum
Open: April to Sept: daily 1130–1630, Oct: daily 1200–1600, Nov to Mar by appointment only
Price guide: Free

BLYTHBURGH AND WALBERSWICK

Blythburgh is a tiny village on the A12 that would pass unnoticed were it not for its magnificent church, known as 'the Cathedral of the Marshes'. The view from the north-east is particularly impressive. The road emerges from the trees and sweeps down towards this insignificant little river which suddenly spreads into a wide estuary, flooded at high tide and giving the impression of a lake; and rising above these waters and a cluster of roofs is the majestic silhouette of the Church of the Holy Trinity. At night it is beautifully floodlit, and its reflection in the river should make the traveller pause in admiration.

Why does such a small community have such a large church? The answer lies in the fickleness of the sea. The nave of the church was built in the 15th century when Blythburgh was a busy town. The river was navigable as far inland as Halesworth, and at Blythburgh there were quays

Church of the Holy Trinity, Blythburgh

handling wool and fish, and imports such as salt, upon which dues had to be paid. The town had a weekly market, two annual fairs, its own mint and a jail and courthouse (now the White Hart Inn). But the larger ships sought bigger ports, abandoning the shallow Blyth which silted up. When the priory was suppressed the church's leaden roof was stripped and the church plate was pawned for £20. Then several fires destroyed houses and lowered morale. In 1577 the steeple collapsed in the same violent storm which struck Bungay and gave rise to the legend of Black Shuck, and the north door still bears a scorch mark said to have been caused by the Devil. In 1644 the church suffered a visit by William Dowsing, a zealous Puritan who was appointed to seek out idols – statues, paintings and carvings – and destroy them. He and his men tethered their horses in the nave and used the beautiful angel roof for target practice.

The Angel Roof of Holy Trinity Church

The River Blyth at Walberswick

In subsequent centuries the church suffered from neglect. In 1880 the congregation had to shelter under umbrellas against the rain leaking through the holes in the roof. But an extensive programme of restoration was undertaken and the battle still continues, especially against the voracious deathwatch beetle. The roof has been repaired, using iron

The River Blyth at Blythburgh

bolts where the original carpenter used scarcely a nail, and 11 of the original 12 angels remain, some with new wings. The visitor today is struck by the size and lightness of the interior with its high clerestory windows, and will admire the lovely carved pew ends which show the seven deadly sins and the seasons. A Jack o' the Clock strikes a bell with his hatchet to signal the start of the service – 'As the hours pass away, so doth the life of man decay. 1682'.

Access to Walberswick is from the A12 at Toby's Walks, a picnic area just to the south of Blythburgh. This village, like Blythburgh, was once a thriving port. In the 15th century it traded with Iceland, the Faroes and into the North Sea, and grew in importance as Dunwich Haven silted up. But fires here brought ruin, and the church of St Andrew charts a similar course of high hopes dashed by changing fortunes. At the end of the 17th century the impoverished villagers petitioned for the church to be made smaller because they could no longer support it; and only the south aisle and tower remain in use – the rest is a picturesque ruin.

Walberswick is indisputably pretty, with its open salt-marsh and heath where once the villagers grazed cattle and geese; a National Nature Reserve here covers 1270 acres. The walk through the village passes the green and leads between red-brick cottages to a wide car park on Fishermen's Flats, where once nets were spread to dry. From here you can see the old sheds, once used for kippering herring, and riverside cottages, some on stilts. A ferry runs to the other bank, or you can walk upstream, past the rickety jetties and little boats, to the bridge.

The beach is a dream – fine light sand running smoothly down to the waves. The western edge of the shore is sand dunes planted with marram grass to prevent erosion; Walberswick loses a yard of land each year to the encroaching sea. A high earthen bank now protects the north side of the village. Walberswick is a favourite with visitors, including artists like Philip Wilson Steer, who in the 19th century captured the changing patterns of light and colour we still enjoy today.

Fishing at Walberswick

SOUTHWOLD

Southwold is an elegant seaside resort, and its gentility stems perhaps from its rather isolated position on a sort of island at the end of a winding road which leaves the A12 just north of Blythburgh. This road crosses Buss Creek, once the busy mooring place for busses (herring boats), and climbs up the hill into the heart of the town.

Southwold Jack

The Market Place is triangular, and its centre is marked by a Victorian cast-iron pump. Around it stand buildings such as the handsome 17th-century Swan Hotel, and the Town Hall which houses a marvellously informative Tourist Information Office. Few of Southwold's houses date from before 1659, when a fire fanned by an onshore wind destroyed three-quarters of the town in the space of four hours. Shops, granaries, merchandise and houses were reduced to ashes, and about 300 families were left destitute. A nationwide appeal for funds was launched, and Southwold was the first nationally declared Disaster Area.

The Church of St Edmund, built in the mid-15th century, survived the fire because it stands in a large churchyard next to Bartholomew Green. Inside is a painted pulpit and a magnificent screen. 'Southwold Jack' is the figure of a Wars of the Roses soldier carrying a sword with which he strikes a bell to signal the start of the service. Opposite the church in Victoria Street is the Southwold Museum, a pretty Dutch-gabled cottage. Near the church, too, is the Southwold Summer Theatre, with its programme of drama to suit all tastes.

East Green is dominated by three buildings. The Sole Bay Inn is the oldest; Sole Bay lies slightly north of the town and here in 1672 a great battle was fought against the Dutch. The English fleet was caught unawares, with many of the seamen ashore sleeping off the effects of merry-making on the previous day, Whit Sunday. When battle was joined it was fierce but indecisive. Many thousands were killed, notable among them the Earl of Sandwich, whose body was picked up some time later near Harwich and identified by his Star and Garter and three rings he had in his pocket. Bodies continued to be washed up for months, and anyone finding and burying one was awarded the handsome sum of one shilling. Behind the Sole Bay Inn rises the startling white tower of the lighthouse. Built in 1899, it was set well back from the crumbling cliff edge and stands surrounded by houses – a beautiful landmark. The other side of East Green is occupied by Southwold's most famous commercial enterprise: Adnam's Brewery. The smell of malt often lingers in the air, and you may see a horse-drawn dray making local deliveries.

Walking along by the sea is a delight. Southwards the cliffs rise higher, and little cottages – which include the delightful sailors' reading room of 1864, now a museum – give way to larger houses at Centre Cliff, each with a long, immaculate garden. Beyond, there is St Edmund's Hill, more commonly known as Gun Hill because of the six cannon which stand overlooking the bay. These have nothing to do with the Sole Bay encounter; they are Tudor, and were given to the town in 1745. The Germans considered Southwold to be a fortified town because of these guns, and they bombed the port in the First World War.

The lighthouse from St James' Green

North along the Promenade the road slopes down to the pier and beach. Here wooden groynes have been built in an attempt to stop the sand shifting southwards, a movement which caused the silting of the harbour – one of the factors that led to the decline of Southwold as a fishing port.

Southwold Museum
Open: April to Sept: daily 1430–1630
Price guide: Free

Lifeboat Museum
Open: May to Sept: daily 1430–1630
Price guide: Free

SUFFOLK WILDLIFE PARK, KESSINGLAND

The Park is situated just south of Lowestoft off the A12. It was established in 1969 and has since been enlarged; it now covers some 100 acres. It offers to the visitor The African Experience, concentrating on species whose existence in the wild is under threat.

Modern zoos are a far cry from the concrete jungles of yesteryear, and the collection at Kessingland is a good example of the new ethos. The grounds are spacious: wide meadows lead down to lakes and to woodland walks from where you can see deer, ponies or exotic breeds of cattle. Contact with these animals, whenever possible, is encouraged. There is a walk-through pets' enclosure containing such domestic favourites as rabbits, as well as the more unexpected – wallabies, for instance, and you may be lucky enough to see a mother and her 'joey'. You can watch them at very close quarters. In Farmyard Corner are pygmy goats, pigs, donkeys and chickens, and you may even feed them with the special food you can buy.

We are fairly familiar with even quite exotic animals through seeing them on television, but television is no substitute for seeing them in real life. It is thrilling to see a real camel or a herd of zebras feeding, and chimpanzees swinging in their hammocks and gazing at you with such intelligence; the lions prowl round in a natural wooded valley where you can admire them and appreciate their power from a safe distance. One of the best times to watch them is when they are fed in the early afternoon.

The rare breeds include the Poitou donkey, which, at 14 hands high is much taller than the breed with which we are so familiar. Originating from the Poitou region of France, it was bred as a strong pack animal whose numbers had dwindled from thousands to only 44 in 1977. You will see here other unusual breeds of familiar animals, such as the picturesquely named Vietnamese Pot-Bellied pigs, or Barbary sheep, or the Soay which in the wild in St Kilda, likes to eat seaweed. More exotic animals include the Japanese Sika deer, a fishing cat from the Far East, petite Squirrel monkeys from South America, and endangered Lemurs from Madagascar, where only 10% of the original forests remain. Follow in the footsteps of the great African explorers, Stanley, Baker and Livingstone, and take one of the colour-coded trails around the park, through Flamingo Walks or past Lemur Islands. For those who find such a safari too arduous, the Safari Road-Train, a charming motorised vehicle will take you on a 20 minute ride down into the valley, allowing you to see in comfort the further reaches of the Park.

And the wildlife is not the only attraction here. There is a large playground, a bouncy castle and crazy golf for the youngsters; young and old alike may take tea in the Explorers' Cafeteria or browse amongst the treasures in Livingstone's Storeroom, which stocks some genuine African handcrafted articles, such as baskets, beads and musical intruments, so that you may take a little of your African experience home with you.

Finally, some intriguing facts about a few of the creatures to set you thinking. Did you know that a full grown lion weighs 225 kg and measures 11 feet from nose to tail? That a male chimpanzee can eat over 50 bananas at a time? That Bactrian camels live up to 25 years? Or that in the wild the mortality rate for baby cheetahs is 90%, many of them falling prey to pythons? If you want to find out about such things, this wildlife park will fascinate you.

Wallaby with 'joey'

Suffolk Wildlife Park
Open: All year: Jan to Mar: daily 1000–1600, April to June: daily 1000–1700, July to Oct: Mon to Fri 1000–1730, Sat & Sun 1000–1800, Nov to Dec: daily 1000–1600
Price guide: C

LOWESTOFT

Lowestoft is one of East Anglia's survivors. A century ago it was the centre of a vast fishing industry. Today it is equally well-known as a seaside resort. This major shift has not been without hardship, and the problems and uncertainties continue to the present day, but if past form is anything to go on, Lowestoft will be thriving a hundred years from now.

The town is divided by a bascule bridge across the River Waveney. To the north is the main shopping centre and the fishing port. It was in the early 1800s that the fishing industry brought prosperity to the town, and the fish concerned was the herring. This was caught by great fleets of sail drifters, and brought into port where it was gutted and packed for the London market. The transition from sail to steam enhanced the port's growth, and it is likely that at the time of greatest success – just before the outbreak of the First World War – over 700 fishing boats worked from the quays and jetties. It was a boom town, and with hindsight was creating the seeds of its own downfall. In those days it must have seemed impossible that fish stocks could be exhausted, but now we know all too well the danger of overfishing. Fewer than 50 trawlers use the harbour today, and they catch plaice and cod. The fishermen still feel that their livelihood is threatened, but this time the uncertainty is directed towards EU quotas which restrict the size of catches.

The Lowestoft and East Suffolk Maritime Museum is situated in the Sparrow's Nest Park and tells the story of the herring fleets of Lowestoft. There are many interesting exhibits, including some models of boats which operated from the port, but the most telling signs of Lowestoft's decline as a fishing port are the photographs of the fleets setting out into the North Sea. The museum also chronicles the stirring history of the lifeboat.

The town retains some of its old street plan, and the small, tightly packed houses create lanes called 'scores' leading to the foreshore. Of more recent creation is the Britten shopping complex, which reminds us that here was the birthplace of one of England's finest composers. The main street is a pedestrian precinct, allowing leisurely shopping.

South of the bridge is the holiday resort, heralded by the pier, which provides amusement arcades, bingo, refreshments and a platform for fishing on a more modest scale. The sandy beach is safe for children, who will find more than enough to entertain them, including a traditional Punch and Judy show. The East Point Pavilion Visitors' Centre has The Lowestoft Story, a multi-sensory experience telling the history of the town, as well as 'Discoverig', an imaginative play platform for younger children. This is a real family resort and the entertainment offered will let everyone enjoy themselves.

To the west of the town is Oulton Broad, linked to Lowestoft and the sea by Lake Lothing. The Nicholas Everitt Park is a lovely place to sit and observe the water-

The harbour

The beach

Bygone Lowestoft, when the herring fleets were in their heyday (photograph by courtesy of Mr. David Moyse and Lowestoft Maritime Museum)

sports which take place there, or to embark on a short cruise. On some evenings there are powerboat races.

Transport of a slower kind is to be found in the developing East Anglia Transport Museum at nearby Carlton Colville.

To the north of Lowestoft is Pleasurewood Hills American Theme Park which makes children of us all. Among the attractions are two miniature railways, sea-lion shows, an exciting Waveswinger, a Dinosaur Park and lots, lots more. Lowestoft still has a great deal to say for itself.

Oulton Broad

Lowestoft and East Suffolk Maritime Museum
Open: May to Sept: daily 1000–1700
Price guide: A

Fishing Industry and Harbour Tours
Mon to Fri: details from Harbour Office

East Anglia Transport Museum
Open: May to Sept: Sun & bank holidays 1100–1700, June also Sat 1400–1600, July to Sept: daily 1400–1600
Price guide: B

Lydia Eva Steam Drifter
Lowestoft Harbour
Open: April to June: daily 1000–1700
Price guide: A

SOMERLEYTON HALL AND GARDENS

Somerleyton Hall is situated to the north-west of Lowestoft, and is approached by roads which become more minor with each turn. The red-brick boundary wall is the first sign of the great house and it runs for miles. The drive is lined with young lime trees planted to honour the marriage of the Prince and Princess of Wales.

Somerleyton Hall

The origins of the Hall are Elizabethan, but what the visitor sees today is early Victorian and dates from the 1840s. Sir Morton Peto was a successful builder whose achievements included the Houses of Parliament and Nelson's Column. He bought the Somerleyton estate and proceeded to rebuild the Hall in the popular Italian style, importing many treasures to embellish its interior. By 1863 Sir Morton had sufficient financial troubles to oblige him to put the whole estate up for sale, and with great sadness he saw it pass to Sir Francis Crossley, a carpet manufacturer from Halifax, who was also known for his philanthropic work among the poor. The Crossley family continues to own and occupy the Hall, and the present Lord Somerleyton inherited the title in 1959.

The Maze

Whichever way the visitor approaches the Hall it offers a splendid sight, being set above manicured flower beds aglow with colour and encircled by great sweeps of lawn. The stone of the Hall is complemented by many steps, statues and terraces in the grounds. There is a pleasing lack of symmetry, making each angle of view a refreshing experience. To one side is the elegant campanile tower from which it is possible to glimpse the lofty spire of Norwich Cathedral. From another approach one comes upon the cloister-like simplicity of the Winter Garden.

Although the Hall is grand it retains the scale of a family home, which is what it is. The Library is comfortable and offers pleasing views of the garden; the Dining Room contains several paintings of interest. But it is to the gardens that the visitor will wish to return, for quite simply they are without equal. A team of three gardeners tends these 12 acres of lawns, shrubs and flowers – a world which should only belong to 17th-century opera or dreams of Heaven. The excellent guide book tells of the 17th-century historian William Fuller who thought the name of Somerleyton appropriate, 'for there summer is to be seen in the depths of winter'. Even the unusual green-houses are worth inspecting, as they were designed by Sir Joseph Paxton, architect of the Crystal Palace in London. Here the disasters of the October 1987 storms are turned to some advantage in a display of cross sections from some of the more substantial timbers.

The Maze is one of the best in Britain, and was designed by William Nesfield in 1846. It is formed from yew and at 400 yards from start to centre it makes for quite a walk. Success here means finding the middle and sitting in a raised pagoda, listening to the frantic cries for help from those still lost, and knowing you have yet to get out. It is good fun.

The pergola

There are so many other features worth mentioning, but the visitor should try to see the beautiful, 300-foot-long iron pergola wrapped in roses of gorgeous scent and colour. The Clock Tower was designed for the Houses of Parliament, but their Lordships rejected it, so Sir Morton built it at Somerleyton. It could have been as famous as Big Ben! A miniature railway runs round a quarter-mile track in the grounds, and this is popular with children of all ages.

Open: April to Sept: Sun, Thur & bank holidays 1400–1700, July & Aug also Tues & Wed. Gardens from 1230
Price guide: B

Above The River Crouch at North Fambridge flats, Essex
Below left Thaxted, Essex
Below right Countryside near Stonham Parva, Suffolk

Cavendish, Suffolk

Above left Carved figure on de Vere House, Lavenham, Suffolk
Above right Woodbridge Tide Mill, Suffolk
Below The River Deben at Ramsholt, Suffolk

Above Thurne Mill, Norfolk

Below Cromer, Norfolk

84

Above Boats at Cromer
Below left Norwich Cathedral
Below right The beach at Great Yarmouth

Wimpole Hall, Cambridgeshire

Newmarket Races

FRITTON LAKE AND COUNTRY PARK

The country park at Fritton lake is part of the Somerleyton estate which has been opened to the public; it is available to all seeking rest and recreation. It is to be found on the Norfolk–Suffolk border near Great Yarmouth, just off the A143.

Fritton Lake is two miles long and is surrounded by attractive wooded countryside. It is thought that the lake was formed, like the Norfolk Broads, by peat cutting in the Middle Ages. Later it became a focal point for wildfowlers, because here there were decoys – special netted channels used to trap ducks. The decoy-man would lure the ducks to swim up the narrowing channel by offering them grain or by enticing them to follow his dog which he had trained to run up alongside. Ducks are apparently very curious creatures, and eventually they would find themselves in the narrowest part of the net where their exit was barred. As many as two thousand ducks a day might be caught in this way, and they were dispatched to the waiting London markets. This activity continued for three hundred years, only coming to an end in 1960.

For centuries, then, people have lived and worked in this valley. Now it is open to even greater numbers as busy town-dwellers search for the beauty and peace of the countryside.

The Snake slide in the adventure playground

The first impression is one of space and light. Even if the huge grassy car park seems full, you are never aware of crowds. To whet the appetite of intending visitors there is a video presentation just outside the reception area which allows you to sample some of the pleasures of the country park. The park has attractions for all the family: for the children there is a fine and imaginative adventure playground which will keep them amused for hours with its snake slide, Noah's Ark and animals, and giant toadstools. There are popular tyre swings, nets to climb and a sandpit to play in. If that is not enough, there are pony rides, or pony and trap rides for the less ambitious. The rest of the family can explore the woodland or walk through the beautiful formal gardens – a mass of colour across which you can see the blue of the lake. In one of the gardens stands a bronze statue in memory of five men killed in the war who had spent their childhood at Fritton.

Pony and trap ride

You can take a boat trip, or hire a rowing boat and find the more isolated parts of the park. An angler will enjoy a visit here, as there are more than a thousand yards of bank set aside for him, and he may be lucky enough to catch tench, bream or carp. There is a putting course, and a 20-acre pitch and putt course. And when the activity is over the visitor may eat in the tea room or enjoy his own picnic or barbecue in the grounds.

The Visitors' Information Centre has a very interesting display about the lake itself and about the surrounding area. There are special features on the flora and fauna of Fritton Lake, and specimens of fish and birds which can be seen here.

In the Visitors' Centre you may also see basket-making demonstrations. It is fascinating to watch, and amazing how many different kinds of basket there are, each with its special name and use. You may buy any of them.

But it is to the lake that your attention will be drawn, whether you go fishing or boating, or simply admire the view. There is something here for everyone, except for dog-owners – please note that your pet is not allowed into this country park.

Open: April to Sept 1000–1700
Price guide: B

THE WAVENEY VALLEY

The River Waveney rises in Redgrave Fen, five miles from Diss, and flows almost due east before turning north to meet the Yare and finally reach the sea at Yarmouth. It is not a grand river; on the contrary, it meanders lazily through the countryside, but it is important in that it forms more than half of the boundary between Norfolk and Suffolk.

The tower of St Michael and All Angels, Beccles, rising over the valley of the Waveney.

The roads and villages keep a respectful distance from the river which is liable to flooding, even now when so many drainage ditches have been dug. In its upper reaches the valley is largely inaccessible; but it is peaceful and attractive, with its rich green pasture grazed by cattle and dotted with willows. Only isolated villages, farms and old halls dare to occupy the valley bottom, and the main Yarmouth to Bury St Edmunds road keeps sensibly to the higher ground to the north – across the border in Norfolk.

The first Suffolk town of any size is Bungay, where the Waveney loops northwards like a horseshoe around Outney Common. Bungay is an ancient town, once a settlement on the Roman Stone Street, and enriched in the 12th century by a massive castle built by Roger Bigod, later Earl of Norfolk. It stands on an eminence overlooking the river valley. Ownership swung between kings and the Earls, and when the latter sided with rebels they had to buy their royal pardon with 1000 marks. Henry II insisted that the castle be demolished, and you can still see the tunnel made to undermine one of the towers. But it was not utterly destroyed, and although in later centuries the facing stones were carted off to be recycled by the townspeople, today's visitor can see the two huge towers and part of the keep, and for a view of what it once must have looked like there is a model in the Council Offices in Earsham Street. The castle is tucked away to the north-east of the main road, and is best approached along the lane beside The Swan Inn.

In 1688 a great fire consumed all but half a dozen detached houses, and the heat was so intense as to melt the bells in St Mary's Church Tower. As a result, most of the older houses in Bungay date from Georgian times. In the Market Place stands the Butter Cross of 1689 which commemorates the fire. It is a pretty structure, octagonal and with a dome surmounted by a figure of Justice. Appropriately, a cage underneath used to hold local felons for public ridicule.

The River Waveney was made navigable as far as Bungay in the 17th century, and the town enjoyed considerable trade in flax, leather and printing. The last-named continues to thrive in the form of Richard Clay Ltd. In Georgian times the town became a spa. No evidence of this remains. What we see today is still a market town with fine churches – St Mary's, and the older Holy Trinity with its round tower – and some picturesque buildings, mainly with more recent shop fronts. Bungay is proud of its long history, and a network of walks sharing the collective title of 'The Bigod Way' remind both visitor and resident alike of the debt owed to that powerful (and belligerent) family. But the town has dwindled in size and importance over the years, and it has escaped the harsher changes of the 20th century.

One incident from Bungay's past is still famous in Suffolk. On a stormy Sunday morning in August 1577, the congregation in St Mary's Church were terrified by the apparition of a monstrous black dog, who killed two of their number, scarred others with burns and frightened the rest half to death. This beast, 'Black Shuck' – the Devil himself, as the parishioners believed – made other appearances in the county, notably at Blythburgh where it burnt an imprint into the church door. The more prosaic would say that

Bungay Market Cross with the tower of St Mary's Church.

Looking through Bungay Castle's twin towers to St Mary's Church

Beccles town sign showing Elizabeth I presenting the Charter

lightning had struck, but the superstitious still report the occasional sighting.

Bungay shares many features with its larger neighbour downstream, Beccles. But whereas Bungay seems not to have kept pace with progress, Beccles has adjusted to change, and it is still thriving. One reason is that Beccles is still accessible by water, and in the new leisure industry has a place as a pretty extension to the Broads. Many pleasure craft moor at the Quay, whose facilities are ever expanding. An excellent new Broadland Information Centre gives details of cruises and angling on the Waveney and in the Norfolk Broads, as well as information about local and natural history. There are wide greens by the river, and the red-brick buildings – some old maltings tastefully converted, and others brand new but in traditional style – enhance the beauty of this spot. In August the Carnival and Regatta bring even more fun and bustle.

Lining the streets of Northgate and Puddingmoor are many attractive houses, most of them with pretty back gardens leading down to the water's edge. Up the hill on the left is the old market place which has now been abandoned in favour of New Market, at the top. Part of this area has been paved and allows better access to the shopper. Dominating the town from every point of view is the high tower of St Michael and All Angels. It has recently been restored by the local council who purchased it for a nominal price of £1! The tower stands apart from the church, whose magnificent two-storeyed south porch must be seen. The view from here across river and floodplain is stunning.

Beccles, too, has an ancient history and many of the street names are resonant of past times: Ballygate, Smallgate, Peddars Lane. Several town trails guide the walker, and there is an unusual Marsh Trail which concentrates on the wildlife of Beccles Fen, a large area to the north-east of the town which was given to the inhabitants by Queen Elizabeth I – a gift recalled in the town sign. The museum in Newgate has a collection of local interest, covering domestic, agricultural and industrial aspects. One of the exhibits is a printing press of 1842, a reminder that opposite the museum is the printing works of William Clowes, which prints books as diverse as *Hymns Ancient and Modern* and the tales of Beatrix Potter. The town, indeed, has a flourishing industrial area, and a heliport which is the largest in Europe; but the industry is inconspicuous, and Beccles presents a friendly and optimistic face to the world.

Beccles Quayside

Bungay Museum
Open: All year: Mon to Fri 0900–1600
Price guide: A

THE MUSEUM OF EAST ANGLIAN LIFE, STOWMARKET

The Museum of East Anglian Life occupies an attractive open-air site which includes a pretty, tree-lined lane, a meadow and a mill and windpump beside a little river. Yet this rural setting is, in fact, only a few minutes' walk from the centre of the busy town of Stowmarket.

The museum was established in 1964, and the site and the collection have since grown. The museum is well signposted from the main road, so motorists need not worry about navigating around the one-way system of the town; they will, however, have to share the paying car park at Meadow Centre with the brand new supermarket. In 1988 a new reception area and shop were opened. The shop has the attraction of being open when the museum itself is closed during the winter months, and it stocks a huge array of crafts, books and comestibles, all with an East Anglian connection, including such diverse merchandise as wooden jigsaw puzzles, corn dollies and Norfolk lavender products. Here, too, old photographs and a commentary give a fore-taste of the museum, and the excellent handbook gives the visitor a guided tour of the site and detailed background information which makes interesting reading.

The Woodturner in his shop

The exhibits are grouped according to themes. 'The Farming Year' is represented in Abbots Hall Barn (an ancient tithe barn, parts of which date from the 13th century) by old-fashioned carts and carriages, and displays of the machinery and tools once used. There is also an early farmhouse re-erected on the other side of Crowe Lane. Another theme is domestic life at the turn of the century, with re-creations of typical rooms, a classroom, and some little shops cluttered with their wares. The 'Travellers and Sporting Men' exhibition contains gypsy caravans, show-men's vans and a variety of gruesome traps.

Moving away from the main huddle of buildings near the entrance, the visitor follows a rather uneven path to the Eight-Acre Meadow. Here is the huge Boby Building, housing locally-built engines and a variety of small craftsmen's shops which include basket-weaving, woodturning, harness-making and printing. There are occasional demonstrations, and video films of some of the craftsmen at work. Outside at the top of the field is the Grundisburgh Smithy, a mid-18th century building containing all the tools for repairing farm machinery and domestic ironware, as well as for shoeing horses.

Alton watermill

At the bottom of the meadow stands Eastbridge Windpump, brought here from the Minsmere Level after it collapsed in 1978. It was reconstructed exactly, and will turn when there is wind enough. Further along is Alton Watermill, relocated here when its site just south of Ipswich was threatened by the building of Alton Reservoir in the 1960s. It is a pretty, white weatherboarded building, and visitors can watch the giant cogs and wheels as they turn. Flour is sometimes ground here.

This prides itself on being a 'living museum', and to see it at its best, you should choose a time when demonstrations or special events are taking place. A calendar of these is available, and it includes sheep shearing, spinning, lacemaking and duck decoy making. Wonderful traction engines, perfectly restored and working as they were intended make such a splendid impression that the noise and smoke become quite bearable! Such activities bring the Museum to life and make it an exciting place to visit.

The Museum has links with the Long Shop Museum in Leiston, a former engineering works which illustrates the history of this local industry. A visit to Leiston confirms that engineering to the highest standards took place in Suffolk even before the First World War.

Museum of East Anglian Life, Stowmarket
Open: April to Oct: Tues to Sun & bank holiday Monday 1000–1700, July & Aug: daily
Price guide: B

Long Shop Museum, Leiston
Open: April to Oct: Mon to Sat 1000–1700, Sun 1100–1700
Price guide: A

ICKWORTH PARK

Ickworth is the creation of an extraordinary, not to say eccentric, gentleman – Frederick Hervey, fourth Earl of Bristol (1730–1803). After 1768 he became Bishop of Derry, a piece of good fortune which probably owed less to his piety than to the fact that his brother was Lord Lieutenant of Ireland. His devotion to church matters was peculiar; on one occasion he is reported to have organised races for curates, with the winners receiving vacant benefices! The income from the diocese permitted him to indulge his passion for architecture, and in 1787 he set about creating a very special house at Ballyscullion. Nothing of it remains today, but it is important as it anticipates the design he was later to use at the family home at Ickworth, three miles south-west of Bury St Edmunds.

His greatest delight was in travel – he had a passion for Italy – and when in 1779 he succeeded his brother to the title of Earl of Bristol, he could induge his whims to the full. He had the income from 30,000 acres of land to spend, and he knew exactly what he was going to do with it. Since the first years of the 18th century his family had thought about building a new home. The first earl had even employed Capability Brown to landscape the park, and today the visitor can enjoy the fruits of his labours by walking along Albana Walk, through lines of magnificent trees, to a deer park. A summer house and a formal canal were built, but the plans for the house stayed on paper until the earl-bishop came to Ickworth in 1792. He rejected the first earl's plans but resolved to build a house on the site. He then returned to his beloved Italy. Incredibly, he was not to visit Suffolk again.

In Italy he eventually engaged Mario Asprucci as architect for Ickworth. He, too, never crossed the English Channel, and so when work began in 1795 both of them were forced to work from the papier mâché model which is now on show in the house. The earl-bishop was very clear about what he wanted: a great rotunda, 100 feet high, to contain the main residence and the state rooms. Curving away from this, both east and west, were corridors to display sculpture, and at the ends were two great galleries, where he planned to present a collection of Europe's great paintings. So dedicated was he to this worthy aim that he even bought works he did not like, but felt should be included! The entire house was to have a frontage of 600 feet, and be surrounded on three sides by a stone wall and box hedges.

The outbreak of war between France and England brought disaster: in 1798 Napoleon invaded Italy, and the earl-bishop's entire collection was confiscated; he spent nine months in prison. So the house holds paintings collected by previous earls, and they are a sample of all that is best: works by Reynolds, Gainsborough, Titian, Velasquez and Hogarth. After his release the earl-bishop resumed his travels until 1803, when he died in a hovel in Italy.

At the time of his death only the rotunda had been built, and even that lacked a roof. It was left to his successors to complete the house. It is our good fortune today to see what he was denied: a sumptuous folly, bursting with beautiful furniture, sculpture, paintings and some of the finest silver in England, and set in magnificent parkland.

National Trust
House open: Mar to Nov: Tues, Wed, Fri, Sat, Sun & bank holiday Monday 1300–1700 Price guide: C
Gardens open: Nov to April: 1000–1600, April to Nov: 1000–1700
Price guide: A Park open: All year: daily 0700–1900
Price guide: Free

BURY ST EDMUNDS

Visitors to Bury St Edmunds have always admired the town: 'the neatest place that ever was seen', wrote Cobbett, and Dickens echoed this sentiment: 'a handsome little town of thriving and cleanly appearance'. The same impression greets today's traveller. It may not seem so from the A14 which by-passes Bury and sweeps under the chimneys of the giant sugar factory, but the heart of Bury St Edmunds is a fine, well-ordered place. One of the factors may be the geometric pattern of the streets, laid out as long ago as the 11th century – an early example of town planning! Although progress has demanded modern chain stores and deference to traffic, Bury still retains many buildings of architectural interest and importance.

Abbeygate Street

The delightfully-named Angel Hill faces the great Abbey Gateway. In truth it is more of a slope than a hill, but it is, nevertheless, a fine open space once used as the site for the Bury Fair, until rowdyism in the last century brought it to an end. It is a pity that this has now become a large car park, and the ugly signpost detracts from the view. On Angel Hill stands the Angel Hotel, an old coaching inn, covered in Virginia Creeper. Mr Pickwick stayed here in Dickens' *Pickwick Papers* because this is where Dickens himself stayed when he gave readings at the Athenaeum,

almost next door. This elegant white-painted building became the town's social and cultural centre. The Ballroom still attracts large gatherings. Angel Hill also has the Tourist Information Office. At Manor House Museum on Honey Hill is a fine collection of exhibits, including the John Gershom-Parkington Memorial Collection of time-measuring instruments. Bury had a tradition of making timepieces, and this marvellous collection was presented to the town in memory of a son killed in the last war.

The road leading away from the abbey is Abbeygate, and it has some interesting shops, many of them old but refronted during the 17th and 18th centuries. Here is The Nutshell, one of Britain's smallest pubs.

The Corn Exchange, at the top of the street, was to have been demolished in 1958, but a public outcry saved this gracious building with its decorated portico and colonnades. Now divided into two storeys, it has shops on the ground floor and a concert or conference hall above. The Market Cross, up the road on Cornhill, is another elegant building, redesigned by Adam in 1774. Originally a corn market below and a clothiers' hall above, it became a theatre and is now the venue for the town's art gallery. The exhibits are not permanent, so there is always something new to see. The roads open out at Cornhill and Butter Market; Bury is still a busy market town and the stalls are set up on Wednesdays and Saturdays. There is a livestock market, too, but it is no longer held in this square – once called Beasts' Market. On the corner of Cornhill is Moyses Hall, a pair of Norman houses which served various purposes before becoming the town's museum in 1899. It has a collection dealing with local archaeology and history, including mementoes of the Red Barn murder.

On Westgate Street stands the Theatre Royal, a magnificent Regency theatre with all the elegance and style we expect from that period. It has known bad days, when the coming of the cinema in the 1920s led to its closure; it was used as a store for beer barrels for the brewery opposite until 1965, when an appeal led to its refurbishment and reopening. It provides all kinds of entertainment for a wide area of Suffolk, and its intimate atmosphere and beautiful decorations make a special event of any performance. The furnishings are dark red, and the ceiling is painted with wispy clouds. There are two tiers of boxes all around the stalls, enabling everyone to have a first-class view. Now in the care of the National Trust, it is, we hope, safeguarded for the delight of future audiences.

Modern Bury has sports facilities for all, and of particular note is Rollerbury, the town's roller-skating rink which has a national reputation.

Manor House, Honey Hill
Includes Gershom-Parkington Collection of Watches and Clocks
Open: daily: 1000–1700, Sun 1400–1700 Price guide: B

Art gallery
Open: All year: Tues to Sat 1030–1630
Price guide: A

Moyses Hall
Open: All year: Mon to Sat 1000–1700, Sun 1400–1700
Price guide: A

Theatre Royal
National Trust
Open: Any reasonable time
Price guide: Free

Bury St Edmunds Abbey

King Sigebert, the first Christian king of East Anglia, established a religious community at a place known as Bedericsworth in the 7th century. In 870 King Edmund was martyred for his faith by the Danes, who tied him to a tree, and fired arrows into his body. After lying in a number of resting places, the bones of the saint came to this Suffolk town, which by the time of Edward the Confessor was known as St Edmund's Bury.

Following the Norman Conquest, work began on a new abbey, and in 1095 the bones of St Edmund were placed with great ceremony just behind the high altar. For centuries pilgrims flocked to the shrine, and their gifts made the abbey one of the richest in England. Even today the scale of the ruins is impressive; the west front was said to be more magnificent than its contemporary at Ely. Today there are houses built into these arches.

King John refused to appoint an abbot to Bury, and instead took the revenue for himself. It was to prevent actions such as this that 25 of the leading nobles met in November 1214 and swore on the high altar that they would protect certain basic liberties. Within a year the King was forced to grant Magna Carta. For this reason the motto of Bury St Edmunds is 'Shrine of the King and Cradle of the Law'.

The Abbey ruins

The Abbey dominated the town – it had the power to appoint all the officials and receive all dues – and its heavy-handed methods caused bitterness which occasionally led to violence. In the summer of 1327 there were riots in the streets, culminating in the destruction of most of the abbey and the death of some of the monks. The town was punished severely: 19 men were executed and massive fines were imposed. Some of the money was used to build the Great Gate, which wisely included many defensive features more often associated with castles.

Although the abbey was constantly at odds with the town, its record of gifts to the poor was good, and far better than most. When Henry VIII's officials inspected it in 1535 they found everything was in order, so assumed the monks had been warned in advance! From this time comes the description by John Leyland: 'A man who saw the abbey would say verily it were a city.' The King's avarice could not be resisted, though, and in November 1539 the abbey was closed. 'We found a rich shrine which it was very cumbrous to deface,' complained a royal official! The townspeople were overjoyed at the abbey's demise, and soon used its buildings as a free source of stone.

The splendid Norman tower was once the gateway to the abbey church, and is still the belfry of the Church of St James – the Cathedral of St James since 1914. This has undergone a number of changes this century, and building work continues. There are many interesting features within it, but the visitor cannot fail to note the beautiful hassocks, which are made by diocesan schools and organisations. Henry VIII's sister, Mary Rose, was buried in the abbey, and after the Dissolution her remains were transferred to the Church of St Mary's, which had always served as the parish church. It has a fine angel hammer-beam roof.

The abbey grounds are now a public park, with the ruins accommodated like some 18th-century folly. The old Abbot's Bridge crosses the River Lark, and there are delightful gardens; the Old English Rose Garden was presented to the town by Sgt John Appleby of Arkansas, USA, who served here during the Second World War, and loved the place.

The Norman tower with the statue of St Edmund on the right

NEWMARKET

Newmarket is described as the horse-racing capital of the world – and it's true. Horses are the obsession of this Suffolk town and everything makes way for them. Stable blocks not only surround Newmarket but have infiltrated the quiet lanes and tree-lined suburban streets. Signs are as likely to be addressed to riders as to drivers, and lines of horses command the traffic to cease until they have passed by. One feels the 20th century must have offended these folk more than most, with its ghastly motor cycles, exhaust fumes and worship of the internal combustion engine. Perhaps that is why it exudes a sense of distance from such things.

Exercising the horses on Newmarket Heath

The place to see the real business of Newmarket is the Heath. Take the Moulton Road from the town centre and almost instantly you are looking across wide acres of grassy heath, dotted with trees and marked out with white fences which are almost a trade mark. There are said to be 20 miles of them! The horses at exercise are a wonderful sight: all the power and character of careful breeding is apparent at a glance; you do not have to be an expert. The riders call to each other, and lean forward off the saddle as with enormous strides their mounts thunder past, throwing up clods of turf and sand. One moment they are upon you, and the next they are a speck in the distance, heading towards the town.

Of course the place to be is at the races. Even if you have never gambled your savings on a horse, know nothing about them, and find the business of racing suspect, you must make the effort to go. From the moment you pass through the gates you are in the world of Dick Francis. The bookies really do stand beneath umbrellas and hang cavernous leather cases from the pole. They stuff money into all their pockets as though it is junk mail, and men scribble transactions in faded ledgers with licked pencils. Their

names are poetry, and summon up images of films of the 1950s in which the good triumph, and the bad hope to do better next time. Socially the scene has changed a great deal, for corporate entertainment has invaded the Turf. Hospitality tents dispense champagne to the chosen few who wear name labels with the pride of campaign medals. Outside, the racing fraternity does not need labels: it seems that head-gear is the thing which marks out owners, trainers and officials. Everywhere the crowd swarms as though to some grand plan – as indeed there is: saddling enclosure; bookie; grandstand; unsaddling enclosure, and so back to the beginning. It is very intimate; you can get as close to the winner as you probably want to.

It was James I who started the royal connection with horse racing, and a later Stuart, Charles II, turned it into an obsession. He is said to have been called Old Rowley after an horse he once rode in a race, and to this day a course bears this name. His mistress Nell Gwynne was provided with a fine house for her visits.

Bookies on the course

In the town is the National Horseracing Museum, which presents a very interesting introduction to the subject. There are said to be about 110,000 thoroughbred foals born annually, and they can all be traced back to just three great stallions: Byerley, Darley and Godolphin Arab. The museum has displays of racing colours, trophies and even

A packed stand watch an exciting day's racing

the head of Persimmon, a great winner. The history of the sport is chronicled in detail. From the museum there are tours of the area which include a visit to the National Stud, and a chance to observe the daily routine of a local stable.

In 1695 Tregonwell Frampton became the first professional trainer and in the years which followed many others took up the task of producing winners, so that it became necessary to supervise the sport. The Jockey Club was established in the 1750s, and administers all aspects of the sport today from its grand headquarters beside the museum. The other Newmarket institution is Tattersall's, where horses are bought and sold for over £1½ million on a nod of the head.

About a mile west of Kentford, on the B1506, is a junction with the road from Moulton to Chippenham. Here is buried a shepherd boy who was falsely accused of sheep stealing, a crime which carried the death penalty. He was so frightened by the accusation that he hanged himself, and as a suicide he was denied burial in a proper churchyard. His grave is still marked by flowers, whatever the season.

The stand side

The winners' enclosure

Horse Racing Museum
Open: Mar to Dec: Tues to Sat 1000–1700, Sun 1200–1600
Price guide: B

Newmarket Stud
Open: Mar to Oct: Booking Essential
Price guide: Telephone for details

WEST STOW ANGLO-SAXON VILLAGE

Until quite recently the Anglo-Saxons have received a bad press: when first encountered they are savages destroying the virtuous and noble Roman empire, and they are last heard of being cut down by Norman knights at Hastings, having stupidly offered battle too early. Excavations in Suffolk have shown how unfair these judgements are. At Sutton Hoo, near Woodbridge, we have ample evidence of their power and wealth, while at West Stow, north of Bury St Edmunds, off the A1101, we can discover something about the life they lived.

'Experimental archaeology' sounds very dull, but in reality it is fascinating. Having discovered evidence of an Anglo-Saxon settlement, it was decided to reconstruct some of the buildings with a view to conveying an idea of what life was like over a thousand years ago. The Anglo-Saxons reached this site some time after the Romans departed, in about AD 450. They had no use for towns, villas or fine roads, for they existed in largely self-sufficient rural communities, and the River Lark was their highway. Their way of life was not inferior to that of the Romans – just very different. At West Stow the visitor can make contact with 'the English', and the experience is rewarding.

The main excavation of the site took place between 1965 and 1972, and covered an area of about five acres, which proved to be the entire settlement. Although no timber survived, dark stains in the soil indicated the locations of post holes, and these in turn suggested the size and shape of buildings. Items such as bone combs, loom weights, pots and assorted tools contributed to the picture of a small community of perhaps three or four large families, farming the fields around, and occasionally trading with other settlements. A bronze cruciform-shaped brooch is perhaps the best discovery, and it is one of the objects on display at Moyses Hall, Bury St Edmunds.

Each family seems to have occupied a large rectangular hall, with walls formed of oak planks tongued together. The roof was probably thatched, with no chimney, so the fire which burned on the hearth must have filled the interior with wood smoke. The wooden floor covered a pit which is believed to have been for storage or ventilation. On a pleasant summer day it all looks rather fun, and the agreeable rustic smells are positively inviting, but in winter conditions must have been miserable. Today the houses contain straw beds, looms, lathes, stretched skins and many items of simple craftsmanship. Chickens scatter before the visitors, providing an authentic touch – although they are spared the fate of their ancestors! Around the main hall were several smaller buildings, possibly used for storage or pigs. The reconstructions are being added to every season, and those in the process of being built provide the best opportunity to study Anglo-Saxon techniques.

Nearby was found a cemetery, with evidence of the social order being maintained even in death: thanes were buried with a sword, and freemen with a spear, while the rest had only the humble knife.

The reconstructed village is part of West Stow Country Park. You can explore the park on a nature trail – good footwear is advisable if the weather is poor. In an attractive visitor centre, which echoes the style of the early buildings, the exhibitions include chronological displays of many key stages in the site's evolution, and some unusual souvenir items.

West Stow Anglo Saxon Village and Country Park
Open: All year: daily 1000–1615
Price guide: B

The reconstructions of Saxon buildings provide visitors with a fascinating insight into the daily life of the original village. The houses contain many artefacts and craftsmen's items which the villagers would have used

NORFOLK

BRECKLAND

Breckland is an area of some 300 square miles of sandy heathland and forest situated on the Norfolk–Suffolk border. The word Breckland only came into use at the end of the 19th century; breck is land once cultivated, then allowed to return to the wild. Breckland was at one time very productive: the less fertile areas were used for grazing enormous flocks of sheep, and where possible the land was cleared of forest and ploughed for crops. But this changed. The fragile soil was overgrazed, reducing it to mere sand which periodically engulfed whole villages. There is the tale of a farmer who, asked where his lands lay, replied 'In Norfolk or Suffolk; it depends which way the wind blows'!

At the start of the 19th century measures were taken to protect the topsoil, and scots pines were planted. The Forestry Commission bought its first tract of land in 1922 and now Thetford Forest covers 80 square miles. Add to this the thousands of acres commandeered in the last war and still used by the military, and the picture of dereliction is complete: the villagers were evicted, and can return only to be buried.

The geological variety of Breckland means a wealth of flora and fauna. The alkaline chalklands favour thistles, cowslips and scabious; the acidic heathlands support gorse, bracken and hawthorn. In spring and summer the Brecks are bright with flowers of all colours; you may spot wild pansy, field gentian, maiden pink and viper's bugloss. Birds include the very rare stone curlew which nests on bare and stony ground, and hawfinches, harriers and the endangered red-backed shrike. The meres attract wildfowl; the woodland is home to crossbills, nightjars, goldcrests and golden pheasants. There are lizards, adders and two dozen species of butterflies. You may see a red squirrel or a deer.

Rampart Field picnic area, showing typical Breckland scenery

The Warrener's lodge

Undoubtedly the animal which has made the most impact on the landscape is the rabbit. It was introduced by the Normans and quickly became a table delicacy; licenses were required to farm them, and warreners acted as gamekeepers, trapping the rabbits with the help of lurcher dogs and ferrets, and fighting off poachers. The warreners lived in fortified lodges, one of which may be seen off the B1107 just north-west of Thetford. It is square and built of flint.

The warrener would have lived on the upper floor, protected by a stout door, slits for windows, and a murder hole above the doorway through which he could shower missiles on any poacher. The dense forest now obscures the open view he would have had. The prosperity of the town of Brandon rested for years on rabbits, whose fur was used to make top hats. Now myxomatosis, introduced in the 1950s, has destroyed much of the rabbit population.

Mildenhall is another of the Breckland towns, with an old market cross and a beautiful church whose roof is covered with angels. Near here in 1942 a farm worker ploughed up a 4th-century hoard of beautiful Roman silver, the Mildenhall Treasure, now in the British Museum.

Conservation Trusts in the two counties have created country parks to preserve this fascinating landscape. East Wretham Heath, for example, is an area of 362 acres which includes reed-fringed meres. It is a haven for birdlife and naturalists alike. One of the smallest sites, but one of the most accessible, is at Rampart Field, just off the main road south-east of Mildenhall. Many of the forest plantations have recreation and picnic areas to interest the tourist, and in autumn the changing colours of the deciduous trees are delightful.

Thetford Warren Lodge
English Heritage
Open: Any reasonable time
Price guide: Free

East Wretham Heath
Open: All year, except Tues, 1000 to 1700

GRIMES GRAVES

It is common these days to hear talk of the Technological Revolution, and we may recall similar claims being made for the industrial and agricultural changes which created an entirely new environment in Britain in the 18th and 19th centuries. But there is a site in south-east Norfolk which pre-dates all these, and is arguably the most important, for it marks the place where man first placed his foot on the ladder of progress.

Grimes Graves is surrounded by the tall pines of the Forestry Commission which dominate this part of East Anglia. To approach the site take the A134 between Thetford and Mundford, and turn off along the B1108. The distinctive English Heritage signs will do the rest. It has an excellent shop and exhibition centre, which must be visited if only to pay admission.

The 34-acre site is pock-marked with something resembling 350 shell holes. It was this extraordinary landscape which led to the name; the Anglo-Saxons, who arrived on the scene 2000 years after it was abandoned by its Stone Age workmen, assumed that such a weird place had been created by their god, Grim. Only in 1870 was its true nature revealed when Canon Greenwell excavated one depression, and found it to be a 40-foot shaft with tunnels leading off it. He had found a 4000-year-old flint mine, and it soon became obvious that it was the equivalent of a Stone Age factory!

The use of flint to make tools and weapons represents one of the great steps forward in man's progress. It is called the New Stone Age in the history books, and was also the time when crops were first sown, and certain animals were domesticated.

Grimes Graves exploits an area of particularly high-quality flints, and a trade with other parts of Britain soon developed. Once the flints had been brought to the surface they had to be chipped into useful shapes by a process called knapping. Flint chippings on the site provide evidence that the knapping was done beside the shafts.

You have to wear a hard helmet to descend a 40-foot ladder into the ground, and the temperature drops too. The shaft is quite well lit, and you can see the two seams of small flints which were ignored by the miners as being of no use. The larger nodules were to be found by tunnelling out galleries from the floor of the shaft. When the flints had been chipped free they were hauled to the surface, but not by pulleys, as this was before the invention of the wheel! In one gallery, archaeologists found prehistoric picks formed from deer antlers, and a discarded lamp. It was as though the owner would return the next day.

The statistics of Grimes Graves are in many ways the most impressive feature of the visit. It is thought that 20 men would have taken 80 days to dig a shaft, and that it was a month's work for eight men to dig the flint out. Over 800 tons of chalk had to be mined to obtain just 36 tons of flint. And there were once over 700 shafts dotted over the area.

There are few places in East Anglia which can have a similar effect on the visitor as Grimes Graves, for far from feeling complacent at our supposed superiority, we experience an astonishment bordering on awe that simple people could achieve such feats of engineering. Perhaps the Anglo-Saxons were not so far from the truth.

English Heritage
Open: Jan to Mar: Wed to Sun 1000–1600, April to Dec: daily 1000–1800
Price guide: A

THETFORD

Nun's Bridges over the River Ouse

In the 1950s Thetford was designated an overspill town for London; its population was enlarged in a very short time, and many new estates sprang up. It still has the look of a

The Abbey Gateway

modern town, with pedestrian precincts, bright glass-dominated shops and a predominantly young population. In the centre a three-way bridge spans the Little Ouse, and gives access to the shops from the main car park. Close by, Bridge Street crosses the river in a more graceful fashion, and the houses and shop fronts proclaim their place in a much older Thetford.

If history had worked differently, Thetford could have been the greatest city in Norfolk, and Norwich might have remained a village! Since prehistoric times, the site had been important because the Icknield Way crossed the river at this point. Today the riverfront is one of the prettiest parts of the town, and the Spring Walks follow the bank to where the many arches of Nun's Bridges span the rivers Little Ouse and Thet. The Iceni tribe which followed Boudicca is believed to have had a large settlement here, but it was the Anglo-Saxons who made it into a town, and Viking armies frequently attacked it. It was burnt down in 1004, rebuilt and then burnt again in 1016!

The Normans raised a great mound, 80 feet high and nearly 1000 feet in circumference, on which they established a castle. Hugh Bigod, an East Anglian magnate, made the mistake of opposing Henry II, and his defeat was followed by the destruction of the castle in 1173. The Castle Mound is one of the landmarks of the town. In front of it runs Old Market Street, once a wide open space but now infilled with housing. The Old Gaol is suitably forbidding. There may have been as many as 20 parish churches in the Middle Ages, and when the cathedral was established here in 1071 there seemed no barrier to Thetford's progress. But Norwich acquired the See in 1094 after a misdemeanour by the Bishop of Thetford.

The 12th-century Priory of Our Lady served the Cluniac Order. It was founded by Roger Bigod, who fought at Hastings, and after a life of bloodshed appreciated the need to do something creative. The foundation stone was laid on September 1st, 1107, and the founder died one week later. At one time the priory boasted a miraculous statue of the Virgin. The Howard family, who rose to become Dukes of Norfolk, were later patrons. Today the ruins give only a hint of the glory that once dominated the town. Flint columns stand like misshapen monsters from the past, bereft of their facing stones, and denied a roof over their heads. The gatehouse stands in a private garden, but may be visited. The priory was dissolved in 1539 and the town moved in to use the stone. Car parking is awkward and it is best to walk from the town centre.

In White Hart Street is the Ancient House Museum, a former merchant's house, dating from 1500. The ex-

St Peter's church in King Street

terior timber work is fine, but inside there is a carved ceiling beam which is in a class of its own. The museum displays material to do with the town and Breckland.

Near the Bell Hotel in King Street is a gold-painted statue of Tom Paine, the radical writer of *The Rights of Man*. He was born in White Hart Street in 1737, the son of a corset maker, and attended the Grammar School. In 1774 he went to America where he urged the colonists to rebel. His writings were regarded as treasonable in England – all the more so when he went to Revolutionary France and incited rebellion there. His statue was paid for by The Thomas Paine Society of America.

Picturesque river scene off Bridge Street

Feeding the ducks from Spring Walks

Thetford Priory
English Heritage
Open: Any reasonable time
Price guide: Free

Ancient House Museum
Open: All year: Mon to Sat 1000–1700, June to Sept: also Sun 1400 –1700
Price guide: Free

THE PEDDARS WAY

The origins of the Peddars Way are a mystery. About 7000 years ago most of southern England was covered in dense forests of native oak so the people came to appreciate the chalk soils whose poor quality did not permit the growth of large trees. Travel across the land was much easier. The Icknield Way was a track, passing between the heavy Essex clay and impenetrable Fenland. Just east of Thetford the Icknield falters and becomes the Peddars Way which continues north to the coast.

The Romans soon appreciated the advantage of such a route and they improved it, adding a metalled road which is believed to have continued south to the regional capital of Colchester. It may be that following the revolt of Queen Boudicca in AD 61, the Romans wanted a road which effectively surrounded the Iceni tribesmen. We shall probably never know what they called it, but the first use of the words Peddars Way occurs in 1587, taken from the Latin *pedester*, to go on foot.

The forty miles of the Way are ideal for recreational walking, and some parts of it are so well managed by the Countryside Commission that disabled or infirm people can confidently undertake a modest trek. The official southern end is at Knettishall Heath Country Park. A mile or so north, and on the Norfolk side of the river Thet, the trail begins its attractive line of advance from Brettenham, a pretty village without, however, school, pub or shop. From here the route is very clear, proclaiming the military precision of the Romans. It is appropriate that after Wretham the sound of soldiers can again be heard for it crosses the modern army training area which dominates this section of the great Thetford woodland.

At Lowster Hill the trail ceases to impress the map, but it struggles on, returning to prominence near South and North Pickenham, where the river Wissey flows. To the

east of Swaffham it is once again shy, but the signposts point the way north, and the best is yet to come. Today's neat, well managed path is misleading: in the olden days (before modern field boundaries) such a trackway would suffer from both over-use and neglect and so individuals would create their own routes, often resulting in scores of parallel tracks heading in the same general direction.

Castle Acre on the river Nar is a timeless crossing point, and from here there are some of the finest stretches to be walked. In the true spirit of the Legions the Peddars Way cuts through the landscape with ruthless simplicity for a distance of almost seventeen miles, but now as minor roads and grass-covered footpaths. Great and Little Massingham are well worth a detour, and as the pedestrian approaches the grandeur of Houghton Hall it is interesting to recall that here the village was destroyed to improve the view from the Hall! Oliver Goldsmith's poem, *The Deserted Village*, is supposed to commemorate the deed.

At Anmer, which abuts the Royal estate at Sandringham, tradition has it that Boudicca fought the Romans, and certainly there have been Roman remains found. From Fring to Ringstead the Way is truly across the fields and finally reaches the coast at Holme-next-the-Sea. The prevailing wisdom is that from Holme the Romans had a ferry service which carried them across the Wash to Lincolnshire, and from thence to York.

For those hearty walkers whose boots have not given out, turn right, and follow the Norfolk Coast Path to Cromer, where you may bask in the satisfaction of having completed a walk of 93 miles without the boredom of cities or the anguish of hills.

BRESSINGHAM GARDENS AND STEAM MUSEUM

As you drive out of Diss on the A1066 towards Thetford, the road follows Freezen Hill – a grand name for what is in fact only a slight rise – and there, on the left, are neat rows of colourful plants and bushes. These are the famous nurseries at Bressingham Hall. Prospective purchasers may want to visit the Plant Centre, open daily and with a great many varieties on show, as well as expert horticulturalists to give advice; but those wishing for a closer look at the world of Bressingham will need to follow the main road until the next turning after the Garden House pub. Here they will be led down a rather rocky lane, past the church, to a giantic field car park. This may well already be crowded, for these nurseries are renowned throughout the country and have a great deal to offer the visitor.

The Dell Garden

The main entrance offers enticing views of nursery beds, and as you walk through what was evidently a farmyard you will see and hear steam engines at work. This combination of gardening and steam may seem rather odd, and to understand the link between them you will need to learn a little about the central character of Bressingham: Alan Bloom.

He came from a horticultural family; his father was a market grower of flowers and fruit. Bloom bought 200 acres at Bressingham Hall just after the war and set about developing this difficult land – it was partly waterlogged peat-diggings near the River Waveney, and partly sandy rabbit warrens. Severe weather and floods undermined his hard work, but by constant efforts he built up the business. Space was at a premium in those early days, and an old chicken shed was used for raising the seedlings. Gradually, Bloom's skill at re-introducing older varieties and developing new ones – a hundred plants bred at Bressingham may be seen in a flower bed outside the museum – the nursery grew to be the biggest of its kind in the country. It produces plants for direct sale to the public, for garden centres and

'Beryl' the traction engine

for our public parks, and it has a thriving mail-order business, too. One of Bloom's sons has established a 50-acre conifer plantation stocking 70 varieties. Alan Bloom is now in his eighties, but he continues to take an active part in both museum and nursery, and personally tends the more delicate plants. Here at Bressingham you may wander freely through his famous Dell Garden beside the Hall, where Bloom made island beds to show off his first love: hardy perennials. You can admire the beautiful colours and forms in a natural and tranquil setting.

So what of the steam engines? As a boy, Bloom wanted to become an engine driver. In the 1950s he bought and renovated a traction engine as a hobby, and from there the collection grew to include many other steam traction engines and fire engines, and Bloom himself laid the first length of track for a narrow gauge railway in the grounds. Now there are three such railways on a total of five miles of track, and these give the public a closer look at the nursery beds which are otherwise inaccessible. The longest ride also runs alongside the river and through woodland. Standard-gauge engines include *Royal Scot*, *Oliver Cromwell* and *Duchess of Sutherland*, all maintained on site. You can realise a dream and ride on the footplate of *King Haakon VII*, a 1919 engine from Sweden, or ride on the steam-driven carousel with its swirling painted horses, lights and fairground music, and its proud claim 'Built by Norfolk craftsmen when Victoria was Queen'.

The Victorian Gallopers

Bressingham Steam Museum
Open: April to Sept: Tues to Sun & bank holidays 1000–1730
Price guide: B

Banham Zoo and Monkey Sanctuary

Banham Zoo is in the Norfolk countryside, off the B1113 about seven miles north-west of Diss. A relatively new collection (it was opened in 1968), it cares for species at risk of extinction, concentrating on the primates. These are endangered because the tropical forests they inhabit are rapidly being destroyed as man searches for land to cultivate. Monkeys suffer particularly because their reproductive rate is slow, and also because in the past they were hunted for their pelts. Two million black-and-white colobus monkeys were killed, for instance, when fashion favoured

Feeding the squirrel monkeys

their fur, and the species almost died out. Here at Banham we can see such rare animals as the Madagascan ring-tailed lemur, whose native forests have been all but destroyed; the emperor tamarin which sports long white moustaches and the pygmy marmoset, the smallest of all monkeys. There are, too, the more familiar chimpanzee and gibbons. Banham prides itself on its breeding record and many of the animals born here are sent to other zoos throughout the world.

The flamingos

The zoo has extensive and well-kept grounds, and the park-like setting reinforces the informal atmosphere. Visitors see more than ever before: glass panels round the sea lion pool ensure that even the smallest child has a view of these graceful creatures, and many enclosures have glass rather than the more conventional bars or wire mesh. At Banham shy animals cannot escape our gaze because windows allow us to see into their sleeping quarters. Open paddocks permit close contact with animals such as zebras, llamas and deer.

The Woodland Walk is an enclosure covering several acres of what was once brick workings. This area serves as a natural backdrop to the elegant flamingos and to wallabies. In the centre, the Monkey Jungle Island is populated by Bolivian squirrel monkeys. These tiny, timid creatures live at liberty in the trees and are hard to spot, except at the twice-daily feeding times when they are tempted into the full view of the gathered public. At any time after noon there are likely to be animals being fed; a board at the zoo entrance gives details.

The enclosures are well-signposted and accessible even to those in wheelchairs. Each cage carries information boards about its occupants, and also the names of members of the public who have contributed towards the cost of the animals' upkeep. Banham Zoo relies entirely upon public subscription, and those who wish to help to finance the conservation work are encouraged to join the 'animal adoption' scheme. For as little as £15 a year you can adopt a black swan, a giant land snail or a pink-footed tarantula!

Banham Zoo caters especially for the young. There are opportunities for amusement, to be sure, but there is also an education department. First opened in 1986, it aims to increase awareness of man's effect on wildlife and the need to conserve species for future generations. There is a lecture and exhibition hall. Introductory talks are given, work sheets provided, and members of staff from the zoo go out into the community to address schoolchildren and youth groups. The zoo's links with the Scouts and Guides are especially strong.

Everyone has their favourite memory of a visit to such a place. For many it will surely be the majestic gaze of the snow leopard: perhaps the most spectacular creature at the zoo, but no more important than the others. Every animal at Banham is under threat in the wild, and all are equally cherished here.

Open: All year: daily: Jan to Mar 1000–1600, April to Jun: daily 1000–1700, July to Oct: Mon to Fri 1000–1730, Sat & Sun 1000–1800, Nov & Dec 1000–1600 Price guide: C

Burston Strike School

Burston is a tiny village, situated four or five miles from Diss and approached along narrow country lanes. A single episode has given this rural backwater an international reputation.

In 1911 Tom and Annie Higdon arrived in Burston to run the school. Annie, the better qualified of the two, was the Schoolmistress; her husband acted as her assistant, taking the older children for classes. They were both strong-willed characters, firm Christians (Tom was a lay preacher at the Methodist Chapel) and had earlier campaigned for better conditions for schoolchildren and their families. They were good and well-respected teachers, believing in a broad education. They taught astronomy, photography and knitting as well as the usual subjects. At Christmas Annie provided the ingredients for the girls to make plum puddings; the children danced around the maypole on the green to celebrate May Day. These sons and daughters of agricultural workers were encouraged to better themselves; they had elocution lessons and Annie brought her typewriter and sewing machine to school so that the girls could learn useful skills.

Soon there was conflict with the Rector, the Reverend Charles Eland. He was relatively wealthy and so did not understand or sympathise with the labourers. As a school manager, he disapproved of the Higdons. He thought that they set a bad example by not attending his church; he was annoyed that, without his permission, Annie would light the fire in school to dry the children's wet clothes; he was angry when Tom set up a branch of the Agricultural Labourers' Union in Burston and was elected to the Parish Council in his place. Matters came to a head when two new pupils falsely accused Mrs Higdon of beating them. There was an enquiry, and the Higdons were given two days' notice of dismissal. The villagers, knowing that the charges were false, took immediate action.

Violet Potter, aged 13, organised her classmates, and at a public meeting on the Green it was decided that the children would go on strike. On April 1st 1914 they marched

Annie and Tom Higdon

round the village with banners and flags, singing songs and demanding that their teachers be reinstated. The parents were summoned to court at Diss and fined. Feelings ran high, and support grew. Lessons continued on the Green, then in the shop of Ambrose Sandy, a blind carpenter. The congregation deserted the church, and the Rector retaliated by withdrawing the glebe land leased to villagers, including Sandy, who was forced to sell up and leave Burston.

This oppression made the parents even fiercer in their demands. The farm workers, united and confident of their worth, claimed higher wages – and got them. Burston became a centre for socialists and trades unionists, who brought moral and financial support. Collections raised £1000 to buy a plot of land for a new school, and a modest building, its stones engraved with the names of the societies and individuals who subscribed to it, was opened in 1917. The strike lasted 25 years, until Tom Higdon's death in 1939, but the school continued to serve its purpose until the 1960s.

Now an annual rally and picnic are held in September, and the schoolhouse has an exhibition and mementos of the Higdons: on the wall hangs their picture of Daniel in the Lions' Den, and a board giving the names of all those children who took part in the strike. The foundation stone reminds us of the purpose of the Burston Strike School; 'to provide a free school to be a centre of RURAL DEMOCRACY and a memorial to the villagers' fight for FREEDOM'.

Strike School Museum
Open: All reasonable times
Price guide: Free

Earsham OTTER TRUST

The otter is one of those animals which is assured of a positive response from the public. It is not just that writers and film makers have chosen to bring them centre stage, but they have that indefinable quality which is only touched on by the word 'anthropomorphic' – in short, we attribute to them human emotions. The sight of an otter emerging from the water kindles recognition of a sort reserved for old friends. We feel we know them on our own terms. But it is not quite that simple, for as the notices at the Otter Trust warn: otters bite.

The Otter Trust at Earsham is one mile west of Bungay off the A143. There is ample parking, and the River Farm site, which was purchased by the Trust in 1975, makes an ideal setting for an introduction to these interesting creatures.

The Trust was set up by Philip and Jeanne Wayre in 1971, and now houses the largest collection of otters in the world. This is no zoo, however, but a well-considered reaction to a serious problem, for throughout the world otters are in decline. The danger of extinction for some species is a very real prospect. Once the threat came from

Otter pens

hunters who traded in their pelts, but now the problem is even more difficult to counter, for the habitat itself is being eradicated. Otters not only need fresh river water but also the fish which share it with them. The Trust breeds otters with the intention of releasing them into the wild to repopulate suitable rivers. While visitors and educational parties are welcome and well provided for, the animals are not exhibits, and the intention is that they should remain wild. The policy of release into waterways is proving to be a success.

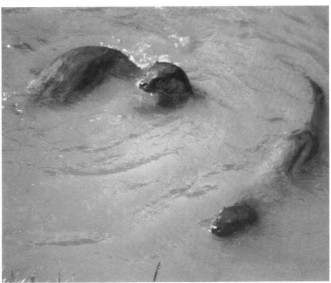

The Visitor Centre provides the background information necessary to get the most out of a tour of the Trust. In addition to the otters there are other things to enjoy, such as the willow-lined banks of the River Waveney which are home to wildfowl, including geese, herons, swans and many kinds of duck. In the wooded enclosure there are muntjac deer. But the otters are inevitably the stars.

These are to be seen in authentic riverbank settings close to the River Waveney. The otters have a stretch of 'river' to themselves, and make their home in the tree-lined bank. It is not always possible to see them as they are not obliged to perform for the public! The visitor should try to be there for feeding time, which occurs at noon and at about 4pm. This is when they are a constant delight, diving into the water in search of food and scrambling to the bank with their catches. Then they become our firm favourites; they seem to take a delight in each other's company, and they really do play.

In the wild, the otter can require as much as 12½ miles of unpolluted river to sustain life. Modern intensive farming with its use of chemicals, together with the removal of riverbank vegetation, have made the otter's future precarious. The Trust is encouraging landowners to protect the habitat necessary for the otter's survival by establishing otter havens on 11 rivers in East Anglia.

There is a moment of sadness when the time comes to leave the otter pens, for one of the qualities of these lovely creatures is that in a short time we feel we know them. We don't, of course, but it is impossible to end a visit here without resolving that they must be saved at all costs.

Open: April to Oct: 1030–1800
Price guide: B

BURGH CASTLE

When Burgh Castle was built by the Romans, Great Yarmouth did not exist. The coastline then was completely different: the rivers Yare and Waveney flowed into a wide estuary where now sandy beaches give pleasure to holidaymakers. With all the changes that have taken place in the area, it is all the more surprising that so much remains of the castle.

Burgh Castle is three miles south-west of Great Yarmouth. It is well signposted from the roundabout marking the junction of the A12 and the A143 to Beccles. The route is along minor roads and gives a superb view of Breydon Water, which in Roman times was the river mouth that the castle was built to guard. There is a car park by the church, and visitors will need to walk about a quarter of a mile along a field track.

The castle

View across Breydon Water to Berney Arms Mill

The first view of the walls of Burgh Castle is both impressive and confusing: impressive because a great deal of them survives; confusing because they lack the grandeur of a conventional castle. To appreciate the remains it is necessary to understand the Roman strategy, and that means a quick history lesson.

The Romans came to Britain in AD 43, and soon conquered East Anglia, moving off north and west to fight fresh campaigns. Towards the end of the 3rd century Roman power was in decline and the south-east of Britain was raided by Saxon pirates who sailed up the rivers to plunder and burn the settlements. To counter these attacks the Romans built a network of defences around the coast from Portchester in Hampshire to Brancaster in Norfolk. Burgh Castle was one of these. It was built in about AD 285 and would have had a garrison of cavalry ready to ride to the defence of a settlement under attack. It was also a base for

a fleet of warships which could intercept the Saxons before they landed.

The fort as seen today has walls about 15 feet high, and that is probably close to their original height. The enormous turrets would have held *ballistae* – giant crossbows and catapults which would have kept the enemy at bay. The combination of flint and layers of brick is a feature of Roman masonry work. The main gate to the fort is in the centre of the east wall. The west wall collapsed into the river long ago.

In AD 410 the Romans gave up the struggle and withdrew their forces from Britain, and the Anglo-Saxons poured in and settled. At first our ancestors were pagans, but Christianity eventually gained a foothold and tradition says that Sighebert, king of East Anglia, permitted Burgh Castle to be the base for St Fursey, a monk who came from Ireland to convert his kingdom. All of this was swept away by the Vikings in the 9th century.

The Normans arrived in 1066 and used the strength of the surviving walls. A knight called Ralph built a great mound with a keep on top and so the fort became a castle. No trace of the keep survives, but it occupied the south west corner where the Roman wall has fallen over in spectacular chunks.

Today Burgh Castle is isolated and still. There is a great sense of history in this region, and although Breydon Water is now the realm of holiday boats it requires little imagination to see sleek Roman galleys at anchor. For family picnics the field inside the walls is ideal, and the view across to Berney Arms Mill is unrivalled. This mill was a water pump designed to drain the marshes, and is in working order. It has seven floors and is 70 feet high. It is in the care of English Heritage and open to visitors, but inaccessible by car.

English Heritage
Open: All reasonable times
Price guide: Free

Berney Arms Mill
English Heritage
Open: Mar to Sept: daily 0900–1700
Price guide: A

GREAT YARMOUTH

The many thousands of holidaymakers who visit Great Yarmouth each summer would no doubt agree with a description of the town given by the nurse Peggotty in Dickens' *David Copperfield*: 'upon the whole, the finest place in the universe'. The five miles of sandy beach have become the focal point for fun and entertainment while each of the two piers provides the familiar ice creams, seaside postcards and silly hats, as well as its own theatre. Children can enjoy Punch and Judy shows on the sand, trampolining, or boating on the Venetian waterway beside North Drive. The sporting may take up tennis, rollerskating, squash or snooker in the splendid modern Marina Centre. Horse-drawn landaus will take you along Marine Parade at a more leisurely pace than the streaming traffic.

The sea front is all lights, colour and noise, with its cinemas, amusement arcades and shops galore. There are so many attractions: a model village with landscaped gardens and waterways, echoing the town with its miniature version of a fairground, all illuminated at dusk. There is also the Sea-Life Centre, offering a marvellously close view of our native marine environment, as well as a captivating display of sharks and tropical fish.

Bowling green on the sea front

A short excursion from Yarmouth might take the form of a boat trip from the beach or perhaps inland to Breydon Water Nature Reserve where there are opportunities for bird watching, or up the River Bure to the Broads; one of the boats used is the *Elizabeth Simpson*, formerly the Gorleston lifeboat. Six miles from Yarmouth is Thrigby Hall Wildlife Gardens, and not far from Thrigby is the Bygone Village at Fleggburgh, where you will see cottage work-shops and a variety of traditional crafts. But a visitor need not stray far from Yarmouth; it is delightful just to stroll along the seafront and watch the various activities. North of Britannia Pier there is a discernible difference in the resort: the lively funfairs and amusements give way to a gentler sort of activity, and the beach is suddenly wider and sheltered by low sand dunes.

But there is much more to Great Yarmouth than a modern resort – it has a long and distinguished history as a port. Situated on a sand spit at the confluence of the rivers Bure and Yare, with its sheltered harbour and favoured position at the extreme eastern tip of England (it is closer to Rotterdam than to London), Yarmouth became an ideal trading centre for Europe. Even now, when the fishing fleets which brought its richest days are disbanded, Yarmouth remains an important base for oil and gas exploration in the North Sea.

A rig supply ship

Since Norman times, herrings were fished offshore in autumn, and their abundance brought great prosperity to the port where they were landed, cured and packed for market. The annual Herring Fair attracted merchants from all over Europe, and the trade continued until the 1930s when overfishing was found to have almost wiped out the shoals. There are reminders of this once most flourishing of trades: there is a smoke room which survives in the south east tower of the town walls, and perhaps more evocatively, the *Lydia Eva*, the last steam drifter built to fish for herring from Yarmouth. For part of the summer season she is moored just downstream from Haven Bridge on the river Yare, and a tour of her cramped decks gives some idea of the living and working conditions of her ten member crew. She also ties up at Lowestoft.

As well as its fishing fleet, Yarmouth had great shipbuilding yards. It sent so many ships to help Edward II at the Battle of Sluys in 1340 that the King granted a new coat of arms to the borough: his own royal arms halved with the town's traditional herring. It is this curious emblem which you will still see today.

The naval history which is so vital to Yarmouth is well documented in the Maritime Museum on Marine Parade. The building itself is interesting: it was founded as a home for shipwrecked sailors in 1861, and developed as a museum because the seamen displayed mementos they had brought back from foreign parts. Now, much enlarged, it contains models of ships, toys and ornaments made by sailors including wooden dolls, carved whales' teeth and ships in bottles, paintings and a fascinating display of life-saving equipment designed by the Norfolk-born Captain George Manby. It was he who invented the mortar appara-tus after witnessing a shipwreck only 150 yards from the shore at Yarmouth when the seas were so heavy that no line could be got aboard to save the men, women and children. He later invented the breeches buoy, as well as a boat having buoyancy chambers to help it float even when over-whelmed by the waters. This remarkable and ingenious man became Master of Yarmouth Barracks in 1803 and on his retirement settled in nearby Gorleston, where he died in 1854.

The town's past prosperity is reflected in the magnificent buildings on the riverfront at South Quay, particularly the Custom House of 1720. Number 4, behind a Georgian façade, is part of a fine Elizabethan mansion, with panelled rooms, finely-carved chimney pieces and moulded plasterwork ceilings. The exhibits in this domestic museum include furniture, Lowestoft porcelain and silver from the town's regalia.

The Tolhouse Museum is the town museum, and is housed in a 13th-century flint building which has variously served as courthouse (where the crime of piracy was tried as late as the 1820s) and gaol. The cells were in the Hold, or dungeon, and reached by a ladder; the cells we see today date only from the early 1800s, following reforms made in the prison conditions. Outside, a staircase leads up to the hall on the first floor: the Heighning Chamber, where herring merchants had to hand over to the Corporation one half of the profits they had made on their sales. The Tolhouse was badly damaged during the war; fire bombs gutted it in 1941 and it has been restored with a modern annexe, a library and exhibition galleries. There is a brass rubbing centre here, with replica brasses of knights and ladies on which you may try the art.

Bomb damage did much to destroy a feature unique to Yarmouth: the Rows. These were a series of more than a hundred narrow alleyways running eastward from the quayside. Some in Row 111 have survived and are open for inspection in the summer.

There are some remains, too, of the town walls. These were begun in the 13th century and took over 100 years to complete. Two towers still exist, at the north-west and south-east corners, and the restored walls can be traced, enclosing the town as it then was: a port facing inland towards the River Yare. Not until the 1800s did Yarmouth become renowned as a resort and the town turn to face out to sea.

Interior of the Elizabethan House Museum

Sea-Life Centre
Open: All year, daily, dawn–dusk
Price guide: C

Thrigby Hall Wildlife Gardens
Open: All year daily: 1000–1800
Price guide: C

Fleggburgh Bygone Village
Open: Mar to Oct: daily 1000–1730. Nov & Dec: Sun to Thur from 1000
Price guide: C

Lydia Eva Steam Drifter
Yarmouth Quay
Open: July to Sept: daily 1000–1700
Price guide: A

Maritime Museum for East Anglia
Open: April: Mon to Fri 1000–1700, Sun 1400–1700, May to Sept: Sun to Fri 1000–1700
Price guide: A

Elizabethan House Museum
Open: April: Mon to Fri 1000–1700, Sun 1400–1700, May to Sept: Sun to Fri 1000–1700
Price guide: A

Tolhouse Museum
Open: April: Mon to Fri 1000–1700, Sun 1400–1700, May to Sept: Sun to Fri 1000–1700
Price guide: A

Nelson's Monument
Open: July to Oct: 1400 to 1700, Oct 21st 1000–1700
Price guide: A

The Tolhouse

On the South Denes is Nelson's Monument, built in homage to the admiral in 1819, and set in the middle of a race course in open fields; now it is surrounded by factories and houses. Nelson looks inland towards his birthplace of Burnham Thorpe, and the visitor who climbs the 217 steps to the top will be rewarded with a stunning panorama.

CAISTER CASTLE

Just north of Great Yarmouth, off the A149, is Caister Castle, which combines an interesting medieval fortification with a car museum of some distinction. The castle remains are set amid beautiful grounds and flower gardens, while the Motor Museum is modern and well-presented.

Sir John Fastolfe who built the castle has done rather badly out of history – or more precisely, literature, as Shakespeare appropriated the name and a bit of his career for one of the greatest comic characters ever created: Sir John Falstaff, the drunken braggart in *Henry IV*. But the builder of Caister Castle was no coward, as his military career confirms.

England's wars with France began in 1346, and few of the next hundred years passed without bloodshed. It was a time when you could achieve fame and fortune if you were a brave man like Sir John Fastolfe. He commanded the English archers at the battle of Agincourt, and went on to other battlefields, gaining distinction and honour. He brought his military career to an end in 1432, and spent the rest of his life building Caister Castle to his own plan, and doing good works with his fortune.

During the building of his castle Sir John kept meticulous records, and these documents have survived. He had experienced warfare in Europe, and saw that the invention of gunpowder had marked the end of the castle as a totally secure base. But not every army had gunpowder, and he lived in troubled times, so a sort of castle was still worthwhile. What he did was to build a fortified home able to withstand the small armies of marauding pirates who were quite common at the time, but which was still spacious and comfortable. It had a moat and drawbridge; it had arrow slits as well as gun ports; but it also had large glazed windows. The great tower which survives today is 98 feet high, containing five floors, and could have served as a keep in time of trouble. Unusually, Fastolfe used locally-made brick rather than stone for its construction. The completed castle had 40 rooms, and at most a garrison of 40 soldiers. In 1458, the year before he died, Sir John fought off a raid by French pirates; the records say 'many gonnes' were 'shotte', so the castle did its job.

Following Sir John Fastolfe's death the castle passed to the Paston family. They have earned a place in history because their letters to each other give a vivid picture of what life was like during the Wars of the Roses. The Pastons' title to the castle was opposed by the Duke of Norfolk, and he issued an ultimatum to them to quit. The castle was hardly in a state to defend itself. In March 1468 John Paston wrote that the walls needed repair: 'If it be not done this year many of the walls will lie in the moat ere long'. The next year the Duke and 3000 soldiers besieged Caister Castle and John's mother, who was in charge during his absence, was obliged to surrender. But the family regained possession in 1476, and remained there until 1599 when they moved. The castle then became a ruin.

The castle today offers a delightful setting of warm-coloured brick walls, towers and gateways. Inside are lawns surrounded by flower beds of great beauty, while surrounding it is the moat which now supports a flourishing population of waterfowl.

The Motor Museum occupies a purpose-built showroom and houses scores of interesting old cars and assorted vehicles, including a steam-powered car dating from 1904. Wherever you turn in this museum there is something of interest. No doubt Sir John would have approved.

Motor Museum
Open: May to Sept: Sun to Fri 1030–1700
Price guide: B

THE EAST COAST OF NORFOLK

Norfolk's east coast is relatively unknown to the visitor; there are no main roads to afford easy access, and although a number of camp-sites have sprung up, they look even more temporary than usual. Farms stand in isolation on the windswept plain. The North Sea has made its indelible mark on these communities, for whereas the coast to the south is yearly built up with shingle spit, here the land is being eroded, and with it the villages on its margin. Eccles-on-Sea has all but disappeared: only a huddle of little beach houses remains. Tales of drownings and inundations stretch far back into history, and within living memory the floods of January 1953 served to remind us of man's frailty. In 1959 eight miles of sea defences were completed between Happisburgh and Winterton – sand dunes planted with marram grass to give them extra stability.

Winterton-on-Sea beach

North of Great Yarmouth is Winterton-on-Sea, dominated by its giant church tower. It is an impressive landmark for mariners and landlubbers alike. The church has a fascinating memorial to those lost at sea: Fisherman's Corner is composed of maritime objects and was set up by the Reverend Charles Porter, who was himself subsequently drowned while rescuing a boy in difficulties. The village houses were at one time built of old ships' timbers, since ships wrecked on the Hazeborough Sands were often washed up here. Bathing is sometimes dangerous, and visitors are asked to use paths over the dunes to avoid unnecessary damage to the village's only defence. To the north is a nature reserve.

Happisburgh has a beautiful church in a dramatic setting, on a low cliff overlooking the pounding waves. In the churchyard are buried many mariners who perished on the treacherous sands seven miles offshore. A mound marks the grave of 119 crew members of HMS *Invincible*, which went down in 1801. Airmen and merchant seamen from the last war are also buried here. So is Jonathan Balls, who enjoyed a local reputation as a poisoner and who died in 1846 after accidentally imbibing one of his own lethal potions. He stipulated that he was to be buried with a plum cake, a Bible, a poker and a pair of fire tongs, presumably to cope with the Everlasting Flames. Local gossip led to his body being exhumed, along with those of several of his

Happisburgh beach

supposed victims, and all were found to contain high concentrations of arsenic! The high tower of the church once acted as a landmark to seafarers; a later beacon is the red-and-white striped lighthouse of 1791.

To the north the road skirts the sea at Walcott Gap, where the marvellous vista eastwards across the waves is not matched by the view inland to the caravan site. North again is the former Bromholm Priory, now a farm, famous for once having a relic of the True Cross brought back from Constantinople by a wandering priest. By its healing power, the monks at Bromholm were able to raise 39 people from the dead and cure many of blindness and leprosy. These tales of miracles contrast strangely with the atmosphere of the nearby village of Bacton, where the road passes between the barbed wire fences of the natural gas terminal.

Paston is famous as the home of the Paston family who left us such a moving account of life in the times of the Wars of the Roses. The thatched Elizabethan barn near the road was built by a descendant, Sir William Paston. It is of flint with an alternate tie-beam and hammer-beam roof. This is one of the lovely old barns to be found in the region; another, recently restored, is at Waxham and was one of the monastery buildings.

The pretty seaside town of Mundesley owes its development to the railway. There is quite a steep ramp down the cliff to a promenade beside the wide, firm sand. The High Street runs inland, and at the top on the left is a pleasant white Georgian building, now called Cowper House. The melancholy poet spent some of his happier moments here.

Mundesley beach

THE NORFOLK BROADS

For many, a holiday spent on the Norfolk Broads serves as an introduction to East Anglia; each year some quarter of a million visitors cruise along the waterways, and to that number must be added those who tour the area by car or on foot. The combination of water, mills and wind-swept marshland has become the epitome of all that is Norfolk, and the beauty of the Broads makes it a true paradise for the tourist.

It comes as something of a surprise to discover that this landscape which seems so timeless and natural is quite artificial, and, in geological terms at least, very recent. The origin of the Broads was long misunderstood, and it was not until a detailed and exhaustive study was undertaken in the 1950s that it was proven beyond doubt that they were created by man's activity – the digging of peat for fuel in the Middle Ages. At one time East Anglia was the most densely populated region of England, and since the natural woodland had mostly been felled, the people turned to an alternative source of fuel in the peat-rich land close to the rivers. Each parish had its own workings, and the digging and drying of the peat became an industry which brought prosperity. Thousands of acres of peat were removed in this way; an amazing feat considering that it was all done by hand. But the low-lying land soon flooded, forming many shallow lakes. These lakes are what we now call the Broads. There are almost 50 of them altogether, though some are too shallow or overgrown to be navigable. Together with the rivers Bure, Ant and Thurne which meet here and flow out to sea at Yarmouth, there are 125 miles of channel available to the sailor.

The Broads attract more than the sailor; this unique region is rich in wildlife of all kinds, much of it rare and therefore precious, and there are rare ferns and fen orchids and water violets for the botanist's delight. The swallowtail butterfly, largest of all British species with its wingspan of three inches, is found only here where its caterpillars feed on milk parsley. The Norfolk hawker dragonfly is seen more often, if only because the Broads Authority has chosen this rare insect as its emblem. The carr woodland attracts purple emperor and white admiral butterflies. In secluded spots you may be lucky enough to hear the booming call of the bittern or glimpse a visiting marsh harrier. Fishermen can catch bream, tench and pike, some of record-breaking weights. Prospective anglers should obtain a licence, remembering that certain broads are private and a charge may be made; but if you are lucky enough to catch a big fish, you may be in line for the Silver Freshwater Fish Award, made from time to time by local newspapers.

This part of Norfolk attracts all sorts and conditions of folk, who spend many happy hours on or beside the water. Paradoxically, however, the very success of the Broads has brought about their gradual destruction. Agricultural development has meant the draining of valuable wetlands, and has relied heavily upon fertilisers which encourage the growth of algae. These not only cloud the water and inhibit the growth of those species indigenous to Broadland, but also produce toxins to threaten fish and wildfowl. Pollution, too, caused by effluent and the spillages of the amateur cruisers has taken its toll. Holiday-makers who dream of meandering peacefully along the waterways come to the Broads in ever-increasing numbers, and the wash from their motorboats erodes the banks and destroys the landscape they have come to enjoy. We are now more aware of the problems, and conservation centres and nature trails abound, but the Broads still need careful management by both farmers and tourists if we are not to lose this beautiful region.

Barton Broad

The Broadland area is vast and the marshy nature of the terrain means that it is not well served by road. This is not to say that the roads are not crowded in summer with cars full of sightseers, but many will be heading for the towns where they can hire boats, because that is undoubtedly the best way of getting around. The River Bure, whose course is central to exploration of the Broads, is navigable as far as Coltishall, and this pretty village whose wide wooded common leads gently down to the river's edge will be the starting point for many. But most will take the A1151 from Norwich and begin at Wroxham. The narrow river bridge can cause traffic jams, and this is surely the busiest and liveliest of Broadland towns. Here you can take that river trip (some launches have facilities for the disabled), hire a cruiser yourself, or simply sit at the water's edge and admire the passing activity. Wroxham boasts 'the biggest village store in the world' in the shape of Roy's of Wroxham, a conglomeration of shops selling everything you could possibly want. At Barton House on the south bank of the river, two miniature railways take you on a different sort of journey on summer Sunday afternoons; a mile or so to the north is the craft centre known as Wroxham Barns, where a picturesque group of 18th-century red-brick barns has recently been transformed into a series of workshops demonstrating traditional arts such as boat-building, stained glass making, bookbinding and lacemaking. Nearby, too, is Beeston Hall, a Georgian mansion with an art gallery and wine cellars, as well as an interesting family history. Wroxham, then, with its fellow Hoveton on the north bank of the river, provides a touring centre and much of what the tourist seeks in a nutshell.

Just downstream is Hoveton Great Broad. The nature trail here can only be reached by boat, and the course is lined with railway sleepers to save the walker from sinking into the depths of its oozy mud. The broad itself is not navigable, and the half-mile trail passes through dense fen woodland, so this is a rare opportunity to see an unspoilt part of Broadland.

The river passes through marsh and sedge fen and loops north to the village of Horning. This is perhaps a more elegant place than Wroxham, with large houses backing on to private inlets, and thatched boathouses. The double-decker Mississippi paddle boat *Southern Comfort* is moored here, and a ticket can include the day trip from Norwich. To the south, around Woodbastwick Marshes, the roads are liable to flooding at certain times of the year.

The Pleasure Boat Inn on Hickling Broad

A nature trail at Cockshoot Broad, which, as its name suggests, was once a haunt of wildfowl and wildfowlers, is accessible by car from the end of Ferry Road, north-east of the village of Woodbastwick, and here the visitor sees how a broad has been reclaimed. By the 1970s this eight-acre expanse had become so silted up that all the birds had deserted it and only six inches of polluted water remained. The Broads Authority has restored this broad to its condition of a century ago by isolating it from the nearby river Bure, source of the pollution, and pumping out thousands of gallons of mud. The results were dramatic: seeds buried years ago in the unproductive mud suddenly germinated, the waters cleared and the birds returned.

Cottages at Ludham

Ranworth church is exceptional and has a marvellous 15th century painted rood screen. The tower allows fine views over the surrounding countryside. A short nature trail leads through a variety of habitats to the Broadland Conservation Centre, ingeniously housed in a thatched building on a pontoon. The problems of conservation are highlighted and there are exhibitions about Man's influence on the Broads as well as the natural history. Upstairs, the Riviere Gallery overlooks Ranworth and Malthouse Broads and binoculars are provided for birdwatching. Just to the south is the pretty village of South Walsham; here the Fairhaven Garden Trust has opened to the public woodland and water gardens exhibiting many rare species of plants and shrubs.

The Bure is joined by the river Ant. Barton Broad, fed by its waters, is one of the smaller and least visited of Broads, and there is only limited parking next to the parish staithe. It is tranquil and the air is full of birdsong. You may see herons, the elusive bittern, or the bearded tit, another of the Broads' most characteristic birds. The village, Barton Turf, has flowers in abundance and a lovely old church. How Hill is just south of here; it is the Environmental Centre for the Broads based at Toad Hole cottage, formerly inhabited by eelcatchers. A museum displays Victoriana dealing with the marshman's way of life, and the centre offers residential courses to give insights into Broadland. The landscape around How Hill includes reeds, sedge fields, marshland, carr and open water, and there are windpumps to visit and nature trails to follow. One is a 50 minute river trip in the *Electric Eel*.

East of where the Ant meets the Bure are the ruins of St Benet's Abbey, a landmark for all those cruising on the Broads. The Abbey of St Benedict was established a thousand years ago and at one time the monks grew rich by buying up the peat-digging rights to a dozen parishes and controlling all the revenue. But the abbey stood on such low-lying land that it was more than once overwhelmed by floods. After the Dissolution the peasants carried off most of the stone (rare as a building material in these parts) and all that is left is the gatehouse to which a 19th-century mill – now also in ruins – was added. An annual service is still held here on the first Sunday in August, when the Bishop of Norwich arrives by boat; there used to be a causeway to the abbey from Horning, but access is now only from the river.

The Thurne adds its waters to the Bure just downstream from this point. The Thurne is fed from several sources and these include two of the most important of the Broads. In 1958 Hickling Broad became a National Nature Reserve. It is the largest of the Broads and covers 1361 acres, but the water is only about three feet deep. Here there are open reed and sedge beds, woodland and scrapes attracting many species of waders. You may see avocets and spoonbills, and this is also a haunt of the swallowtail butterfly. It is a good place for fishing, too, with a record 31 lb pike having been caught. There are two walking trails starting from the warden's house in Stubb Road (to the north of the broad), and a water trail lasting 2½ hours which starts twice daily in the summer from Pleasure Boat Inn Staithe.

Potter Heigham Bridge

Horsey Mere, to the east, is another secluded Broad, situated only a mile from the sea and often threatened in the past by inundation – it is only 3 or 4 feet above sea level. In the 1938 floods the area was cut off for more than 4 months and the inhabitants of the little village had to be evacuated. Horsey Windpump is in the care of the National Trust and from four storeys up the view is superb. This is a wonderful spot for the car-bound to study life afloat. The river path away from the Windpump is well worth exploring too.

The Thurne rises at West Somerton, where the churchyard has the tomb of Robert Hales, the 19th-century Somerton Giant, who measured seven feet eight inches and weighed 33 stone. Smugglers coming ashore at Somerton Gap would look anxiously at the sails of the windmills, because the angle at which they were set informed them whether the coast was clear of revenue men! Close to West Somerton is Martham Broad, where there is a sailing school. The village of Martham is lovely, with wide greens and pretty houses. The churchyard has a tombstone in memory of Alice Burraway, 'my sister, my mistress, my mother and my wife'. To appreciate the complexity of the unfortunate Mr Burraway's position, you must see the stone!

Downstream is the village of Potter Heigham, with its low stone bridge arching across the river. The clearance at high water is only 6½ feet, and a pilot service is available for the inexperienced. This is a good vantage point for the landlubber; it is also a centre for boat hire and there are

Cut reeds at Thurne

trips upstream to Hickling Broad and Horsey Mere, and downstream to St Benet's Abbey. A little downriver is the Helter Skelter House, formed from the top of a fairground ride brought from Yarmouth Pier.

The Weavers Way follows the river bank from Potter Heigham southwards. The charming village of Ludham is nearby, and this is joined to the Broads system by Womack Water, where the Norfolk Wherry Trust keeps the *Albion* moored. She is one of the last of the wherries, boats that were specially designed for the Broads. Manoeuvrable even in shallow water and under low bridges, at one time they were the chief carriers of cargoes in this inaccessible region. There were once more than 300 wherries on the Broads and their black sails and painted hatchcovers were a distinctive part of the local scene. Now the *Albion* can be chartered and you can experience a real Norfolk tradition which was almost lost.

The river runs south to the secluded village of Thurne. Here is a village store, a pub, a telephone kiosk, and nothing much besides. But the dyke is very picturesque, lined with boats (many of them occupied), and finished off in a very satisfactory way by a small white-painted windpump which contains a display detailing the role of windpumps in the Broads. The River Thurne flows into the Bure near here, and united they wind their way past Palmer's Hollow Post Mill; under Acle Bridge, where criminals were once hanged from the parapet; past the delightful village of Stokesby, and Stracey Arms Windpump, built on piles sunk deep into the mud – and thence to Yarmouth, in a slower and less dangerous fashion than the Acle Straight, notorious for accidents caused by speeding motorists.

There remain only the Trinity Broads, once joined to the Broads system by the aptly named Muck Fleet, which has long since silted up so that they now sit in splendid isolation at the eastern edge of Broadland. Ormesby, Rollesby and Filby Broads are crossed by two main roads and thus allow good views to the motorist. At Filby Bridge you can hire rowing boats for fishing or simply for getting away to explore the more secluded parts of this reed-fringed expanse; or you can sit and feed the mallard, geese, coots and swans which throng the lakeside.

Horsey Windpump

Ormesby Broad

Barton House Railway
Open: April to Oct 3rd Sunday of month 1430–1730
Price guide: A

Broadland Conservation Centre, Ranworth
Open: April to Oct: Sun to Fri 1030–1730, Sat 1400–1700
Price guide: A

Fairhaven Garden Trust
Open: April to Oct: Tues to Fri 1100–1730, Sat 1400–1730, Sun 1100–1730
Price guide: B

Toad Hole Cottage
Open: April to May: Mon to Sat 1100–1700, June to Sept: Mon to Sat 1000–1800
Price guide: Free

Hickling Broad Water Trail
Open: May & Sept: Tues, Wed, Thur, June to Aug: Mon to Fri dep 1030 & 1400
Price guide: Telephone for details
Advance booking essential (01692 598271)

Horsey Windpump
National Trust
Open: Mar to Sept: daily 1100–1700. July to Aug: 1100–1800
Price guide: A

Thurne Dyke Windpump
Open: May to Sept: Sun, bank holiday Monday, Sat in school holidays 1500–1800
Price guide: Free

Stracey Arms Windpump
Open: April to Sept 0900–2000
Price guide: A

NORWICH

'A fine old city', wrote George Borrow a century ago, and most would agree that Norwich retains that indefinable quality today. It is proud of its past, its present status and its appearance. At a time when urban centres are condemned as embodying all that is worst in architecture, Norwich stands like a beacon, proclaiming what can be done with imagination and courage. It was one of the first cities to create pedestrian precincts, and by night it is floodlit to perfection.

In medieval times Norwich was one of the greatest cities in England. The wool of East Anglia passed through its markets and was shipped from the quayside, bringing prosperity and confidence. In the 13th century four miles of flint boundary wall were built, and to this day incongruous chunks of it survive. It is said that there was an inn for every day of the year, and a church for every Sunday. The oldest inn is 'The Adam and Eve' at Bishop's Gate, which served its first customer in 1248. Much later, it operated a wherry of the same name which supplied all the pubs with sand for their floors. If support for pubs has remained constant, though, church attendance has declined. Many churches have closed for good, or have reopened for other purposes: St James' is now a puppet theatre.

No visitor to this city should fail to see Elm Hill. A cobbled lane winds down past tightly packed pretty houses, many of them timber-framed. Trees are everywhere, and the warm colours of the buildings make this an

Elm Hill

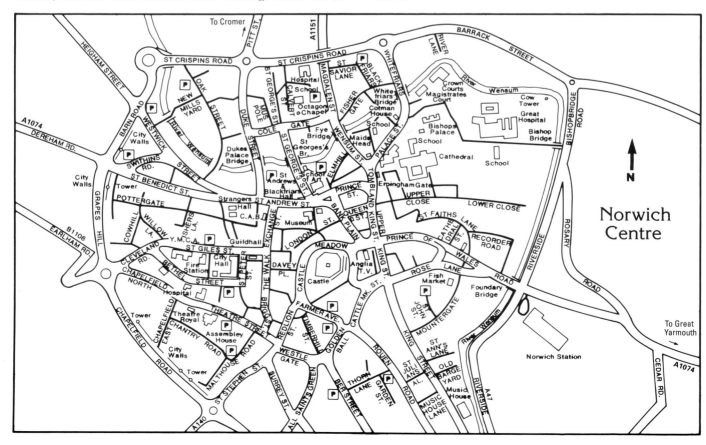

Norwich Centre

The Castle

enchanting spot. Tombland Alley nearby has a wonderful 15th-century half-timbered house, but its calm seclusion is misleading – during Kett's rebellion in 1549 it was the headquarters for the King's forces, and Elm Hill saw fierce fighting.

Market Place still stands below the stern gaze of the Norman castle, and hundreds of stalls dealing in every imaginable commodity continue to trade beneath their great

The Arcade

Castle Mall

expanse of brightly coloured canvas. There are so many covered pathways it becomes a labyrinth, but each change of direction offers further pleasurable surprises. To the north stands the Guildhall, a resplendent example of flint flushwork and a centre of city government from 1413 down to the 20th century. It is now the Information Centre. On the other side of Market Place is the beautiful church of St Peter Mancroft, a glorious tribute both within and without to the craftsmen who worked in the Perpendicular style.

The Assembly Hall in Theatre Street, with a fountain in its forecourt, possesses all the elegance of an 18th-century gathering place for the city's well-to-do. Now it is a restaurant and art gallery. Almost next door is the Theatre Royal, which not only offers a varied programme of entertainment, but manages to make a modest profit, too!

In Bridewell Alley is Colman's Mustard Shop. It sells many varieties of mustard and is also a museum, telling the story of the company who first moved to Norwich in 1814. It has over 110,000 visitors a year! Many of the lanes and alleys Jeremiah Colman would have known are still lined with small shops, although there are also very modern pedestrian precincts with famous store names and tempting merchandise. The prestigious and exciting Castle Mall shopping centre is but the latest to open its doors.

The River Wensum joins the Yare east of the city. A river walk runs beside the river which is used as much for pleasurable purposes as for trade. The Music House (Wensum Lodge) is the oldest house in the city, dating from the 12th century, and if its stones could speak one hopes they would still recognize and approve of Norfolk's capital.

NORWICH MUSEUMS

The Norwich Castle Museum was recently acclaimed as one of the best museums in Britain, and it is a verdict few visitors would quarrel with. The Castle Museum houses a number of collections, all of them rich in interest and well presented. Leading off from an attractive rotunda are galleries containing exhibitions on Norfolk's archaeology, natural history and ecology. The Norwich School of painting occupies two galleries; the works of John Crome, John Sell Cotman and their colleagues were enormously influential on their 19th-century contemporaries, and their views of Norwich and Norfolk endure while the scenes they painted have often vanished. Other galleries display modern art and special exhibitions.

Puppets in Stranger's Hall

The Great Norman keep of the castle continues to be the most impressive exhibit! A gallery runs round the walls, and the overall size of the building is astonishing. It houses cabinets of medieval archaeology, and has a fine collection of arms and armour. The story of how Norwich began and prospered is well told. When the Normans arrived they forced the Saxons to construct for them a great mound on which they erected a wooden fort. In 1100 the present stone keep was constructed, with a splendid Norman doorway at first-floor level and a well over 100 feet deep. Although refaced in 1830, the external appearance of the keep is probably accurate. After a rather undistinguished career it ceased to do service as a castle in 1220, and became the city's gaol, a role it held until 1894. Executions took place at the end of the Castle Bridge, and the museum displays a number of death masks! The moat was always dry; it now has flower-lined walkways, and is a site for occasional entertainments.

Stranger's Hall Museum in Charing Cross bears the name given to some refugees to the city, although there is doubt as to whether these were Flemings in the 16th century or French aristocrats in the 18th century. The Great Hall is admirably simple, with stone floor, dark oak table, Flemish tapestry and large lead-paned windows. Other rooms are furnished in later periods, and the visitor will choose his own favourite. Children must see the toy collection, which ranges from rocking horses to all sorts of dolls.

The Bridewell Museum in Bridewell Alley was once a gaol for vagrants, who exercised in the courtyard. It used to be a merchant's house: one owner was William Appleyard, the first Mayor of Norwich in 1404. Now its collection of bygones is of special interest to local people. The crafts and industries of Norfolk are imaginatively presented.

The 15th-century church of St Peter Hungate, near Elm Hill, is now a museum of church fittings and a brass rubbing centre. In 1900 it was derelict and ready to be demolished, so its fate should not occasion too much regret. Once it was the smallest parish in the city, a mere three acres, but its congregations were wealthy. The magnificent hammer-beam roof supported by carved angels was a gift from John and Margaret Paston in 1460. There are many things to see, including church silver, religious statuary and a wonderful collection of musical instruments used to accompany worship before the organ boomed them into submission.

The 9th Regiment of Foot soldiers was raised in 1685, and later became the Royal Norfolk Regiment (now part of the Royal Anglians). The Regimental Museum in Shirehall tells its story. From this building on Market Avenue a tunnel, built by prisoners, passes to the Castle.

Castle Museum
Open: All year: Mon to Sat 1000–1700, Sun 1400–1700
Price guide: B

Stranger's Hall Museum
Open: All year: Mon to Sat 1000–1700
Price guide: A

Bridewell Museum
Open: All year: Mon to Sat 1000–1700
Price guide: A

St Peter Hungate Church Museum
Brass Rubbing Centre
Open: All year: Mon to Sat 1000–1700
Price guide: A

NORWICH CATHEDRAL

Norwich has not always been home to the See of East Anglia. At first it resided in Dunwich, then moved to North Elmham, spent a few years at Thetford and finally was brought to Norwich in 1096. The great cathedral was begun in 1096 by Bishop Losinga, but the consecration of the completed building only took place in 1278. The task of bringing stone up to the site was simplified by the digging of a canal from the River Wensum. It has since been filled in, but Pull's Ferry marks the spot where the barges left the river to approach the cathedral.

In the Middle Ages a monastery stood in the shadow of the cathedral. About 60 monks would have lived within its walls, their lives entirely dominated by the daily routine of prayer and good works. Henry VIII dissolved the monastery in 1539, an act which probably earned him the praise of the Norwich citizens as the relationship between church and city was never smooth, sometimes leading to violence in the streets. But all this is far removed from the tranquil scene presented from the south-east, beside the River Wensum, where the slender 15th-century spire – at 315 feet the second tallest in England – soars free of the finger-like buttresses and overlooks the next generation playing cricket on the school fields.

The nave is cool and quiet. This is no museum, and worship continues as it has done since the days of Bishop Losinga. Fire destroyed the roof in 1463 but the medieval craftsmen excelled themselves in rebuilding it. The bosses depict biblical scenes, and those with good eyesight may be able to detect four naked sinners being devoured by the jaws of Hell, or Pharoah's army being engulfed by the rushing waters of the Red Sea.

The choirstalls possess tip-up seats with carvings underneath (misericords), which supported weary worshippers during long periods of standing. It was common for such carvings to depict irreverent scenes, and these include a man riding a pig, a woman pursuing a fox and even a monk beating a pupil. The bishop's throne behind the high altar may be 1000 years old.

The Cloisters

The cloisters of Norwich are the largest in England, and even have a floor above them. They were built over quite a long period so the arches reflect changes in architectural taste. Benedictine monks walked here, and it is easy to sense their continued presence. The vaulting seems effortless, and the filtered light falls in shafts which illuminate the worn paving stones. More than anywhere else, this is where the modern tourist glimpses the religious ideal which inspired the work.

The Ethelbert Gateway, Norwich Cathedral

Edith Cavell served as a nurse in Belgium during the First World War. The Germans accused her of helping British soldiers to escape, and shot her. Her last words have become her epitaph: 'I realise that patriotism is not enough. I must have no hatred or bitterness against anyone.' Her simple grave and stone cross are in the churchyard, east of the cathedral. A more emotional memorial stands outside the Erpingham Gate.

The Close has some lovely houses, and tall trees rise from well-tended lawns. Nelson was a pupil at Norwich School which occupies the Old Bishop's Palace, and statues of Nelson and Wellington stand guard at either end of Upper Close. Two fine gates lead to Tombland, the old market place. The Ethelbert Gate was built in 1316 to replace one destroyed in riots during the Trinity Fair; the citizens had to bear the cost. Opposite the cathedral's west door is the Erpingham Gateway of 1420, recalling the good knight who fought with Henry V at Agincourt.

BLICKLING HALL

The B1354 from Aylsham to Saxthorpe is exceptionally pretty, and winds between the fields of good farming country, but the first sight of Blickling Hall is unexpected and never to be forgotten. In any list of England's most beautiful houses, it would vie for the highest rank. A long striped lawn, parted by a gravel drive, stretches between tall yew hedges and warm Dutch gabled brick outbuildings towards the majesty of a turreted brick and stone Jacobean mansion. East Anglia offers no finer view than this. A grand bridge, guarded by stone lions, crosses a dry moat and gives access to a courtyard and the Great Hall beyond.

Sir Henry Hobart bought the estate in 1616, and his architect Robert Lyminge pulled down the medieval moated manor which stood on the site and created Blickling Hall. The Boleyn family had owned the old house and the ghost of Anne is said to drive in a carriage through the grounds! Sir Henry died three years before Blickling was completed in 1628. Today, the south view from the road is still very much as Lyminge intended, except for the white wooden clock tower, added in 1830.

The gardens

The gardens are beautiful and varied. In 1872 a parterre of four flower beds was created around a central fountain. The flowers are carefully arranged according to colour. A raised walkway extends along one side and in summer the border is a blaze of gold and purple. The shrubs are labelled and will give inspiration to would-be gardeners. Hedges are clipped into elaborate, graceful shapes and the effect of this garden with the soft colours of the Jacobean brick in the background, accompanied by the gentle swish of the fountain is truly idyllic. No wonder seats are provided! A wide lawn called The Acre slopes down to a crescent-shaped lake which curves between fields of grazing sheep and cattle. Woodland walks extend for miles, and at the end of the east avenue is a Doric temple of simple elegance, its steps leading between the columns to a small, cool room illuminated through large clear windows which reveal even more park beyond. The orangery on the south side of the park was built in 1782.

The south view

In the mid-18th century the house passed to John Hobart, second Earl of Buckingham, a man of refined taste who employed the Norwich architect Thomas Ivory to carry out extensive alterations. The Great Staircase was removed to the Great Hall and enlarged, producing the double flight arrangement we see today. There are paintings by Canaletto and Reynolds, and a portrait of John Hobart by Gainsborough hangs in the Peter the Great Room. Hobart was ambassador to Russia for three years and Catherine the Great presented him with the fine tapestry showing one of the Tsar's victories. Restoration of tapestry and furniture takes place in the Hall, and visitors may see work in progress.

The Long Gallery has not been greatly altered since its creation in 1620. It became the Library in 1745 and has a collection of 12,000 books, some of them rare. The plasterwork was executed by Edward Stanyon, who charged £96 for his work. It must be one of the finest ceilings in England; 120 feet long, it incorporates the Hobart arms, its detail perfectly picked out by the light from the line of full-length windows.

Everything at Blickling is memorable – even the car park is a pretty orchard, and the ice creams are in a class of their own!

The Doric Temple

National Trust
Open: Mar to Nov: Sun, Tues, Wed, Fri, Sat & bank holiday Mon:
Gardens 1100–1700, Hall: 1300–1700
Price guide: B (Gardens), C (Hall)

MANNINGTON HALL GARDENS

The emblem of England is a rose, and for many it is a symbol of perfection with its delicate form, colour and perfume. Gardeners will know that roses come in many different varieties, and that new roses are always being developed; but you don't have to be an expert to appreciate the charms of Mannington Hall Gardens.

Mannington is hidden away off the main road, south of Holt and two miles from the village of Saxthorpe. This part of Norfolk is rich and rolling, and Mannington Hall occupies a hollow in the landscape. The approach is across green lawns and under fine old cedar trees, and our first view of the Hall is a surprise. It is an unusual and asymmetrical building of grey flint, which dates from the late 15th century. Later it was sold to the Walpole family and it was the fourth Earl, an enthusiastic connoisseur of the antique, who set up the classical temple on the south lawn and the 'follies' near the ruined church. The Walpole family still live in this house.

The ground floor is open only on special occasions in the summer, but you are invited to cross the narrow footbridge over the moat and wander around the gardens on the other side. Here are roses and statues to enhance the tranquillity of the scene, and a modern ornamental garden whose scented flowers and shrubs are planted according to the design of the Dining Room ceiling.

In a walled garden to the north of the Hall lie the Heritage Rose Gardens. These were established fairly recently in an acre of former kitchen garden which had been neglected and overgrown. Some of the fruit trees still stand, but the rest of this sheltered area is given over to roses planted in different sections according to their date of origin, as far as is known. Over a thousand roses were planted in one year alone, and the variety of species is quite marvellous. Here we see the Medieval Garden with its herbs and damask roses; the Knot Garden which incorporates the initials of each of the members of the present Walpole household; the Classical, Victorian and Trellis Gardens, and so on up to the present day. Each section has its own style, reflecting the taste of the time, and each is enchanting.

One of the excellent booklets available at the entrance to the Gardens gives detailed information about each rose, and most of the bushes are labelled. If you find it daunting to encounter Latin names, or impossible to distinguish between a hybrid tea and a musk rose, don't be put off: merely to stroll around the gardens and take in their colours and fragrance is a delight.

You may buy rose bushes in the shop, or choose from a variety of pots pourris with enchanting names like Elizabethan, Musk Rose or Tea Rose.

The Mannington Countryside Project was set up in 1986 to protect the estate and its wildlife, and to encourage the public to enjoy the countryside. Running round the Hall and beyond are many footpaths, and these have been incorporated into three nature trails which concentrate on different aspects of country life. In all there are 20 miles of walks taking in woodland, meadows and wetlands along the River Bure. Each trail is clearly marked and leaflets are available at the information centre. This also has an education room where children are taught what to look out for on their ramble. Throughout the year there are special events such as the Rose Festival – not to be missed by either expert or amateur.

The Heritage Rose Garden

Open: April to Oct: Sun 1200–1700, June to Aug: Sun, Wed to Fri 1100–1700
Price guide: B

FELBRIGG HALL

We all know architectural tastes change, but at Felbrigg Hall, to the south-west of Cromer, the fact is vividly displayed, and a mere 50 years produces two totally different styles abutting on one another. The effect is not disturbing, but it is certainly striking.

Simon Felbrigg, standard-bearer to the unfortunate King Richard II, was first to build a hall on this site. His first wife died in 1416 and was buried in the nearby Church of St Margaret. She lies beneath an almost life-size brass depiction of herself and her husband. It is considered to be very fine, if rather misleading, as Simon is buried in Norwich beside his second wife.

Thomas Windham was the man responsible for the building we see today, which was begun in 1621. He employed as his architect Robert Lyminge, who was at the time working at Blickling Hall. By 1624 the south front was complete, with its impressive porch tower and a stone balustrading which proclaims 'Gloria Deo In Excelsis'. Through the door and to the left was once the Great Hall, the centre of family and estate life.

In the 1680s Thomas's son William added the west wing. Rejecting the predominantly stone facing favoured by his father, he chose to build in red brick. His son completely remodelled the house in the mid-18th century, influenced by his extensive Grand Tour of Europe. He had returned with so many fine paintings that he made the Cabinet Room into a veritable private gallery. Van der Velde's *The Battle of the Texel*, which hangs in the Drawing Room, was especially prized: 'My great V. Velde I cannot trust to the seas, so that alone should go by land'. He loved his books too, and the Library contains many of his collection, including some left to him by his friend Dr Johnson. William also took up bookbinding, and some 300 are his handiwork. In 1994 eleven ground floor rooms were opened to the public.

The East Wing

The orangery to the west was built in 1705, and has seven large windows which overlook what was once a formal garden. A walled garden was laid out in the early years of the 18th century to provide the house with fresh vegetables, fruit, herbs and cut flowers. The herbaceous borders and clipped box hedges were within the protecting brick wall, against which climbed peaches, plums and pears. The house guests would have enjoyed their rambles along the neatly-tended paths, probably pausing to enjoy the activity at the dovecote, built in about 1750 and capable of accommodating 2000 birds. The poor birds ultimately fed the house, while in life they manured the soil! The National Trust, which cares for the property, has restored the garden to its former glory.

Felbrigg is only two miles from the coast, and to act as a windbreak generations of Windhams have planted trees. The woodland today is magnificent, and in autumn a carpet of gold leaves sweeps between proud timbers. Before the age of refrigerators, ice was collected from the surface of the park lake in winter, and stored in the cold depths of the ice house. Felbrigg's was built in 1820, and is in the wood to the north of the Hall. The storage chamber is 28 feet below the ground.

The Windhams lost the estate thanks to 'Mad' Windham, who was forced to sell both house and contents to the Ketton family in 1863. He had a passion for trains: refusing to be a mere passenger, he insisted on driving the engine, collecting the tickets and being the guard! No wonder *Punch*, hearing he had won a legal action on the subject of his sanity, wrote: 'Windham is sane; but England must be cracked.'

The South Porch

National Trust
Open: Mar to Nov: Mon, Wed, Thur, Sat: Gardens 1100–1700, Hall 1300–1700
Price guide: C

CROMER

Cromer calls itself 'the gem of the Norfolk coast', and the narrow streets and elegant boarding-houses at the centre of this former fishing village lend it such a comfortable air that the visitor feels instantly at home. The resident population of Cromer is a mere 6000, but in summer its beach and roads are thronged with tourists. Its popularity brings traffic jams, and the day-tripper is advised to arrive early to secure the best parking place – but the heart of Cromer is never far away.

Cromer is situated at the extreme north-easterly point of Norfolk, and is set on high, crumbling cliffs. The best view is from the beach; the town piles up most picturesquely against the backdrop of the sky, and the wide shore leads to a horizon unbroken by any landfall. North of here is the Arctic, and the severe storms which sometimes batter this coast have always caused problems. Cromer, for instance, was originally some way inland from the village of Shipden, which was mentioned in the Domesday Survey, but washed away soon afterwards. Cromer developed as a resort at the end of the 18th century, when favourable reports were given of 'the beautiful scenery and pleasant walks in the neighbourhood, the excellence of the beach at low water and the simple manners of the inhabitants' (*White's Directory*, 1845). It quickly became a fashionable resort, and one of Jane Austen's characters described it as 'the best of all the sea-bathing places'. Grand hotels were built in the 1850s and the railway made the town flourish, so that by the mid-19th century Cromer made its living from tourism.

The cliffs and sea front

Cromer is inextricably linked with the sea. Cromer crabs are still considered the most delicious in England, and are for sale both fresh and dressed. The town was also a trading port, with the boats being pulled up on to the beach where at low tide carts came down to unload them. The dangerous nature of the seas necessitated the building of a lighthouse, but successive structures were washed away; the present building to the east of the town dates from 1833, and the white-brick tower may be visited. But it was the massive tower of the Church of St Peter and St Paul which for many years served as landmark to seamen. At 160 feet high, this is the tallest tower in the county, and its flint and freestone decorations are very fine. The interior has been restored since Cromwell's troops used it as a barracks.

Behind the church are a number of little fishermen's cottages which have been made into a museum. You can see how a typical cottage looked at the turn of the century, and learn about local history. A second museum deals with another important facet of Cromer's history: the lifeboat. The new lifeboat is launched from the end of the pier, but in the old lifeboat house is an exhibition concerning the exploits of the lifeboatmen, particularly Captain Henry Bloggs. This extraordinary man saw 53 years' service and assisted at the rescue of 873 men – and a dog. He won the Gold Medal, the RNLI's highest award, three times, as well as the George Cross and the British Empire Medal. His courage was exemplary, and earned him the title of 'Cromer's Greatest Son'. A bronze bust commemorating him gazes out to sea from North Lodge Park.

These are Cromer's past glories. What attracts today's visitor? The scenery is still magnificent, and the beach and cliff tops make for marvellous walks. The Pavilion Theatre offers genuine old-fashioned seaside entertainment, and there are summer shows on the pier. It is an excellent place to visit – but do arrive early to beat the traffic!

Cromer Museum
Open: All year: Sun 1400–1700, Mon to Sat 1000–1700
Price guide: A

Lifeboat Museum
Open: May to Oct: daily 1000–1600
Price guide: Free

Lifeboat House
Open: May to Sept: daily 1000–1700
Price guide: Free

SHERINGHAM

Like its near neighbour Cromer, Sheringham is a small fishing village which has developed into a resort. Its narrow, crowded streets lead to little fishermen's cottages on top of precipitous cliffs, and brightly-coloured fishing boats are drawn up on the shingle near the old lifeboat house; you can watch fish being landed here and it is on sale everywhere, as well as cockles, whelks and prawns. Over a million crabs are bought here every year. At one time a hundred Sheringham boats made a living from the sea, and until as late as 1920 cargoes such as coal were brought in by ship. The bustling activity is still very much in evidence, although the seamen have given way to holidaymakers who find this a congenial centre for touring north Norfolk.

A North Norfolk Railway Steam locomotive

The town faces north and the high cliffs shade the beach for much of the day, but this pleasant mixture of sand and shingle is perfect for walks and games. Swimming can be dangerous, so there are lifeguards on duty. Like Cromer, Sheringham has a proud lifeboat record and for almost 70 years had two working lifeboats, one private (given to the fishermen by the Upcher family who made such a great contribution to the town) and one RNLI boat. The new RNLI inshore lifeboat, the first and the fastest of its kind, the *Manchester Unity of Oddfellows* is housed at the western end of the Promenade. To the east, beside the Fishermen's Slope which runs underneath the new concrete bridge, is a shed containing the old lifeboat, the *Henry Ramey Upcher*. This remarkable oak boat was built without plans or drawings, and is one of the last rowing and sailing lifeboats on show in this country.

Sheringham is an ideal shopping centre. At the heart of the town, where the three main streets converge, stands a Victorian brick and flint Town Clock. Sheringham's popularity means that the seaside car parks are often full, but there is plenty of space at Station Road – except on Saturday when this is the venue for the market. Enthusiasts of steam railways will find this place ideal, because the station serves the North Norfolk Railway, and from here steam and diesel trains run as far as Holt. Sheringham station is very picturesque with its displays of old railway

signs and advertisements; it also has a buffet and a small museum housed in the signal box. Sheringham station once saw 64 trains daily, and business is still brisk during the regular runs from April to October, and at Christmas. Engines such as *Fireless* and *Brighton Belle* may be inspected at close quarters, and the five-mile journey to Holt passes through some beautiful countryside.

Another glory of the past is Sheringham's Little Theatre, home to Britain's only surviving weekly repertory company. For many years now the Theatre Society has shown films, put on musicals, pantomimes and puppet shows and hosted lectures by celebrities. All the members are volunteers, and they deserve the support and praise of the holidaymakers who crowd their theatre of an evening.

August sees Sheringham Carnival with its myriad stalls and sideshows, its Fun Run and beach sports, and the Raft Race to Cromer, where prizes are awarded as much for originality of costume and raft design as for winning the race!

Sheringham is surrounded by high ground which affords marvellous views. The aptly named Pretty Corner, off Holway Road, is a 70-acre site of woodland, perfect for walks and picnics. To the east of the town is the Sheringham and Beeston Regis Common, rich in botanical interest and insect life, where you can wander freely or follow a guided walk with the warden. Sheringham Hall has grounds designed by Sir Humphrey Repton which he considered to be his finest work; they are now open to the public, and the magnificent rhododendrons and the lovely sea view delight the eye.

Within easy distance of Sheringham are other attractions, including the Norfolk Shire Horse Centre at West Runton, 2 miles east of Sheringham, where you may see these gentle giants at work, and the Muckleburgh Collection, housed in the former NAAFI building of the Weybourne Military Camp on the A149 coast road. Here the visitor passes through a sandbagged guard post and finds himself surrounded by vintage military vehicles and weapons in a real wartime setting.

RNLI Lifeboat
Open: daily 1000–1700
Price guide: Free

Henry Ramey Upcher Lifeboat
Open: Easter to Whitsun: Sat & Sun 1430–1630, Whitsun to Sept: Wed, Sat & Sun, July & Aug: also Thur and Fri
Price guide: Free

North Norfolk Railway
Open: Mar to Oct
Price guide: C

Sheringham Park
Open: All year daily
Price guide: A (car parking fee)

Norfolk Shire Horse Centre
Open: April to Oct: Sun to Fri 1000–1700
Price guide: B

The Muckleburgh Collection
Open: Mar to Oct: daily 1000–1700
Price guide: B

HOLKHAM HALL

Even before you catch sight of Holkham Hall there is an air of expectancy, for the signs are all about you that the experience will be something altogether breathtaking. So indeed it is. The Holkham estate is a few miles to the west of Wells-next-the-Sea, and the encircling red brick wall which runs for nine miles will be the first indication of the scale of the property. The visitor approaches by way of a drive between charming country cottages, which lead to a magnificent gateway through which we pass into a landscape almost entirely created to the wishes of its builder.

Early in the 18th century Thomas Coke inherited a fortune at the age of ten, and in time was sent off on the obligatory Grand Tour, taking in all the sights of Europe. He was captivated by all he saw, and during his travels made the acquaintance of two men who were to exert an influence over him for the rest of his long life (he lived to be 88); the designer William Kent, and the connoisseur Lord Burlington. Holkham Hall, the child of their shared dreams, was begun in 1734, on a stretch of sandy shoreline which was formerly of interest only to rabbits.

The visitor's first view of the Hall is the north façade, which proclaims itself to be the home of a well-bred and much-travelled gentleman, being rather severe and classical. To the side is the lake, and a view of well ordered parkland.

The Entrance Hall is famous, and rightly so, for it makes an extraordinary impact upon the visitor. A cool amphitheatre of marble, it conveys a love of the classical period and the values which inspired it. A grand staircase leads up to the principal rooms. These are opulent, a cornucopia of 18th century aristocratic education. The exquisite elegance of the North Dining Room is a preparation for the treasures of the Statue Gallery, in which are displayed two of Holkham's finest exhibits: the bust of Thucydides and a statue of Diana. The sense of space makes this a room to linger in.

Gainsborough's portrait of Thomas William Coke, first Earl of Leicester, hangs in the Saloon. It shows a young country gentleman with his gun dogs at his feet. This is appropriate, for here is 'Coke of Norfolk' whose interest in farming and husbandry resulted in innovations of truly revolutionary importance. He was no absentee landlord, but devoted himself to understanding the problems of farming and finding solutions to them. When his tenants erected a monument to his memory, they chose to depict the hallmarks of his achievement: an ox, a sheep, a plough and a seed drill – an unconventional but accurate tribute.

You will need time to discover the treasures of Holkham Hall. The state rooms are only some of the rooms to be seen. The 'below stairs' aspects are not neglected either, and an exhibition of bygones comprises 4000 domestic and agricultural objects, housed in the former stable block. In the grounds are more places to visit. There is a pottery workshop which sometimes allows you to watch the creative process, and buy the product, too. An extensive garden centre even tempts you to indulge in creating your own landscape.

But the final view of Holkham is likely to be the most enduring, and it is from the south, looking back down the drive, to a noble palace which is exactly what its creator desired: a tribute to the power of thought and order.

Holkham Hall and Bygones Collection
Open: May to Sept: Sun to Thur 1330–1700
Price guide: B

THE NORTH NORFOLK COAST

The 40-mile stretch of coastline between Holme-next-the-Sea and Sheringham has rightly been designated an area of outstanding natural beauty. It is one of the most unspoilt parts of East Anglia, and great efforts have had to be made to protect this landscape and preserve the wildlife it harbours.

This region is not all flat, despite the common prejudice about Norfolk. Certainly the marshes are, cut by winding creeks and channels left muddy and quiet by low tide, and the reclaimed land criss-crossed by drainage ditches; but behind the coastal plain rises a ridge of rolling chalk hills; once sea cliffs but long since abandoned by the water. This pleasant hilly ground affords an often spectacular prospect of the saltmarshes and the strip of sea beyond. But this is no idyll: the marshes are unprotected from the north or east winds except by shifting dunes or banks of shingle, and the air is at best bracing, and at worst icy and bleak. Yet even when a glacial wind is sweeping off the sea with a force to take your breath away, the experience is magical. Whether it be the rustling of marshland grasses and reeds, the calling of seabirds, the clarity of the light on a bright day or the grandeur of the sunset, the skies here seem broader than anywhere else in the county.

To many, a visit to the north Norfolk coast will mean an opportunity to view a landscape now sadly almost unique: saltmarsh and reedbeds, sand dunes and shingle spits. Man has battled against the sea for centuries, endeavouring to keep it at a respectable distance from his crops and to use it to transport his goods to the commercial markets. On this coast, man has largely lost the battle. In the 17th century, banks and walls were built to stop the encroaching tide and allow the marshes to be drained and cultivated. But the thriving ports found that their channels silted up and they dwindled in importance. The sea surged back in places, notably during the dreadful floods of 1953, and much of the reclaimed land was lost. Now we have come to a rather uneasy alliance with the elements, we are aware of the need to preserve this vanishing land.

A more detailed look at the coast reveals the attractions it has to offer. We begin in the west, at Holme-next-the-Sea, just east of Hunstanton. Here is a 500-acre nature reserve and bird observatory from where have been spotted almost 300 species of birds. Nearby Titchwell Marsh, once cultivated, has now returned to its natural state.

The name of Brancaster comes from Branoduni castra, the fort at Branodunum, since this was the site of one of the Roman coastal defences against invaders. Nothing now remains of the fort except its name.

Scolt Head Island is distinguished for its colonies of rare terns, and access to the ternery is restricted during the nesting season. The island can be reached by boat from Burnham Overy Staithe. This village is one of six Burnhams in the area. As late as the 19th century it was a busy port,

Holkham Bay Nature Reserve

Wells-next-the-Sea

It is possible to walk to Blakeney Point from Cley, a distance of four miles; but perhaps it is better to take a boat from Morston Quay or from Blakeney itself. This is a charming village. It used to be a commercial port from where Norfolk's wool was exported; nowadays it is a picturesque sailing centre. A steep and narrow lane leads down between pretty cottages from the main road to the quay, and you may walk for some distance beside the water.

Cley-next-the-Sea has completely lost its access to the sea, which is now half a mile from the village. The beautiful 18th-century mill once stood on the quayside; now its red brick tower rises up from the waving reeds and stands out sharply against the sky. The village is very pretty with its narrow streets of cramped cottages. The marshes here are freshwater, and sheltered by a high, steep shingle bank.

The village of Salthouse, as its name suggests, was once a warehouse centre for locally-produced salt. The marshes stretch out as far as the eye can see, but more accessible are the ducks and seagulls which gather near the roadside to be fed. You can buy samphire here: a succulent rock plant which can be cooked and served with butter as 'the poor man's asparagus'. All along the coast shellfish are caught and sold, including the cockles known as 'Stewkey Blues' after the village of Stiffkey near where they are found. And while in the area it is well worth making the detour to explore some of the charming inland villages.

Cley-next-the-Sea Windmill

but competition from the railway robbed it of its commercial role. Now it is a sailing centre, where the brightly-coloured boats are left high above the waterline at low tide, and where the clanking of rigging sounds like music in the air. There are picturesque old fishermen's cottages in brick and flint – the typical building materials in this part of the country where stone is scarce – and they have been modernised and are inhabited no doubt by those not native to this coast, but who have come to pursue the peaceful recreation of boating.

Next along the coast is the Holkham National Nature Reserve, the largest coastal reserve in England, covering 10,000 acres of dune and saltmarsh and home to some rare species of bird. In the 19th century hundreds of pines were planted to try to stabilise the sands which stretch in a long arc along Holkham Bay. There is access to this beach down Lady Ann's Drive, opposite the entrance to Holkham Hall.

Wells-next-the-Sea scarcely lives up to its name, and certainly not at low tide when the sea recedes by a good mile or more; the beach, therefore, is some distance from the port, and is reached either by walking along the harbour wall, or by road, or by taking a little railway. The beach may be wide and sandy, but the tide comes in quickly, and may trap unsuspecting walkers, and there are dangerous currents. But warnings are freely given on notice boards and by the lifeguards, and the prudent bather should find it a safe place to swim. The resort will suit all the family; apart from the obvious attractions of the beach, the harbour with its distinctive grain loader affords a pleasant walk beside sailing and working boats, and there are pretty houses and shops. At Wells you may also take a sea trip or join a fishing party; or if you prefer to remain on land, the Wells and Walsingham Light Railway runs steam trains daily along a four-mile track.

Blakeney Point is a shingle spit which reaches out westwards along the coast. It has been a nature reserve since 1912 and covers about 1400 acres. Here there are nesting colonies of terns, oystercatchers and redshanks, among others – indeed, this reserve is home to more species of bird than any other reserve in the country. As well as the more familiar native seabirds, there are summer migrants to spot from one of the observation hides. Children may like to follow the nature trail designed for them. Seals colonise this part of the coast.

Holme
Open: all year
Visitors should contact the Warden on site
Price guide: B

Wells and Walsingham Light Railway
Open: April to Sept: daily 1000–1800
Price guide: B

Cley Marshes
Open: April to Oct: Tues to Sun 1000–1700
Price guide: Permit charge

Cley Windmill
Open: April to Sept: daily 1400–1700
Price guide: A

NORFOLK HERO

Biographers attach considerable importance to discovering the influences on their subjects, particularly while young. In the case of Horatio Nelson this is made more difficult because the closed rural world of north Norfolk offers few obvious preparations for becoming England's greatest naval commander. Now only pub names such as the Lord Nelson and Norfolk Hero provide a tangible connection with his roots.

He was born on Friday September 29th 1758, the sixth child (and fifth son) of the Rev. Edmund Nelson and his wife Catherine. Burnham Market likes to claim that the birth took place in a barn beside their pub, but it is more probable that Nelson came into the world at Burnham Thorpe Parsonage.

The name Horatio was given to him to please the Walpole family who were distant and superior relatives, but the boy preferred Horace, which he described as 'an English name for an Englishman'. The baptism took place on October 9th in the font of Purbeck marble which still serves in the Church of All Saints less than a mile from his home. The church now has a lectern made of timbers from the *Victory*.

The Parsonage at Burnham Thorpe was really two large cottages joined together and when, as a half-pay naval officer, Nelson and his new wife lived there, he said it was the coldest place he had ever experienced. About 30 acres of glebe land belonged to the Rector but he failed to farm it

Nelson's Monument (by courtesy of Norfolk Museums service, Great Yarmouth Museums)

profitably, although he enjoyed trying, saying his garden was the place where 'Nature will meet you smiling'. Among their servants were the delightfully titled 'Will Indoors' and 'Peter Without'. The Parsonage was pulled down in 1802, and a plaque beside the road now marks the site.

The coast is only four miles away, and it is fair to assume that the young Nelson soon grew familiar with the numerous creeks and wide expanses of marshland, and the wildfowl which lived among them. Local tradition says he learned to sail his first boat at Brancaster. Entertainments in such a country parish were few and far between for people of their humble rank in society, and was probably confined to festive occasions at Norwich, King's Lynn and Aylsham.

Nelson's mother died on December 26th 1767, aged 42, having given birth to 11 children in the space of 17 years. Although only nine years old at the time of her death, Nelson remembered of his mother that 'she hated the French'. This was not entirely unexpected, for her side of the family had a strong naval tradition. Her brother, Captain Maurice Suckling, had in 1759 won a victory over the French in the West Indies when he commanded HMS *Dreadnought*, and the date – October 21st – was always celebrated at Burnham, as it still is today! It was while attending his sister's funeral that Captain Suckling promised to take care of one of the boys. The Rev. Nelson now had to bring up his family alone. He was a strict disciplinarian: they had to sit up so straight that their backs should not touch the chair!

Nelson attended Norwich School in the Cathedral Close, staying with relatives. His statue now stands facing the former schoolroom. During this time he was witness to a wedding and signed his name, 'Horace', which his father corrected to 'Horatio'. Next he was sent to the Paston School, North Walsham, where the Headmaster had a reputation for flogging his pupils. The Church of St Nicholas once had a tower and spire 170 feet high, but they collapsed in 1724, so the schoolboy Nelson would have known of the futile appeals and schemes to rebuild it.

Many stories attach themselves to these years, some of them repeated by Nelson's first serious biographer, Robert Southey, writing in 1813. He tells how Nelson and his brother William were riding to North Walsham through deep snow, to start the new term. William wanted to turn back, saying they had done their best, but Horatio reminded him: 'Remember, brother, it was left to our honour', and they struggled on. From these years the school displays Nelson's pencil box, and a brick improved by the initials 'HN'.

The Christmas of 1770 brought exciting news to the Parsonage. Capt. Suckling was to command HMS *Raisonnable* in a probable war against Spain who claimed the Falkland Islands. Horatio urged his brother to write to their absent father: 'Do, brother William, write to my father at Bath and tell him I should like to go with my uncle Maurice to sea'. The Rector wrote to the Captain, and received this encouraging reply:

'What has poor Horace done, who is so weak, that he above all the rest should be sent to rough it out at sea? But let him come; and the first time we go into action a cannon-ball may knock off his head, and provide for him at once.'

In January 1771 a servant was sent to North Walsham to collect Horatio from school, and with his father he set out

Nelson landing at Great Yarmouth (by courtesy of Norfolk Museums service, Great Yarmouth Museums)

for London. The boy was just over 12 years old when he was rated midshipman on his uncle's ship, anchored at Chatham. The rest is, as they say, history.

Nelson's naval career is proudly commemorated on the Norfolk Naval Column which stands at South Denes, Great Yarmouth. It was begun in 1817 and rises to a height of 144 feet. Those prepared to climb the 217 steps may obtain a marvellous view on a clear day, perhaps even to Norwich. Nelson landed at the port on his return from the Mediterranean. The plinth bears the names of the ships he commanded as Admiral: *Captain*, *Vanguard*, *Elephant* and *Victory*, while the coping lists his victories: St Vincent, Aboukir, Copenhagen, Trafalgar. Proudly the Latin inscription proclaims: 'This great man NORFOLK boasts her own, not only as born there of a respectable family, and as there having received his early education, but her own also in talents, manners and mind.'

But it is in Burnham Thorpe that the strength of his presence is greatest. The Lord Nelson pub was then The Plough, and here Nelson spent his last night in 1793 before leaving Norfolk to command his country's ships in the war against Napoleon. He once wrote that he hoped his bones would lie in All Saints Church, beside those of his mother and father, and yet with an eye to greatness his will qualified the wish: 'unless the King decrees otherwise'. And so his death at Trafalgar on October 21st 1805 was followed by a splendid funeral procession to St Paul's Cathedral.

In 1799 he had been created Baron of the Nile and of Burnham Thorpe. Although he could not return to Norfolk it seems to have kept its hold on his affections, and perhaps he thought of those childhood days spent walking the coastal marshes or sailing a small boat up the creeks to Burnham Overy, and Burnham Overy Staithe. He was kind to his crews in an age known for its cruelty, and achieved a unique relationship with his officers and men as a result. His character was formed in Norfolk, and was not found wanting. On the church door today is a notice: 'All who enter of your charity pray latch these doors lest a bird enter and die of thirst'. This is still a special region.

Burnham Overy

Nelson's Monument, Great Yarmouth
Open: July to August 1400–1700, Oct 21st 1000–1700
Price guide: A

LITTLE WALSINGHAM

There can be few places in East Anglia where the streets are thronged with visitors from all parts of the country whom it would be inaccurate to call mere sightseers. Walsingham is different from anywhere else, for in spite of being a pretty little town, with flower baskets hanging from the beams of timber-framed houses, it owes its fame to a phenomenon almost as remote from our times as the horse-drawn plough. It is a place of pilgrimage.

In 1061 the Lady Richeldis de Faverches had a vision of the Virgin Mary. She felt compelled to build by a well in Walsingham a wooden replica of the house in Nazareth she had seen in her vision. Soon the shrine was attracting pilgrims, and their reports of miraculous healing ensured Walsingham's rise to the status of England's Nazareth. It became a place of such veneration that from the 13th century few kings of England omitted to make at least one visit. In 1511, Henry VIII walked the last mile barefoot, but did not trouble to return when in 1539 he closed the abbey and seized all its property.

There are a number of buildings worth seeing in Walsingham. In High Street is the fine gateway to the Augustinian priory which stood on the site of the holy well. Its closure by Henry VIII led to neglect and ruin. Only the east window remains to provide some indication of its original splendour. The grounds are very beautiful, especially in spring when they are a carpet of snowdrops and daffodils. The old packhorse bridge over the River Stiffkey makes a perfect scene.

The Common Place is one of the two market places in Walsingham. Around a 400-year-old pump are pretty houses, many of them decorated with flowers. The museum is housed in the Old Courthouse, complete with lock-up. The Bull Inn provides a lovely backdrop to the excitements which occur at times of special pilgrimage. Close by is the Anglican Shrine of Our Lady of Walsingham, which was rebuilt in the 1930s.

Friday Market is worth seeing; it contains many fine buildings, including the Black Lion Hotel, whose emblem commemorates the visit to Walsingham in 1328 of Edward III's Queen, Philippa. From this square the coaches to London used to depart at 6.30 in the morning. It is easy to imagine you hear the posthorn sound, as this part of the town seems so timeless. Here are located some of the organisations which help pilgrims find their way about – geographically and spiritually!

The Abbey ruins in Spring

The Slipper Chapel

The Holy Mile leads from Walsingham to the Slipper Chapel, the Roman Catholic shrine. It was one of the features of medieval pilgrimage that the last mile was walked barefoot, and today you will see many people walking the narrow road. The Slipper Chapel was built in 1350 and was one of the objectives of all the royal pilgrims. Following the Reformation it was closed down, and it even spent some time as a cowshed. It was reopened in 1921, and the Chapel of Reconciliation was added in 1981. All the Christian denominations are represented in Walsingham, and all make visitors welcome.

Walsingham is a place not to be missed, for it provides a unique experience. It seems to have captured the essence of Chaucer's Canterbury pilgrims: it explains how people could be cheerful and devout at the same time. It is as much a place of money and laughter as prayers and incantations. Do go to Walsingham – follow in the footsteps of kings to England's Nazareth.

The Common Place

Shrine of Our Lady of Walsingham
Open: All year: daily 0730–1930. National Pilgrimage Spring bank holiday, Pilgrimage for sick and handicapped August bank holiday Monday
Price Guide: Free

Abbey Grounds
Open: April: Wed 1400–1700, May to Sept: Wed, Sat, Sun. Aug: Mon, Wed, Fri to Sun 1400–1700
Price guide: A

Shirehall Museum
Open: Mar to Sept: Mon to Sat 1000–1700, Sun 1400–1700. Oct: Sat 1000–1700, Sun 1400–1700
Price guide: A

Slipper Chapel
Open: All year: daily. Winter 0800–1600, summer 0800–1800
Price guide: Free

THE THURSFORD COLLECTION

What could be finer than to save from extinction an important aspect of our history and at the same time provide entertainment for hundreds of people? Such is the success story of George Cushing who has established the Thursford Collection in a group of renovated farm buildings off the A148 north east of Fakenham. As a boy he was taken to see the fair at nearby Walsingham, and was captivated by the beauty and power of the steam traction engines and organs he saw there. For several decades he has rescued and restored the machines, once condemned to the scrapyard, which now form this most unusual and lively of museums.

The Marenghi Showman's Organ

The visitor enters the collection as if walking into an Edwardian village with its bow-fronted shops and red postbox. There is the Corner Shop, which stocks a wide variety of goods, including recordings of the organ music played here, and the Thursford Pantry which caters for the sweet tooth! Through double doors you pass into a covered arcade where you may sample home-made ice cream in the period parlour, take refreshment in the Norfolk Barn, or buy souvenirs at the Old Stable Shop. The collection is through

the swing doors, and what sights and sounds greet you as you enter! First there are the engines: the agricultural traction engine used for threshing or hauling timber; the road locomotive used for crushing stones and levelling the road surface: and most spectacular of all, the showmen's engines, resplendent in bright colours and golden embellishments. All these engines have been restored to full working order.

Against the walls are eight static organs, gorgeously painted and decorated, many with moving figures. There is the street organ, 'De Leeuwin', the oldest in the collection. The Marenghi showman's organ, made in Paris at the height of organ manufacture in 1911, is a dance hall organ which stuns the visitor with its ornate decoration including a scantily-clad Parisian lady apparently riding two horses out of the top of the façade. The opulence of the Marenghi contrasts with the plainer geometric design of the Gebrs. Decap organ of 1938 which has a display of flashing lights. One of the more amazing fairground organs is the Carl Frei organ of 1910 which can play for half an hour. It has figures (some almost life size) which beat time with the music. Another fairground organ is the Gavioli organ which has been incorporated into the gondola switchback ride in the collection. This is a magnificent sight with its ornate gold decoration, bright lights and colours. The ride operates at intervals through the afternoon, and it will stir in any visitor a nostalgia for the gaiety of the fair.

The centrepiece of the collection is the Wurlitzer organ, played as often as three times a day for half-hour sessions. This is a real spectacle with spotlights and screens showing films which the organist accompanies, or a close-up view of the keyboards so that the audience can marvel at the performer's quick fingers. Communal singing is encouraged, and you may make special requests for songs. The organist will even autograph his records for you! The special concerts here are very popular: midsummer musical evenings, Easter concerts and carol concerts, but you will need to book your seat early!

Outside the collection there are other attractions, including a narrow-gauge steam railway engine, the *Cackler*, which takes you on a short ride through the fields, past the children's adventure playground.

Open: April to May: daily 1300–1700, June to Aug: daily 1100–1700, Sept to Oct: daily 1300–1700
Price guide: B

THE NORFOLK WILDLIFE PARK

there are no barriers or wire enclosures, giving an uninterrupted view. Many of the animals and wildfowl share the areas with you! You can walk through some of the aviaries, which is a wonderful way of seeing the birds. Every enclosure has a clearly-labelled description of the inhabitant

There really is no substitute for seeing animals, birds and suchlike in the fur or feather! It is a great thrill to see exotic species we would never naturally encounter in Great Britain, but it can be just as exciting to study those species native to our country, like hedgehogs and rabbits, which we are told live all around us but which we seldom meet. The Norfolk Wildlife Park gives us the opportunity to see a wide range of European mammals in their natural surroundings, and the visitor will find the experience enjoyable and instructive.

In 1961 the naturalist Philip Wayre founded the first wildlife park in Great Britain, with the intention that, unlike a traditional zoo, the animals should be seen in enclosures which resembled as far as possible the conditions found in the wild. The venture was a success, and subsequently was transformed into a charitable trust. It is entirely supported by income from admissions, and has established a reputation as a breeding centre, winning many prestigious awards. The trust has been the first to breed in captivity plovers, curlews, choughs, and many other threatened species.

The Norfolk Wildlife Park is 12 miles north-west of Norwich on the Fakenham road. It is well signposted and has a large car park. Children are particularly well looked after, with education sheets and work packs. Schools are even offered the loan of slide sets prior to their visit. On Saturdays children get in free – with a maximum of two per adult. Dogs are not permitted to enter the 40-acre park.

There are no set routes, and the enclosures are well spread throughout the park areas. Wherever possible

which is often vital if you are to find him, because warm, sunny weather, while excellent for visitors, tends to drive animals into the shade and out of sight. Feeding time is likely to find them all at their best, and these times are displayed at the admission building. The excellent handbook to the park is full of statistics about the feeding habits of the animals, involving thousands of rabbits or tons of fish . . .

Everybody will have their favourites, and it is quite impossible to do justice to the sheer variety of species to be seen. It is wonderful to see your first red fox, tawny owl or badger. This last animal can be watched through a glass window in the intimacy of its underground sett. The breeding record is good, and badgers from here now roam free in the Norfolk countryside.

Rather less likely to be seen the other side of a Norfolk hedge are animals such as Barbary apes, wild boar, European bison and the Arctic fox. The Scottish wild cat is deceptive, for while it looks at first glance like everyone's friendly tabby, it is in reality ferocious. Asleep it does not seem to warrant the wire cage which surrounds it, but when it wakes that's another matter! The European lynx, too, is a magnificent animal. For many it will be the high spot of the visit.

Others will recall the reindeer. These are to be seen in stables and a large enclosure; they cannot eat grass and are fed on specially imported lichen. They give sleigh rides, but not on very hot days.

Open: April to Oct: daly 1030–1800
Price guide: B

THE NORFOLK RURAL LIFE MUSEUM GRESSENHALL

Gresssenhall lies three miles north-west of East Dereham on the B1110 Fakenham road. The Rural Life Museum is housed in an imposing 18th-century red-brick building. This is the former Mitford and Launditch Union workhouse. At most it accommodated 700 people from the 60 parishes it served but its numbers were reduced by an outbreak of cholera and scarlet fever in 1834 which carried off a sixth of the inmates, and by the middle of the century there were scarcely 250, each of whom was fed and clothed at a weekly cost of 2s 4d.

The museum was established in 1976. Its aim is to give us a vivid picture of country life, with particular emphasis on the agriculture which has played such a large part in Norfolk's history. The principal hall contains displays on this theme. Here we see various tools and machinery, all explained and illustrated by old photographs and interesting extracts from a farmer's diary of the 1920s.

The museum guide takes the form of a folder of well-presented leaflets which deal with each topic in detail. The farmer's year is examined, and every month highlights a certain task, beginning in October when the land is prepared for the following year's crops and moving through such diverse subjects as lambing, sowing barley and vermin control. We can read the remedies used by the ploughman to cure his horses' ailments, or see the re-creation of the hut where the shepherd slept during the lambing season. In the centre of the hall is the gigantic threshing machine, with two old bicycles dangling from it, because the driver of this machine and his mate moved from farm to farm and had to ride home at night. There are models of the Norfolk Horn sheep, now almost extinct, and fascinating posters from the Norfolk Show (in 1878 you could win a silver cup or £2 for the best cart stallion). Then an evocation of the final event in the farmer's year and the culmination of all his hard work: the harvest and its 'horkey' or special harvest supper.

Other aspects of country life are not neglected. You can enter the seed merchant's shop, or the dairy with its wooden churns, butter presses and wide-necked milk bottles. Pass through the dusty ironmongery to see the school

Norfolk Horn Sheep with clipping machine

certificates and samples of children's needlework, and the cobbler's shop, whose owner was a former soldier of the Norfolk Regiment, blinded on active service and retrained at a school for the blind in his new skill. At the end of the corridor is the building trades room, with examples of thatching, carpentry and plumbing work. One interesting display features about 200 razor blade packets!

In the outbuildings are re-creations of more craftsmen's workshops: the gigantic loom of the linen weaver, the saddler's shop, the smithy and the bakery and, perhaps most fascinating of all, the village shop bright with the clutter of biscuits, chocolate, mineral waters, boot polish, patent medicines . . . and just about everything else!

After seeing the places where the country folk worked, we are shown a typical home. Cherry Tree Cottage is a low, red-brick dwelling with only four rooms: the parlour, seldom used, but where the best china is left on display; the homely kitchen, with whitewashed walls, cast-iron stove and religious texts for pictures; and two small bedrooms, with crooked iron bedsteads and handmade furnishings. The cottage garden is as it should be: a neat vegetable plot (complete with scarecrow!) and a wealth of colourful flowers.

The seed shop

Gressenhall Museum
Open: April to Oct: Tues to Sat 1000–1700, Sun 1200–1730
Price guide: B

HOUGHTON HALL

Houghton Hall is the largest country house in Norfolk. It stands deep in the countryside, midway between King's Lynn and Fakenham. The Hall was built in the Palladian style in the early 18th century by Sir Robert Walpole, England's first Prime Minister. To provide himself with an unspoilt view, he had the village of Houghton pulled down (he was good enough to rebuild it elsewhere) and this has resulted in one of the grandest parks imaginable, complete with peacocks and white fallow deer. The long approach is through wooded grounds. The car park is neatly concealed behind a screen of trees, and from there the visitor has a short walk across the lawns to the West Front.

The West Front

The Hall was built over a period of 13 years, and although the original designs were the work of Colen Campbell, by the time building began in 1722, Walpole had engaged the services of Thomas Kipley, Chief Carpenter to the King's Works. Creamy Aislaby sandstone was chosen for its toughness and appearance, and shipped from Whitby to nearby King's Lynn, and so on to the site. Beneath the grand stone façade is locally produced brick.

The State Rooms are splendid and classical. The Stone Hall has an elaborate ceiling, balustrades and busts; the Marble Parlour is equally grand, but with a touch of Sir Robert's humanity in the alcove, where stands the bowl in which he used to cool his home-brewed beer. The Cabinet Room is hung with exquisite hand-painted Chinese wallpaper, and there are two magnificent bedchambers, complete with four-poster beds and their elaborate hangings. Houghton Hall is fortunate in having retained most of its original furniture. The Tapestry Dressing Room was designed to house the Mortlake tapestries, and these are still vividly coloured; they feature the Stuart kings with their palaces. Between them are small medallions showing their children; one medallion, rather touchingly, is left blank in memory of a stillborn son.

Entrance to the Hall is by the little door beneath the grand flights of steps. It is a curious point of interest that a nineteenth century owner of the Hall had them removed when the cost of their repair became too demanding. They were reinstated in 1973 in memory of the 5th Marquess of Cholmondeley.

Once inside we proceed up the Great Staircase to the State Rooms which are all on the first floor. Walpole called in William Kent to decorate the Hall, and our eye is immediately drawn to the dark, finely carved mahogany, the bronze statue, and the murals, designed and painted by Kent. The tone is set for the rest of the house: it will be stately and opulent, with Kent's work giving integrity to the whole.

Of equal (if not greater) interest to some will be the collection of model soldiers to be found in the north wing of the Hall. There are about 20,000 soldiers in this collection, which was begun in 1928 by Lord Cholmondeley – Sir Robert's direct descendant – whose family still lives in the Hall. The model soldiers are most ingeniously set out in realistic situations ranging from the Battle of Culloden to a skirmish in the Western Desert. The whole is accompanied by martial music. Lord Cholmondeley has devoted much time and effort to setting up this collection, and it is most enjoyable.

Stable courtyard

Finally, the Stable Block is well worth a visit. Built in 1730 of red brick, it is most elegant, with its herringbone patterned floor, its high arched ceilings and its wooden stalls.

Houghton Hall
Open: April to Sept: Thur, Sun and bank holiday Mon. Telephone for times
Price guide: B

HUNSTANTON

Hunstanton is unique in East Anglia: you can sit on the beach and watch the sun go down over the sea. This is the only coastal resort in East Anglia where such a thing is possible, since Hunstanton is alone in facing west.

The beach and cliffs

This location brings another benefit and one which makes Hunstanton ideal for families, and that is the resort is well sheltered from the keen east wind and therefore safe for bathing. The beach is of firm sand, shelving almost imperceptibly. At low tide the water recedes a great distance, and swimmers and windsurfers must prepare themselves for a gentle stroll. Those who prefer to stay at the top of the beach will find plenty to occupy themselves, if it is only searching through the rock pools and making elaborate sandcastles.

The other remarkable feature of Hunstanton is the cliffs. These are extraordinary not just because the shoreline on either side of the resort is of sand dunes and marshland, but because they are striped in vivid colours – brown, red and white. For those who worry about such details, they are composed of carrstone and chalk and rise to a height of 60 feet above the beach. On top are stretches of open grassland, extending from the golf course in the north to the Esplanade Gardens and The Green in New Hunstanton. 'New' because this resort was developed over the last 100 years or so. Old Hunstanton still exists; it was a fishing village, and some of the cottages are quaint and picturesque. But the resort proper was an 1860s creation of the Le Strange family, local landowners who saw the opportunity to attract Londoners to this pleasant seaside town via the newly-built railway line from King's Lynn. The Le Strange family still exert an influence over Hunstanton; thanks to an ancient law they have a claim to everything on the beach or in the sea as far as a man can ride at low tide and throw a spear into the water!

The Victorian and Edwardian buildings give Hunstanton a period charm which is emphasised by the rather old-fashioned seaside attractions: donkey and pony rides, treasure hunts, beach competitions, band concerts on the Green on Sundays and shows at the Princess Theatre. But the resort has certainly not turned its back on the 20th century. The new Oasis Leisure Centre on the Promenade has all the modern facilities, including two swimming pools, one with a 35-metre water-slide, jacuzzis and opportunities for all kinds of energetic sports. It offers a focal point for the young holidaymaker.

On the cliff you will see the former lighthouse, made redundant by modern technology and transformed into a private home, but a landmark nonetheless. Nearby are the remains of St Edmund's Chapel, reputedly built by that saint in the year 850 to mark his safe arrival in East Anglia where he was to be crowned king. Some have questioned why St Edmund landed here, far from any large settlement, but a few miles away is the northern end of the Peddar's Way, an ancient trackway leading south-east to the regional capital at Thetford. The Peddar's Way can still be traced on the map and in reality, and makes for a long, straight walk through some unspoilt countryside.

The Green

Whatever you look for in a seaside holiday, Hunstanton will suit you, because it offers to all ages a marvellous variety of activities in friendly, relaxed surroundings.

NORFOLK LAVENDER

Imagine if you will a garden filled with lines of flowering bushes in colours ranging from white, through pink and mauve to a dark blue–purple; add to this the buzzing of bees and the heady summer scent of lavender. Such are the sights and sounds that greet you when you walk on to the farm at Heacham, on the A149 just to the south of Hunstanton.

It is no surprise that visits to the farm are extremely popular, and the visitor is well catered for, particularly the blind and disabled. This is the only farm of its kind in England, and from its 100 acres of fields hereabouts is made the impressive range of Norfolk Lavender products. Harvesting the lavender takes place during July or August, and the flowers are dried or distilled for their essential oils in the barn here at Heacham.

Caley Mill

The farm is based at Caley Mill. This is an attractive red sandstone building almost 200 years old, formerly a corn mill and now converted into a visitors' shop. The miller's cottage is now a tearoom where the visitor can enjoy a lunch or a cream tea. When the weather is fine, refreshments may be taken at the picnic tables in the garden or by the riverside walk. The abundance of flowers makes the setting ideal.

Entrance to the farm is free, and the visitor is first drawn to the well-stocked herb garden. Here, set out in neat rectangles like a monastery garden, you may see more than 50 varieties of herbs and learn from information boards of their medicinal properties and culinary uses. Some of these herbs are well-known: sage, thyme and the various kinds of mint. But others are fascinatingly novel – sweet cicely, Jacob's ladder, bergamot, hyssop: their very names are redolent of the old-fashioned English garden for which we all have a special place in our hearts. Nowadays we are relearning the healing powers of herbs and their usefulness in the kitchen, and many of us will want to improve our own gardens with their scent and beauty. At the conservatory in the grounds of Caley Mill you may buy seeds or plants of the herbs on display.

To appreciate the lavender farm it is best to take a conducted tour of the garden and distillery. These 40-minute tours take place quite frequently (as many as five in a day in high season) and for a modest charge you will be told all you need to know about the cultivation and use of lavender. Lavender has been grown for its perfume since Roman times and was even then used to scent the water when washing linen. It is well-known how it can be dried and used in a lavender bag or pot pourri; we all know, too, of the pretty smell of lavender water. Perhap it is less well-known that the boiled leaves of the plant help to cure stomach complaints, or that the oil may be used as an effective embrocation.

At Caley Mill they are trying to establish a national collection of all varieties of lavender, and you are invited to study the different colours of such plants as nana alba, lodden pink, grappenhall and royal purple. Other bushes are as yet labelled simply with numbers, since new varieties are being created here. Visitors are encouraged to contact the farm if they have any varieties they can share.

The shops on the farm stock many of the lavender plants as well as dried lavender and the Norfolk Lavender range of perfumes and soaps.

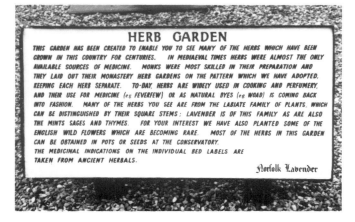

HERB GARDEN

THIS GARDEN HAS BEEN CREATED TO ENABLE YOU TO SEE MANY OF THE HERBS WHICH HAVE BEEN GROWN IN THIS COUNTRY FOR CENTURIES. IN MEDIAEVAL TIMES HERBS WERE ALMOST THE ONLY AVAILABLE SOURCES OF MEDICINE. MONKS WERE MOST SKILLED IN THEIR PREPARATION AND THEY LAID OUT THEIR MONASTERY HERB GARDENS ON THE PATTERN WHICH WE HAVE ADOPTED, KEEPING EACH HERB SEPARATE. TO-DAY, HERBS ARE WIDELY USED IN COOKING AND PERFUMERY, AND THEIR USE FOR MEDICINE (eg FEVERFEW) OR AS NATURAL DYES (eg WOAD) IS COMING BACK INTO FASHION. MANY OF THE HERBS YOU SEE ARE FROM THE LABIATE FAMILY OF PLANTS, WHICH CAN BE DISTINGUISHED BY THEIR SQUARE STEMS: LAVENDER IS OF THIS FAMILY AS ARE ALSO THE MINTS SAGES AND THYMES. FOR YOUR INTEREST WE HAVE ALSO PLANTED SOME OF THE ENGLISH WILD FLOWERS WHICH ARE BECOMING RARE. MOST OF THE HERBS IN THIS GARDEN CAN BE OBTAINED IN POTS OR SEEDS AT THE CONSERVATORY.
THE MEDICINAL INDICATIONS ON THE INDIVIDUAL BED LABELS ARE TAKEN FROM ANCIENT HERBALS.

Norfolk Lavender

Heacham Lavender Fields
Open: daily: 1000–1700
Price guide: Free

SANDRINGHAM

of the loveliest garden prospects in Britain. Lawns and bright flower beds reach down to the water's edge, while scores of trees frame the warm brick and stone of the house

The future king Edward VII purchased the estate at Sandringham in 1862 with the intention that it should become the private country residence of himself and his wife Alexandra. The county of Norfolk made them a wedding present of the magnificent iron gates which grace the entrance to the drive. Edward undertook a huge rebuilding programme to enlarge and transform the original house, wanting to entertain his friends to the weekend parties which were all the rage among the aristocracy. Even today, Sandringham is not a palace; quite the reverse, for it is a retreat away from the formal duties of state, and the Royal Family has great affection for it. 'Dear old Sandringham, the place I love better than anywhere else in the world', wrote George V. The Queen spends the New Year holiday and part of the summer here, and on these occasions both house and gardens are closed to the public.

Sandringham attracts thousands of visitors and the ticket office is often busy. Those wishing to visit the house will find that they are allotted a time for their tour, and will need to queue in the courtyard until that time arrives. This may allow a walk through the grounds.

The 85 acres of garden provide a variety of vistas. The Upper Lake forms the centrepiece of what must be one

itself. Swans and ducks glide from one rock island to another, and the air is full of birdsong and the buzzing of bees. Overlooking the lake is The Nest, a summer house presented to Queen Alexandra in 1913. The York Cottage Lake is larger and just as beautiful, with bursts of colour provided by azaleas, rhododendrons and waterlilies.

The Gates presented by the County of Norfolk

The house has an intimacy unusual in such a noble address, and the rooms are elegantly and comfortably furnished. The largest room is the Saloon, which contains many paintings and fine porcelain. This lofty room also has a minstrels' gallery which recalls the music which was such a feature of country house life. No less a person than Queen Victoria extolled the attractions of the Drawing Room, saying it was a 'very long and handsome room, with painted ceiling and panels and with two fireplaces'. Over one is a full-length portrait of Princess Alexandra who supervised so many of the improvements we admire today.

Tucked away out of sight, but well signposted, is the museum located in the former Coach House. This is well worth seeing. Not quite to everyone's taste, perhaps, is a room full of animal heads – trophies of royal shoots from 1880 to 1930 – but also on show are the fascinating gifts presented to the Royal Family during their travels. One item in particular is most unusual: a Nativity scene presented to the Queen on a visit to Naples, which is simply dazzling in its complexity. In 1900 the Royal Family bought its first car, a Daimler; now the collection on view here is very large. Many of the vehicles are custom-designed.

After a visit to the house and grounds there is still Sandringham church to visit. It has a most unusual interior, with a gilded roof and a solid silver altar. The Royal Family always attends services here when in residence: Edward VII insisted that no sermon last longer than 10 minutes! In the 600-acre country park visitors may study the wildlife of this beautiful region. There are two nature trails for walkers and a woodland drive for motorists with secluded parking and picnic areas.

Sandringham
Open: April to Sept: Mon to Sat (House and Museum) 1100–1645,
Sun 1200–1645, Mon to Sat 1030–1700 (Grounds)
House, Grounds, Museum closed mid July to early Aug
Price guide: B

Sandringham Church

WOLFERTON STATION MUSEUM

For over a hundred years the tiny railway station at Wolferton was famous all over the country. After the purchase of the Sandringham Estate by Prince Edward (later Edward VII) in 1862, visiting royalty travelled by special train to this halt only a couple of miles from Sandringham House. Here they alighted and took refreshments while their luggage was transported to the house. Just imagine the pomp and grandeur of such occasions! No era is more evocative of elegance and ceremony than the Edwardian age, and it is in its depiction of these years that this unusual and fascinating museum excels.

The station platform

But the station's history has not always been glorious; the times were changing and the railways felt the effect. The last royal train ran in 1966, and when the King's Lynn to Hunstanton line was closed in 1969, Wolferton Station was already empty and derelict. British Rail had applied for planning permission to demolish it and build a small estate of modern houses. Happily, these plans fell through and the station buildings and goods yard were bought at auction by an enterprising couple, Eric and Herta Walker. They took over the station as their home, and gradually developed the museum which they opened to the public in 1977. Since the death of the founders, the museum has been run by their son and daughter-in-law, who with their three small children still live in these rooms once visited by all the kings and queens of Europe. In the evening the Walkers remove the corded ropes protecting the furniture, uncover the television neatly concealed behind a velvet hanging, and sit down on beautiful blue sofas made for Queen Alexandra in her favourite colour.

The station buildings we see today were designed for Edward and Alexandra in the 1890s, and their original splendour has been restored. They house a magnificent collection of memorabilia about the railways and about the Edwardian age in particular. To do this museum full justice, the visitor will want to spend several hours here.

We pass first along the platform. There is still a red carpet leading to the double doors into the main hall, but we commoners are not permitted to enter this way; we must go in by the farther door and proceed down a corridor fairly cluttered with interesting curios. Here the emphasis is on the railway itself. There are tickets, photographs and timetables, as well as the more unexpected – the wreaths carried on the last train to use this line, and the clock stopped at 10.29 when it left Wolferton Station. A particular joy, and typical of this friendly museum, is the humour of the captions neatly affixed to each exhibit. These are the work of Mr Walker senior, and they convey his love of the railway. More importantly, they reassure the visitor that this collection is not just for the railway buff; we all share some nostalgia for the unhurried days of steam trains.

The museum is so packed with wonderful things that we can only single out a couple of items for particular notice: Queen Victoria's travelling bed, for instance, made for her in 1828; Edward VII's beautifully decorated toilet; the tea cosy worked by Queen Alexandra. The exhibits are well labelled, and on the walls are anecdotes giving us rare and intriguing insights into the personalities of the Royal Family.

Wolferton Station is well worth making a detour for, if only to hear the cat with the loudest purr in England!

Interior of the museum

Wolferton Station Museum
Open: April to Sept: Mon to Fri 1100–1730, Sun 1300–1700
Price guide: A

CASTLE RISING

William de Albini began constructing Castle Rising in about 1138 to protect a port centred on the tidal estuary of the River Babington. He was not to know that the river would silt up, and the trade would move to the neighbouring port of King's Lynn, leaving Castle Rising

The Grand Staircase

without a role. De Albini created a gigantic earthwork 1000 feet in circumference and as much as 60 feet deep. Around the top of this was a stone curtain wall. The great keep commanded a view over the defences, and stands today at full height, although it has lost most of its roof. The main rooms of the castle were on the first floor, and leading to them is a superb stone staircase. Over the stairs is an aptly named murder hole, which permitted the unwary attacker to be smitten from above! At the top of the stairs is the entrance vestibule, a bright room with a firm timber floor and a 14th-century vaulted roof. The rest of the apartments are not so easily understood, for they lack both floors and roofs.

The Great Hall was where the family and their retainers ate and carried on their business. There would have been unceasing activity throughout the day, and at night it would have resounded to the snores of those who made their beds on the rushes which covered the floor. The Great

Chamber afforded the lord and his family some element of privacy, but by our standards it was dreadfully inadequate. The chapel is very fine, and the Norman arcading which survives indicates the importance attached to this building even in such violent times.

Castle Rising was never called upon to resist a siege, and only once achieved a dubious sort of fame. In 1327 Edward II was murdered, and his Queen, Isabella, was popularly supposed to have approved the deed. Three years later she was incarcerated in Castle Rising by her 16-year old son, and there she remained for 27 years; she was, however, hardly treated as a prisoner and received many distinguished visitors.

The Church of St Lawrence in the village was already being built by de Albini when the construction of the castle began. He was replacing the earlier church whose ruins are within the castle enclosure. The village of Castle Rising is very pretty. The houses are built of red stone, with an attractive pebble line seam at intervals. The gardens are exquisite, and there are lots of green spaces, including a paddock.

The almshouses of the Trinity Hospital were built in 1614 as the result of a bequest from Henry Howard. Only women of good character were eligible: 'no common beggar, harlot, scold, drunkard, haunter of taverns, inns and ale-houses'. The buildings comprise chapel, hall and rooms for 12 residents around the small courtyard, and while recent improvements in facilities have led to the number being reduced to nine, the almshouses retain their Jacobean charm. The ladies are proud of their homes, and each tends the flower bed outside her door. Howard insisted they should attend church on Sundays wearing the heavy blue (now red) cloaks he provided for them. On Founder's Day they also wear a tall black conical hat. Each lady was given a bed, table and chair, and while the beds have failed to command affection, the other furniture is still to be seen in use. A narrow staircase beside the gateway leads up to the treasury, with its original panelling, where stands the iron-bound chest which once held the funds.

The Trinity Almshouses

Castle
English Heritage
Open: April to Sept 1000–1800, Oct to Mar 1000–1600
Price guide: A

Trinity Hospital
Open: see noticeboard
Price guide: Free

KING'S LYNN

King's Lynn is a town to be explored on foot, as the narrow streets and lanes are more suited to a bygone age and many of the finest buildings are hidden behind rather unimpressive fronts and are only glimpsed through gateways or across courtyards.

In the beginning it was called Bishop's Lynn, and made a living as a port at the mouth of the River Ouse serving the towns further inland. The merchants of Lynn grew rich on the trade in wool, fur, timber and grain and their warehouses lined the wharfs (or staithes) of the waterfronts. The street plan they created still remains, and many of the names recall these medieval times. From Fisher Fleet, in the north of the town, fishermen still set sail as they have always done. The many seals in the Wash catch most of the fish, so the fishermen have become adept at harvesting the abundant shrimps, mussels and cockles. Once there were two separate settlements beside the river, one making its living through fishing and the other through trade; King John united the two with a charter in 1204, and Henry VIII honoured the town with the name of King's Lynn in 1535.

A good place to begin a walk is Tuesday Market, a large open space still used once every week as it has been since the 12th century. Then it exhibited a pillory and gallows too, but now it is overlooked by the Duke's Head Hotel of 1683, and the Corn Exchange of 1854.

King Street, which leads off the south-west corner of Tuesday Market, includes many of the town's best buildings. St George's Guildhall, now known as the Fermoy Centre, is the largest and oldest guildhall in England, dating from 1410. The merchants who established it sometimes used it as a theatre, and it is known that Shakespeare's company visited it, so perhaps he did, too! The successful King's Lynn Arts Festival is based there now, and it is once again a venue for performances.

The Purfleet channel marks the point where King Street becomes Queen Street, and is also the old boundary between the medieval settlements. Here stands the Custom House, designed in 1683 by Henry Bell, then Mayor. Its most distinctive feature is the white timber lantern tower with its access ladder. It was originally built as the Exchange, where merchants met to transact business, but by 1718 it had become the Custom House, a role it fulfilled into the 20th century. A statue of Charles II stands in a niche on the north side. Looking at the oily mud of the basin, and the sad state of the vessels moored there, it is hard to imagine it as it once was – the busiest quayside in the port.

Running alongside Purfleet is King Staithe Square, which leads to the wide and still busy Boat Quay. There can be few towns in England which can display such continuity of use. Returning to Queen Street there are more fine examples of modern restoration. Clifton House, with its doorway of twisted columns, dates from the 1400s, although it was greatly modernised in 1718. Through the gateway is a pretty courtyard garden, and the view from the five-storey Elizabethan tower is well worth the effort of the climb.

The Quayside

Nearby is Thoresby College, decorated with splendid Dutch gables. The building was named after Thomas Thoresby who died in 1511. He built it to house 13 priests of the Holy Trinity Guild – obviously not an unlucky number! Today its neat front doors conceal a variety of uses, including a Youth Hostel. The Hanseatic Warehouse with its distinctive levels of brick and timber was begun in 1428 at a time when the Hanseatic alliance of towns was at its strongest, trading with all the ports on the North Sea and the Baltic. Opposite is Hampton Court, a half-timbered building named after John Hampton, master baker, who in the 17th century converted a much earlier timber warehouse. This is one of Lynn's best buildings, and the first to be saved by the indefatigable King's Lynn Preservation Trust. St Margaret's Lane leads down to the waterfront, for we are never allowed to forget that this is a town which depended on sea trade.

St Margaret's Church has magnificent towers at the west end. By the west door there are marks in the wall showing the heights of various tides which have lapped against the fabric. The highest was in 1953. Inside, the church has two memorial brasses which are ten feet long

Tuesday Market

and the largest in England. They date from 1349 and 1369, and besides commemorating two merchants and their wives, they also show scenes of country life in minute detail. Outside the church is Saturday Market, the older of the two market places.

On the other side of Saturday Market stands the ornate flint flushwork of the Guildhall of Holy Trinity. Here you will encounter the 'Tales of the Old Gaol House', a multi-sensory experience which guides the visitor through the 1930s police station and back into the time of stocks and manacles – which you may try for yourself! A personal stereo takes you on this realistic and enjoyable historical journey.

In the undercroft of the Guildhall are the treasures of Lynn. The town has a complete set of charters beginning with that issued by King John in 1204. Among the items of civic regalia on display is King John's Sword, a gift from Henry VIII in 1529! The Nuremburg Cup was made by a goldsmith from that city for a Mayor of Lynn, and dates from 1634. But the real gem is King John's Cup, for it is not only the earliest surviving example of medieval secular plate, but it has a story attached to it of treasure waiting to be discovered. King John visited Lynn in October 1215, when he was at war with his barons, and on the 13th of that month rashly decided to take the short cut across the Wash into Lincolnshire. His entourage escaped the incoming tide, but their waggons had to be abandoned – complete with England's Crown Jewels and much more besides. To this day there are treasure hunters who believe they will locate that long-lost convoy.

Greyfriars Church

The gold and translucent blue enamel cup now in the Guildhall deserves to be part of the treasure, but it is not. It was probably made in about 1340, and has undergone at least four major restorations since then. But the blue enamel is original, and from the tip of the cover to the toe of the foot it is a wonderful object for any town to possess.

The modern shopping area of King's Lynn is close by, and has kept the intimacy of the old street plan. There are several pedestrian precincts, so the visitor may still discover the town on foot. In Tower Gardens stands the tall tower which is all that remains of Greyfriars Church. Expert landscaping has prevented it from becoming a sad ruin, and instead it complements the lawns and flower beds which surround it.

The town is a busy port and a centre for light industry. The tradition of glassmaking is continued in the workshops of Caithness Crystal, where you may see glass blown and engraved. King's Lynn has skilfully managed to retain the best of its past, and has done so without compromising its present.

Guildhall of St George
National Trust
Open: All year: April to Sept: Mon to Sat 1000–1700, Oct to Mar: Mon to Sat 1100–1600
Price guide: A

Regalia Rooms & Tales of the Old Gaol House
Open: Jan to Mar: Fri to Tues 1000–1700, April to Oct: daily 1000–1700, Nov to Dec: Fri to Tues 1000–1700
Price guide: B

Caithness Crystal
Open: All year: Mon to Fri, weekends May to Sept
Price guide: Free

Porch of the Trinity Guild

CASTLE ACRE

The village of Castle Acre is about four miles north of Swaffham and it is well worth seeing. Norfolk has many delightful villages, and this is one of the very best. The excellent village sign on the green is surrounded by pretty cottages in brick and flint, and shaded by tall trees. In one direction is a cluster of priory ruins, and in the other, at the end of a tree-lined path, is an early Norman castle. Straddling one of the streets in the centre of the village is the massive Bailey Gate which dates from about 1200, originally the north gate of the planned fortified town.

William de Warenne fought beside the Conqueror at Hastings, and part of his reward was this manor in Norfolk. The Peddar's Way crossed the River Nar here, so it was a strategic site. De Warenne began the castle in the 1080s, erecting a great earthwork within which he constructed a two-storey stone building. The experts prefer to think of it as a country house rather than a castle, as the defences were slight. Here in 1085 de Warenne's wife Gundrada died in childbirth, and he himself died three years later; it was their son who founded the nearby priory.

In the troubled times of King Stephen's reign the castle was strengthened and enlarged. The stone house was retained, but the walls were reinforced and it became a stout keep. The earthworks were built up, and crowned

The village sign

with a flint curtain wall. Access to the upper ward and keep was controlled by a gateway, which guarded the bridge across the moat. All these features are visible thanks to an extensive excavation programme. Most of us were taught at school about motte-and-bailey castles; well, here is a rare example of one which is almost intact.

The castle ruins

Priory ruins

After 1347 the direct Warenne line died out, and the castle eventually passed to the Coke family. King James I is said to have been reluctant for them to acquire it, believing they were already too wealthy, but a wily courtier assured him it was only an acre! Its warlike past appearance has given way to a peaceful scene of grassy mounds, teeming with grasshoppers and butterflies on a summer day.

South-west of the village, and a very pleasant short walk away, is the priory. This is in the care of English Heritage, and the visitor centre is excellent. It contains a model of what the priory would have looked like in its best days. A covered arcade displays the history of the site, and geographical and geological information about Norfolk as a whole, illustrated by some lovely aerial photographs. Beyond the arcade is a herb garden set out in individual plots, as the monks would have had it. The visitor then walks down a grassy slope beneath aged chestnut and lime trees towards the river and the priory ruins.

The Warenne family introduced the Cluniac order of monks into England, and the priory at Castle Acre was begun in about 1090. The west end of the church is very ornate and stands almost to its full height. In the 15th century a window was cut through the earlier stonework, but the effect is not unpleasing. In its heyday there were probably 30 monks living and working here. The Cluniacs were wealthy, charging pilgrims to view holy relics. The arm of St Philip brought in 10 shillings a year! The Prior lived in great comfort in the Prior's Lodge, and when the priory was closed down in 1537 this part of the complex was taken over, and eventually became a farmhouse. The varied styles do not detract from the beauty of this tranquil spot.

Castle
Open: Any reasonable time
Price guide: Free

Priory
English Heritage
Open: April to Oct: daily 1000–1800, Nov to Mar: Wed to Sun 1000–1600
Price guide: B

Priory ruins

SWAFFHAM

Just as Hamelin has its pied piper, so Swaffham has its pedlar, and both have every reason to be grateful. John Chapman, a poor pedlar of Swaffham, was barely able to provide for his wife and children, and they lived in a small cottage in the shadow of a huge oak tree which stood in their garden. One night John dreamed that if he stood on London Bridge he would discover a great treasure. Excited, he set out for the capital, and made his way to the Thames and the bridge which was lined with shops and houses. He paced up and down, searching for any sign of his treasure. Eventually a shopkeeper came up to him and asked what he was doing, and the pedlar told him the story of his dream. Astonished, the London shopkeeper said that he too had memories of a dream. In his, he went to a town in far-off Norfolk, to a garden belonging to a pedlar, and there, beneath a tall oak, he had found a great fortune in gold. Such nonsense – he would not waste his time doing anything of the sort! At once the pedlar understood, and hastened back to Swaffham. He dug in the shadow of the oak, and sure enough he found a brass pot filled with gold coins. Thrilled, he looked forward to better times, but his old trade was in his blood, so he put the pot up for sale. A customer picked it up, and told him the Latin inscription it bore read: 'Under me doth lie another much richer than I'. Needing no more prompting, the pedlar took up his spade once more, and sure enough found an even larger horde.

The town sign depicting The Pedlar

The Butter Cross and the Church of St Peter and St Paul

In the Black Book which lists those who made donations to the Church of St Peter and St Paul appears the name of John Chapman, who paid for the north aisle as well as making many other gifts. His family pew has carved ends which show him and his wife, for he was a church warden. So there was a John Chapman, and he did come into a fortune, which he used for good works; perhaps the rest of the tale is true, too!

Dr John Botright was chaplain to Henry VI, and began the present church in 1454. His grand tomb is in the sanctuary. The hammer-beam roof of the nave is impressive. No less than 88 carved angels hover from the beam ends, and more line the walls. In 1510 work began on a tower, which today is topped by an 18th-century spire. The churchyard is spacious and pretty, and a narrow lane leads to the Market Place.

The large, wedge-shaped Market Place is still a busy trading centre on a Saturday. At the south end stands the Rotunda, or Butter Cross, supported on eight columns and surmounted by the statue of the Roman goddess of the harvest, Ceres. This was a gift from Lord Orford in 1783 and cost him £400. He loved greyhound racing, and in particular his dog, Czarina. It was while watching her speed to another victory that he became so excited he fell from his horse and died. Nearly all the buildings around the Market Place are of this period, and while many have greatly changed their shop fronts, they remain attractive and at one with their neighbours.

The Assembly Room of 1817 was the hub of Swaffham's social round in the early 19th century, when improvements in transport and roads encouraged the gentry to broaden their social activity and Swaffham became a centre for their soirées, dances, sports and all the other excuses to meet.

At the north end of the Market Place stands the town sign, carved in 1925 by Harry Carter, who was responsible for over 100 more in Norfolk. It shows The Pedlar of Swaffham, eyes closed as though dreaming. His treasure is now ours.

COCKLEY CLEY ICENI VILLAGE

The Romans invaded Britain in AD 43, but it was only in AD 60 that they really had to fight for their new province. Their opponent was a woman, the Queen of the Iceni. Once she was known as Boadicea, but the current version of her name is Boudicca. She is a legendary figure in British history, and at Cockley Cley, three miles south-west of Swaffham, you have the opportunity to glimpse the reality behind the legend. For here, on the estate of the late Sir Peter Roberts, an Iceni village has been recreated on its original site.

The village stands in a field and is encircled by a small moat. A palisade of sticks provides the main protection for those inside, while the gateway is dominated by a precarious platform extending between two towers. The narrow drawbridge is operated by weighted baskets of stone being filled or emptied according to need. A far more effective deterrent would have been the severed heads exposed to view on the poles which sway above the gate! We are assumed to be visiting the village in AD 60, after Boudicca has passed through, but before the victorious Romans arrived and utterly destroyed the site – and probably led the tribesmen off to slavery.

The Elizabethan Cottage

Inside the camp there are a number of wooden buildings, all thatched with the abundant reeds which were one of the compensations for a marshy site. The chief's hut is built around a growing tree, and is much larger than the others. The interior is dark and filled with wood smoke, and the leader's weapons hang from the beams ready for action at a moment's notice. In the evening the warriors would have shared his fireside, and exchanged tales of heroism and wonder. The spring which was the source of water 2000 years ago still bubbles from the ground.

The society of the Iceni was well defined: after the chief in status came the warriors and working men, who lived in the longhouse with their families, and probably their cattle. There were no slaves; the lowest position in society was reserved for the old and infirm.

Prisoners were rarely taken when the Iceni went to war, but Cockley Cley's most popular feature with children is likely to be the adder pit, where captives were lowered and left to be bitten to death. A set of bones helps the imagination to visualise the details! A chariot stands ready in the shed, complete with blades protruding from the axles. A notice admits that the knives are not authentic, but that visitors expect to see them!

There is more at Cockley Cley than just the Iceni village. In the farm barns is a collection of carriages used in the past by members of the estate owner's family. There is a picture of the children in the very donkey cart which is displayed. There are also displays of agricultural machinery and engines of all descriptions. A nature trail, lake and picnic area are all close by.

Across the road is the 'Elizabethan cottage', once a forge but now a museum of prehistory and of Breckland life. It was actually built in about 1450, and the interior has changed very little. An imaginative tableau has been created which shows a family living there in the 1550s. Upstairs is the 5ft 11in skeleton of the prehistoric 'Giant of Cockley Cley' who died long before Boudicca challenged Rome.

Nearby is the small stone church of St Mary's. It has a fine round apse and a Norman doorway. The church may date from AD 628, and could be the oldest in England.

Cockley Cley Iceni Village
Open: April to Oct: daily 1100–1730
Price guide: B

The Gateway

OXBURGH HALL

The Wars of the Roses in the late Middle Ages conjure up images of unremitting danger and almost total destruction. But the evidence of our eyes contradicts this: the prosperous wool towns with their beautiful churches were being created at this time, and while many of the nobility fought and died, there were those who managed to keep in with both factions. Sir Edmund Bedingfeld, the builder of this magnificent house seven miles south-west of Swaffham, was one of these.

Sir Edmund was a supporter of the Yorkist king, Edward IV, and received permission from him to build Oxburgh in 1482. In 1485 the Yorkist dynasty came to a bloody end at Bosworth field, defeated by the Tudor king, Henry VII. Sir Edmund had not been present at that battle, a fact which can only have helped his relationship with the new sovereign. When in 1487 another Yorkist challenged Henry's claim, Sir Edmund fought for his king at the battle of Stoke. His loyalty was now proved beyond doubt, and the stage was set for a royal visit to Oxburgh which took place in August 1497.

The Parterre Garden

The visitor today enters Oxburgh Hall by way of the great north gateway, the earliest part of the Hall to survive. A brick spiral stairway leads up into the King's Room, a solid, comfortable apartment with an enormous brick fireplace, graceful window arches and a four-poster bed. The Queen's Room contains one of Oxburgh's treasures: the Sheldon tapestry, which dates from 1647 and shows a map of Oxfordshire of such size that all the villages are included. Another outstanding tapestry at Oxburgh evokes the extraordinary life of Bess of Hardwick, who outlived her three husbands. There are also examples of tapestry work by Mary, Queen of Scots. The many fine rooms each recapture the spirit of a past age. The Saloon and West Drawing Room have the uncluttered elegance of the early 19th century, while the Library has the delightful luxury of a door concealed by bookshelves.

Sir Henry Bedingfeld was the grandson of Oxburgh's builder and during the reign of Queen Mary he was appointed 'Jaylor' to Princess Elizabeth. This was a delicate task, made even more so when his prisoner became 'Good Queen Bess'. The Bedingfeld family remained Catholics, and were punished for their faith throughout Elizabeth's reign by fines and threats to their liberty. Even more serious consequences would have befallen them had they been caught harbouring Catholic priests. We know they did so because in the gatehouse is a reminder of those frightening times: a priest hole. The poor man who constructed it was later tortured to death on the Queen's authority.

Oxburgh has gardens which are worth a visit. The visitor passes through a brick arch into a walled orchard planted with such unusual trees as quince and medlar. The first view of the Hall itself is enchanting. The moat encircles the rich coloured brick with a necklace of waterlilies. A French parterre garden was created on the east side in the 19th century. It is fascinating in its complexity. Beyond, and screened from the Hall by evergreens, is a walk beside a wide herbaceous border of vivid flowers. Here the exhausted or overwhelmed visitor may rest and wonder at the energy of the gardeners.

Although Oxburgh has been in the care of the National Trust since 1952, the Bedingfeld family continues to live there, and their flag flies proudly from the gatehouse roof, as it has done for 500 years.

National Trust
Open: Mar to Nov: Sat to Wed: Hall 1300–1700, Garden 1200–1730
Price guide: B

CAMBRIDGESHIRE

FENLAND

For many people the Fens are an alien landscape: a flat and seemingly endless expanse of black soil, bereft of trees, enlivened only by lonely buildings and the occasional huddled shapes of workers, bent double, defying the savage winds while they gather potatoes, carrots and cabbages from the land.

summer grazing land. He used his skill to greater effect, but ironically the success of the project brought about its downfall: as the peat soil dried out it shrank, lowering the level and again preventing the waters from discharging into the sea. There is a powerful reminder of the result of such drainage on Holme Fen, south of Peterborough. Here in 1851 an iron post was buried in the soil so that only the top showed. By the turn of the century 10 feet of the post had been exposed, and although the rate of shrinkage slowed thereafter, by 1957 a second post was needed to replace the first, proving that the land had shrunk by 13 feet in all.

Delph Bridge near Welney

Fenland covers an area of 1300 square miles and today represents some of England's most productive farmland. But it has not always been so; the landscape we see today is essentially a creation of the 17th century, though for centuries attempts had been made to reclaim this deep, fertile soil for agriculture. The Romans began the work, and Car Dyke, still visible near Waterbeach, was a 70-mile canal linking the Fens with river and sea ports. They also constructed lodes – drainage channels – such as the one running from Reach to Upware (so remote that the pub is called 'Five miles from anywhere, no hurry!'), and there you can still see the remains of their brick landing stage. Other Roman relics have been found in the area: in the 1920s two Cambridge undergraduates unearthed a complete skeleton in Roman armour, and they bundled it rather unceremoniously into a sack and carried it back to the University on the back of a bicycle!

The Romans did not succeed in their aim because the slow-moving rivers gradually silted up. The Dutch engineer Vermuyden was called in by the fourth Earl of Bedford, who had been empowered to turn the Fens into

The true fenland – a land of water, reeds and sedges – has largely disappeared, together with many species of wildlife. Now nature reserves have been created in this

Ramsey Abbey Gateway

Fenland landscape near Ramsey St Mary's

unique area, so close to towns yet so unknown. A few miles to the south of Whittlesey, near Peterborough, lies Wood-

The Holme Fen Post

walton Fen Nature Reserve, the last surviving British habitat of the large copper butterfly. Birds, too, are attracted to the region; the RSPB holds almost 200 acres at Welches Dam near Manea, where public hides are open at all times. Another key reserve is owned by the Wildfowl Trust, and is situated at Welney, overlooking the Ouse Washes. This is a narrow strip of land some 20 miles long between the Old and New Bedford rivers which has been designated a Wetland of International Importance. During the year many birds visit the Washes, including some species which had stopped breeding in this country, such as the black-tailed godwit, ruff and black tern. Migrating birds may also be seen: wigeon, Bewick's swans, teal and other wildfowl. There are 20 hides beside the wetlands, and one from where, on winter evenings, you may watch the swans by floodlight – a magical experience.

Ploughing near Littleport

Wildfowl Trust Refuge, Welney
Open: All year daily 1000–1700
Price guide: B

THE DEVIL'S DYKE

Devil's Dyke has been called the most impressive archaeological monument in East Anglia. It is the largest of a series of four linear earthworks consisting of a bank and ditch, and stretches south-eastwards from the edge of the fenland at the village of Reach to the forest at Woodditton. It was probably built to defend East Anglia from incursions via the Icknield Way – a prehistoric track running from Wiltshire to Norfolk. In its original form it extended for more than 10 miles, and was up to 100 feet wide. With its steep sides cleared of grass it was a formidable obstacle, and waiting at the top were heavily armed defenders secure behind some sort of palisade.

The earthwork has now been designated a Site of Special Scientific Interest as well as being an ancient monument. A public footpath runs along the top for a distance of about 7½ miles. The chalk grassland supports rare and colourful flowers: yellow rockrose, pink rest-harrow and blue milk-wort. More than a dozen species of butterfly may be spotted here, including the chalkhill blue. This open landscape used to be preserved by the grazing of sheep; recently there have been unwelcome invasions by hawthorn, buckthorn and other vegetation typical of scrubland, but these at least allow cover and nest sites for yellowhammers, long-tailed tits and whitethroats.

Devil's Dyke comes to an abrupt end at Reach, where the last few hundred yards of bank were levelled in medieval times to allow space for a fair – a tradition still continued when, on the weekend of the May Day Bank Holiday the Mayor of Cambridge opens the festivities by showering coins on the eager children. Reach is an ancient village, used in Roman times as a port and important enough to be created a self-governing Kingdom under a charter granted by King John. The coming of the railway in the 1880s reduced river trade, and Denver Sluice, built to control the drainage of the complex waterways of the Fens, cut off access to Reach.

The larger village of Burwell, a few miles from Reach and only five miles from Newmarket, also has a long history. In Burwell Fen was found the skull of a Neolithic wild ox, together with the stone axe which killed it. Much later, Burwell was the place where one of the lesser-known villains of King Stephen's reign, Geoffrey de Mandeville, 'the Devil in human form', met his downfall. This robber baron stormed Ely and starved and burned the peasants into submission. Stephen was forced to face this unpleasant opponent and he built a chain of fortifications, one of which was the castle at Burwell. The rectangular mound and surrounding ditch may still be seen. De Mandeville laid siege to the castle on a warm summer's day; removing his helmet, he was struck by an arrow and later died of gangrene at Mildenhall.

Burwell grew prosperous as a trading port in the Middle Ages, and many handsome houses remain. Boats may still navigate this far, but the canal ends at a T-junction at the bottom of a pub garden.

The splendid church of St Mary is at the southern end of this mile-long village. Its tower is evidently modelled on the lantern at Ely Cathedral. The churchyard has several interesting memorials, in particular a stone commemorating 78 people killed in a fire in a local barn in 1727; they were attending a puppet show, and demand for seats was so great that the doors were nailed shut, with disastrous consequences. Almost 50 years later the arsonist confessed on his deathbed that he had held a grudge against the puppeteer.

WICKEN FEN

There are two nature trails on the reserve. The shorter is less than a mile long, takes about half an hour to complete, and runs over a boardwalk designed particularly for those in wheelchairs and pushchairs. The longer trail is a couple of miles long and sturdy waterproof footwear is advised. Both trails begin at the William Thorpe Building, a modern visitors' centre which also contains a lecture hall and a display about the Fens. As you walk along (studying the admirable Trail Guide), your attention will be drawn to the various types of scenery: sedge and litter fields, pits where clay was once dug for brickmaking, now home to many aquatic plants and insects, and carr, characterised by alder, buckthorn, hawthorn, guelder rose and sallow.

The longer Trail also takes you to the Tower Hide which overlooks water reedbeds visited by many birds. You will see the other two fens which make up the reserve: Adventurers' Fen covers 200 acres and takes its name from the 17th-century investors who ventured their money in the drainage project (the workers who cut the channels were called the undertakers!). This fen was drained in the Second World War when farming land was needed, and now it is mainly wet grassland attracting wildfowl and waders in winter and spring. The smaller St Edmund's Fen includes Poors' Fen, which still belongs to the parish and where on one day a year the poor scrambled for the best spots to dig turf and cut sedge.

The reserve has wildlife in abundance: thousands of species of insects, including fascinating dragonflies, half a dozen kinds of spider found nowhere else in England, and many butterflies such as the large skipper and the yellow brimstone which lays its eggs on the buckthorn. Plants include meadowsweet, yellow flag, bog myrtle and the rootless, carnivorous bladderwort. Of the birds, the hen harrier is a winter visitor, and at other times you may see warblers, tits, finches and wagtails. The Trail Guide clearly illustrates what may be seen, and you will enjoy the unaccustomed loneliness of this watery wilderness.

Not all of Fenland is under the plough, with flat fields of black peat under the wide and dramatic sky; of the 2500 square miles of reeds, sedges and wetland which once existed, there remain a few areas of natural, undrained land. Wicken Fen is one of these. It covers 600 acres and lies to the south of Ely. This was the first nature reserve set up by the National Trust in 1899, and here the drainage process has been reversed: the weatherboarded windpump on the Fen, built in 1908 and resited here in 1956, scoops water back into the reserve rather than helping it on its way to the sea. This is the only survivor of the many hundreds of windpumps which once drained the Fens.

Because the peat of Wicken Fen has not dried out and shrunk, it now stands some eight feet above the level of the surrounding land. The reserve consists of three adjoining fenland areas, and the public is admitted to the largest, Wicken Sedge Fen. Once the Fenlanders (known as 'Fen Tigers' because of their resourcefulness and suspicion of strangers) made a living by fishing and wildfowling, and the peat, sedges, reeds and litter were valuable sources of fuel, thatch and animal fodder. The Fen is not, therefore, untouched by man; man's activity here has created and maintained a habitat for the many species of plants and animals by preventing the encroachment of carr (scrubland) or woodland, and this is the policy which the Trust follows to the present day.

The windpump

National Trust
Open: All year daily dawn to dusk
Price guide: Free

CAMBRIDGE

Cambridge is one of Europe's most attractive cities, and to visit it on a summer day is to experience a rare pleasure. It seems to combine the past with the present more perfectly than any other place in England. There are many versions of how the university was established in this part of East Anglia, but most agree that in 1209 some students at Oxford quarrelled with the townsfolk and moved well beyond their reach to Cambridge. In 1284 the first college, Peterhouse, was founded. Today there are 32 colleges and almost 12,000 students.

Probably the most enduring image of the city is of under-graduates in punts drifting along the River Cam. Even the briefest of tours should begin with the Backs, as the river area is called, and so we shall start from Silver Street Bridge. Punts may be hired from here, and the technique of experienced users should be noted: the pole is not only employed to move the boat along, but for steerage too! Here also is Queen's College, founded in 1448 by Henry VI's Queen, Margaret of Anjou, and added to by the wife of Edward IV, the man who deposed and murdered him. In the courtyard is a most unusual timepiece, a Sun and Moon dial. But the real gem is to be found over the river, for in 1749 the mathematician Etheridge devised and built a wooden bridge which required no nails. To discover the secret of its ingenious construction the bridge was dismantled at the beginning of this century, and then attempts were made to reassemble it; alas, Etheridge had taken the secret with him to the grave and nails had to be used.

King's College Chapel

From Silver Street go up to Trumpington Street, and if time permits, walk away from the city centre to Peterhouse College. Thomas Gray, the writer of the 'Elegy in a Country Churchyard', was a Fellow here. He lived in fear of fire and kept a ladder propped against his window which was to be the cause of misfortune. Some students played a trick on him, calling 'Fire!', at which the gentleman scrambled from his window, down the ladder, and into a tub of cold water. Far from amused, he left Peterhouse and took up residence across the road at Pembroke College.

Retrace your steps past St Catherine's College and you come to the grand view of King's. The gateway dates from the 19th century, and leads through to the courtyard.

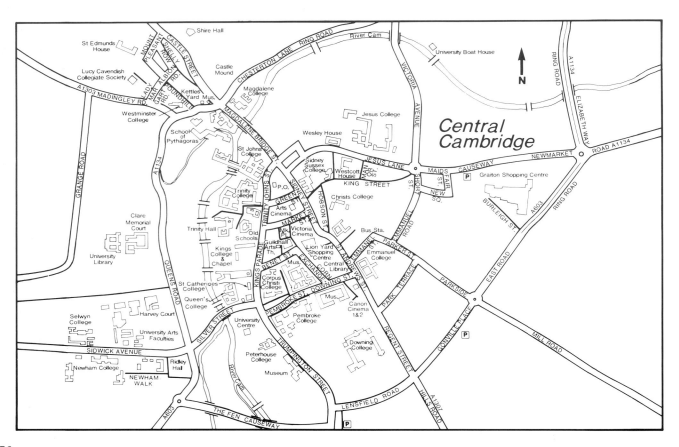

The lawns may only be walked on by the Fellows (tutors), a privilege regarded as compensation in those days when they were required to be celibate! The chapel of King's was begun in 1446 by the pious Henry VI as a sister foundation to his school at Eton. From outside the length and height are impressive, but nothing prepares you for the lightness of the interior. The fan-vaulting is without equal, and effortlessly spreads its fingers across the roof of this graceful building. Henry VIII completed the work in 1515 by adding the stained glass windows which survive in their entirety today. The carved screen is a masterpiece, showing the interwoven initials of the King and Anne Boleyn. So desperately did Henry want the work completed that he insisted the craftsmen work through the night by candlelight. The altarpiece is *The Adoration of the Magi* by Rubens. The Service of Nine Lessons and Carols has made this chapel famous throughout the world.

The Backs at King's college

From King's, walk through to the Backs. Once the port of Cambridge occupied this spot, and in very dry years it is said to be possible to detect the old street plan in marks in the grass. The view of King's College Chapel seen from the Cam is a must for the visitor. Return to King's Gate and walk down to Great St Mary's Church, which is the university church. There are excellent views of the city from the tower. Once all students had to live within three miles of the university, and the measurements were made from one of the buttresses. A pretty alleyway brings you to Market Hill. The busy market survives, but the stone water conduit which once stood here has been moved to Lensfield Road. It was called Hobson's Conduit after the man who hired out his horses in strict rotation, denying his clients any preference – hence they were given Hobson's Choice.

Returning to King's Parade, plunge into the bustling crowds as they sweep past the elegant shop fronts and university buildings. Even in vacations there is no shortage of students, for many colleges offer summer courses. The Senate House building dates from 1720 and is the university 'parliament'. The Senate House Passage passes Gonville and Caius (keys) College, and comes to Trinity Lane, once one of the main roads of the city. Turn left here, and Clare College is on your right. This college was founded in 1326, but soon afterwards was destroyed by fire and was then refounded by Lady Elizabeth de Clare. A second fire in 1521 caused more damage, and the present buildings were begun in 1638. The gardens of Clare are not to be missed. The beautiful gateway to Clare Bridge dates from 1640, and the

surrounding view of lawns, flower beds and grazing sheep and cattle cannot have altered that much. If you have crossed the River Cam, return to the college side by way of Garrett Hostel Bridge, and walk up towards Trinity Street. Heffer's, the famous bookshop, is almost opposite the main gate of the next college.

Henry VIII founded Trinity College in 1546 by merging King's Hall of Edward II and Michaelhouse of Edward III. The tall brick gatehouse depicts the sons of Edward III. The Great Court is two acres of manicured lawn with a noble fountain at the centre. The college clock strikes each hour twice, using separate bells. Isaac Newton lived in rooms beside the gatehouse. Other famous students included Byron, Tennyson and the present Prince of Wales. From Great Court we pass to Neville's Court, with its magnificent library built to designs by Wren in 1676. Many famous manuscripts are kept here, including the original of *Winnie the Pooh*! The lawn of Neville's Court is used for the May Ball which, curiously enough, is held in June.

Hobson's Conduit

From Trinity we are once more on the river path and follow it to Kitchen Bridge. St John's College occupies both sides of the Cam at this point, and its two courts are linked by the lovely Bridge of Sighs, or New Bridge, to use its proper name. This was built in 1831 and was inspired by the much older bridge in Venice which led to the prison, hence the sighing. Walk through to St John's College gateway, which is surely the most magnificent of all. It was built

Trinity Great Court

in the early 16th century by the founder, Lady Margaret Beaufort, mother of Henry VII.

Continue along St John's Street to the Round Church, which was built in 1130, and betrays the influence of the returning crusaders in its unusual shape. A left turn at Bridge Street brings you to Magdalene (maudlin) Bridge, the first crossing point of the river in Roman times and today another place for hiring punts. Magdalene Street and Northampton Street have rows of houses which have changed little in appearance since medieval times. The Folk Museum is nearby. Magdalene College was founded by a courtier of Henry VIII, and Samuel Pepys was a student here. The College Library displays the famous diaries he kept between 1660 and 1669.

The Fitzwilliam Museum in Cambridge enjoys an international reputation, and the visitor to Cambridge is recommended to admire its treasures. The portico is so grand that it is almost overwhelming, but inside there should be something to interest everyone, since its range of collections is vast.

A painting by Joseph Wright shows Richard Fitzwilliam in the gown of an undergraduate of Trinity Hall. It was painted in 1764. Although the family seat was near Dublin, Fitzwilliam spent most of his life in England, and when he died in 1816 he bequeathed to Cambridge his extensive library and fine art collections, with £100,000 to provide a proper home for them. Work began on the project in 1837 under the direction of George Basevi. Unfortunately he was killed when he fell from scaffolding in Ely Cathedral in 1845,

and the work was completed by C.R. Cockerell. The interior is best described as High Victorian, because the coloured marble and mosaic of the staircases dates from 1870. The museum was intended for students; the public was permitted to enter only on certain days, provided they were 'respectably dressed'.

The variety of exhibits provides a clue to Fitzwilliam's personal tastes but the collection now includes many generous donations. The story is told of one director of the museum whose presence at a bedside was interpreted as a sure sign of a fatal illness, because he was always looking for more benefactors! We are all familiar with the practice of historical buildings and suchlike having Friends, who help

St Mary's Church from the market

provide funds and maintain interest throughout the year; the Fitzwilliam Museum pioneered this idea in 1909.

The displays include Egyptian, classical and oriental art, coins, glassware and manuscripts. The Grey-FitzPayne *Book of Hours* dates from about 1300, and is believed to have been produced near Nottingham. These were really prayer books for the aristocracy, and the duller moments of any service would have been alleviated by studying the busy scenes portrayed in the capital letters and margins. The Fitzwilliam Virginal Book is a collection of keyboard music from the 16th and 17th centuries and is quite simply unique. Other original manuscripts include Keats' 'Ode to a Nightingale', Hardy's controversial novel, *Jude the Obscure* and most appropriately, Rupert Brooke's 'Grantchester'.

The paintings in the collection are of the very highest quality. Titian, Rubens, Van Dyck, Gainsborough, Constable, Turner, Blake, Monet – these are all represented, and many more besides. Allow a lot of time to visit the Fitzwilliam Museum, because you will want to linger.

The Fitzwilliam Museum

A very different museum is to be found at the Scott Polar Research Institute, established in 1920 to honour the memory of Captain Scott RN who died returning from the South Pole in 1912. It deals with the history of polar exploration, the geology and geography of the North and South Poles, and the equipment used by explorers, past and present.

Far from the frozen wastes are the Botanic Gardens, founded in 1762 and second only to Kew in national importance. Although primarily intended for research work they are open to the public, and their lawns, flower beds, rockeries and ponds are enormously popular. An unusual idea is the chronological flower bed, with plants set out in the order they arrived in Britain.

St John's Gateway

The shopping area is almost inseparable from the university. There is always something going on in the city: it has a thriving Arts Theatre, a Folk Festival and some of the best restaurants in East Anglia.

Folk Museum
Open: April to Sept: Mon to Sat 1030–1700, Sun 1400–1700, Oct to Mar: Tues to Sat 1030–1700, Sun 1400–1700
Price guide: A

Fitzwilliam Museum
Open: All year: Tues to Sat 1000–1700, Sun 1400–1700
Price guide: Free

Botanic Gardens
Open: Nov to Jan: Daily 1000–1600, Feb to April: Daily 1000–1700, May to Sept: Daily 1000–1800, Oct: Mon to Sun 1000–1700
Price guide: A

ANGLESEY ABBEY

In the middle of bleak and unpromising fenland near Lode, six miles north-east of Cambridge, stands Anglesey Abbey – a stately home with a rich collection of treasures, and a garden which, although a creation of the 20th century, conveys all the elegance of 200 years ago.

The South Front

This is not, and never has been, an abbey. The name Anglesey is derived from the nearby hamlet of Anger-hale, long since disappeared. A priory of Augustinians was founded here in the 12th century, and some 13th-century remains were incorporated into the Tudor mansion built on the site after the Dissolution, and later into the modern building we now see. Anglesey benefited from the generosity of several patrons during its long history, and passed through different families before being bought in 1926 by its greatest benefactor, Huttleston Broughton, son of a wealthy American industrialist. The family had moved to England; Huttleston was educated at Harrow, served with the Life Guards in the First World War and was made Lord Fairhaven in 1929. At his death in 1966 he left the house and garden to the National Trust.

Anglesey originally attracted his interest because it was well situated to satisfy his principal interests of racing and shooting: close to Newmarket, and in fine partridge country. Soon, however, the Abbey became the focus of his dedication to the arts, and he established an enormous collection of books, paintings, silverware, porcelain and objets d'art. To house this collection, Lord Fairhaven re-modelled and enlarged the house, adding a two-storeyed picture gallery linked to the main block by an ingenious bridge, as well as a library wing containing some 9000 volumes.

Despite the evident grandeur and luxury of its contents, this remains a comfortable and welcoming home because of its intimate scale. The Drawing Room has a notable Elizabethan fireplace. The 13th-century Dining Room, once the Monks' Parlour, has stone pillars and a vaulted ceiling. There is a unique collection of paintings of Windsor; Lord Fairhaven was fond of the town and was stationed there with the Life Guards. There are also silver chandeliers, Chinese vases, miniatures, snuff boxes and many early colour plate books, some of which are on loan to the Fitzwilliam Museum.

The glory of Anglesey Abbey is perhaps also its most astonishing feature: the garden. Lord Fairhaven's creation, in the middle of flat and rather dreary scenery, is a place full of colour and pleasing surprises. The grand formal design of the half-mile long Coronation Avenue, planted with horse chestnuts to honour King George VI and Queen Elizabeth, and the traditional vast urns, statues and temple, are contrasted with the informality of woodland and apparently natural landscape. In reality, the whole garden was most carefully planned, and the effect is stunning. Visitors will especially admire the dazzling crescent of the Dahlia Garden, vivid with colour set off by the green hedges which shelter it. The Herbaceous Garden is set in a semi-circle and is graced with stone seats and a statue of Father Time. In spring the Daffodil Walk and Hyacinth Garden with its thousands of blue and white scented flowers should not be missed. Wander down the leafy paths beside a clear stream to Lode Mill, now restored and grinding corn for flour. Everywhere there are magnificent trees of all kinds, many of them rare. Whatever the season, there is something to delight the eye.

The Herbaceous Garden

Anglesey Abbey
National Trust
Open: Mar to Oct: Wed to Sun 1300–1700
Price guide: C
Gardens only
Open: Mar to July: Wed to Sun 1100–1730, Sept to Oct: Wed to Sun 1100–1730
Price guide: B

THE GOG MAGOG HILLS

Near Cambridge there is a range of hills which provide a popular recreation area. The visitors' centre is at Wandlebury Hillfort, four miles south-east of Cambridge, at the side of the A604 where it passes the Little Shelford junction. A car park is provided. The name of this range of hills is ancient: according to the 12th-century historian Geoffrey of Monmouth, Gogmagog was a twelve-foot high brute, one of the race of giants who once populated Britain. This monster uprooted oak trees as if they were hazel twigs but was, of course, finally killed.

Some time around 250 BC invaders from the Marne area of France moved into this area, and the local population opposed them by building great earthwork forts, probably with timber palisades, surrounded by deep ditches. Despite these precautions the invaders were triumphant, perhaps because they used a new weapon – the chariot. The fort at Wandlebury was overrun, and the Marnians, later called Iceni, improved the defences against the Romans. The half-mile circumference of the ditches survives, enclosing about 15 acres.

View from Wandlebury Ring

John Layer, an antiquary, told of a figure carved into the hillside, and in the 1950s it was claimed that a sun goddess, two male figures and a chariot had been found carved into the chalk. The experts are dubious about this, but followers of the occult are both impressed and excited.

The hills have connections with horse racing: James II's Inspector of the King's Running Horses, a man called Tregonwell Frampton, built stables here, and was acknowledged to be the 'Father of the Turf'. Francis, second Earl of Godolphin shared Frampton's love of the turf and built a house within the ancient earthworks in the early 18th century. In 1723 the Earl brought to England Godolphin Arab, a thoroughbred Arab stallion from which nearly all thoroughbreds are descended. When the horse died in 1753 it was buried beneath the arch of the new stable block,

The stable block within Wandlebury Ring

which survives to this day. The cupola has a clock with the unusual feature of one hand only on each of its faces. The house was pulled down in the 1950s, but the site is marked by the raised lawn with a sundial in the centre. The stable block is now private, but has a shop and exhibition centre at the end.

Godolphin had created a park for his pleasure, and the sheep-grazing land was replaced by woodland of beech and elm. Many of the latter fell victim to Dutch elm disease. In 1954 the property passed to the Cambridge Preservation Society who created three nature trails concentrating on the many interesting and unusual species of local plants and wildlife which were in danger of being lost. The longest trail covers two miles. There are 200 species of wild flower, some only just saved from local extinction caused by intensive farming. The cowslip has been reintroduced and other species are making a slow return. Beetles, butterflies, voles, hares, fox and muntjac deer are all to be seen in season by the vigilant walker. Over 150 nestboxes have been provided to attract owls, kestrels, doves and woodpeckers. Also in a tree, but less likely to thrill birdwatchers, is part of the tail of a Wellington bomber which crashed in 1941 to the west of the stable block. The paths are lined with deadman's fingers, beefsteak and earth stars – all fungi!

For many, these hills offer a retreat from the city. A fine weekend sees scores of people walking their dogs, playing cricket, picnicking or enjoying the view. Here you can be as active or lazy as you please.

DUXFORD AIR MUSEUM

No doubt one day some distinguished professor will explain why things to do with war exercise such a fascination for us. The most peaceful of people thrill to tales of epic encounters, and few can resist marching along with the magnificent sound of a military brass band. Nothing at Duxford could be described as corrupting, and indeed it is more likely that the stories it illustrates will induce healthy reflection. The Imperial War Museum at Duxford is south of Cambridge, off the M11 at junction 10, and it is famous for having Concorde 101; but there is much more to see than this graceful supersonic bird.

Concorde 101

Duxford is still in use as an aerodrome, which explains its success as a museum. This is not a place for models of famous aircraft; the real thing is everywhere. The military history of aviation is well documented, from the BE2c which entered service in 1915 and saw action over the trenches of the Western Front, to the giants of our own times: the Vulcan bomber, with its beautiful delta wing, and the American B52D, which is so enormous it seems to defy the laws of aerodynamics. This is the largest aircraft to fly into Duxford. Lining the runway or in the hangars are other celebrated names: Spitfire, Hurricane, Mosquito, Mustang, and the bombers they protected: Lancaster, B17 and B29.

The Superhangar

There are five large exhibition hangars. One is the reception centre for visitors, with a shop which sells books, posters and postcards. A viewing platform enables you to oversee the jigsaw arrangement of aircraft through the years. Everyone has a favourite, but children will probably want to try out the hi-tech simulator capsule which lets them experience the thrill of making a landing on a carrier's pitching flight deck! Lovers of engines are not ignored either, as scores of these are distributed throughout the museum. Everything is well labelled, and the guide book is a constant source of useful background information.

Outside, the airfield has kept its wartime appearance, and is still used by film makers for this reason. It was in 1917 that military flying began here, and during World War Two it was to play a vital part in the air war, first as home to Douglas Bader and his 'Duxford Wing', and later as a base for units of the 'Mighty Eighth', the American bomber Group. Number 3 hangar has a wide-ranging exhibition of the contribution made to the war effort by the US Air Force. Only in 1961 did Duxford cease to be an RAF station, and the Imperial War Museum took it over in 1971.

RAF Shackleton, maritime reconnaissance aircraft

Military vehicles are also on show, and in one hangar there are more famous memories of the past: Churchill and Conqueror tanks, a Saladin armoured car in startling United Nations white, and even a T34 tank as used by the Soviets in their war on the Eastern Front. There are reconstructions of scenes, such as a very realistic evocation of a First World War Bristol Fighter being made ready for action, and from the Second a desert patrol group's camp in North Africa. Among the more unexpected items to be found on display are a coastal motor boat, parts of a midget submarine, a lifeboat and even a V1 flying bomb, complete with launcher!

A visit to Duxford can mean a lot of walking, but trucks offer free rides between the hangars. The really adventurous may wish to take a short flight over the museum in a plane or helicopter. If this is too alarming, then settle down to watch a video of the airfield's long and distinguished history. Sometimes there are special events, and these often include flying displays by international teams.

Duxford Air Museum
Open: All year: Mar to Oct 1000–1800, Oct to Mar 1000–1600
Price guide: C

WIMPOLE HALL AND HOME FARM

Wimpole Hall, near the junction of the A603 and Ermine Street (the A1198), is the largest house in Cambridgeshire. The south avenue is three miles long; 'Capability' Brown lined it with elms, but the ravages of disease caused them to be felled in 1978, and the limes which replaced them have yet to equal their grandeur! Wimpole Hall was begun by Sir Thomas Chicheley in 1640, but his work was refaced and extended in the 18th century by later owners, particularly the first Earl of Hardwicke, Lord Chancellor of England. To this gentleman we owe the grand south front, with its double stairway, imposing entrance and, high up on the pediment, the family crest. The fifth Earl was the gambler popularly remembered as 'Champagne Charlie', whose luck fell short of his expectations, and whose debts of £300,000 forced him to sell the estate. In 1938 Captain and Mrs George Bambridge bought it. She was the daughter of Rudyard Kipling, and at her death in 1976 the property passed to the National Trust.

The entrance hall tiles proclaim 'Salve!' to the visitor, and the interior is large and welcoming. Throughout its history the Hall has undergone changes to suit fashion, such as in the Yellow Drawing Room, where whole floors were removed to enable the insertion of a grand reception room.

There are many fine paintings. Also worth seeing is the chapel with its extravagant baroque decoration, and the bath house, whose plunge bath required over 2,000 gallons of hot water to fill it.

The 300-acre park is landscaped, and even has a Gothic folly: a ruined castle. The stable block, now an admission and exhibition centre, is being restored. From here, for a small extra charge, you can ride across to Home Farm on an old waggon pulled by a Suffolk Punch. Or you can walk through the pleasure grounds and admire the trees and shrubs. There is a walled garden, but the rest is pleasantly informal.

Home Farm was rebuilt at the end of the 18th century when the owner was a pioneer in the new agricultural methods of soil improvement, crop rotation and animal husbandry. He remodelled the buildings and farming continued into the middle of the 20th century. It was the hub of activity, with its storehouses, animal enclosures and workshops. The visitor today sees thatched buildings of black weatherboarding which house a museum and unfamiliar breeds of farm animals, because in 1982 the farm was approved by the Rare Breeds Survival Trust as a centre for endangered species – the only one in East Anglia. Here we see cattle such as the Irish Moiled, British White and the Gloucester. In the piggery are Tamworths and Large Blacks, while in another shed are Golden Guernsey goats and Anglo-Nubians with their distinctive drooping ears. There are also sheep, donkeys, ponies and turkeys. Children will particularly like to see the calves or piglets, and mounting blocks are provided to allow a full view into the pens, although the littlest ones will still need a helping hand! There is also a duck pond, and picnic tables set beside paddocks which enclose a special children's corner.

The centrepiece is Soane's Great Barn, 150 feet long and beautifully restored, housing a collection of farm implements and machinery. Behind the barn is the century-old dairy from where milk and butter were taken to the Hall. The open cart shed is now a covered refreshment area with a film loft where visitors may see a video about the farm.

Suffolk Punches with waggon

The South Front

Wimpole Hall and Home Farm
National Trust
Open: Hall: Mar to Oct: Tues, Wed, Thur, Sat, Sun 1300–1700
      Farm: All year: Sat & Sun 1300–1700, Mar to Oct: 1030–1700
Price guide: C

CROMWELL COUNTRY

Until he was 40 years old Oliver Cromwell had done nothing to ensure his name would endure in Huntingdon, let alone England. He was propelled by events into the very forefront of our history, and it is a mark of his importance that even today opinions about him are as strong as they were three centuries ago. To some he is the tyrant who beheaded his King, while to others he is the champion of religious and political freedom. This part of England represents his roots, and the landscape we see even today provides a clue to the extraordinary vision and determination he displayed. Huntingdon, St Ives and Ely are all associated with his career and we are fortunate that they still offer glimpses of the region he knew.

Cromwell's House at Ely, now St Mary's Vicarage

'I was by birth a gentleman, living neither in any considerable heights, nor yet in obscurity', he was to write. He was born on the 25th April 1599 at The Friars in Huntingdon High Street. Today this is a private clinic, but the Cromwell coat of arms is placed above the door. He was christened at the Church of St John the Baptist (destroyed in the Civil War and now the site of the Garden of Rest), and above the entry in the register, a Royalist sympathiser has written: 'England's plague for five years.' Legend has it that when King James I stayed at nearby Hinchingbrooke House as a guest of Oliver's wealthy grandfather, the five-year-old Oliver quarrelled with Prince Charles, the future king, and gave him a bloody nose! Much later Charles stayed at the house a second time, but as 'guest' of a troop of soldiers conveying him as a prisoner to London. Hinchingbrooke House is now a school.

The Hospital of St John the Baptist had been converted to the town's Free School in 1565. The building dates from the 12th century, and the imposing doorway with its Norman archway is only a fraction of the original structure. Oliver Cromwell began his schooling here in 1610, when the Master was Dr Thomas Beard, a distinguished Puritan. Today the school is the Cromwell Museum, and provides a superb background to any study of his life. It has paintings of the principal characters, and a wealth of objects and

Cromwell's hat

clothing associated with him. There was once a second floor, providing accommodation for Dr Beard. Later in the 17th century another famous pupil was to pass through the door: Samuel Pepys, whose family home may be seen at Brampton.

There is no evidence that Oliver was exceptional as a pupil, but he moved on to Sidney Sussex College at Cambridge in 1616. On his arrival he presented a cup to the college – and it was sold almost immediately to help pay off debts! The Puritanism he encountered during his short time here, coming hard on the heels of Dr Beard's training, may have decisively shaped his future. He was not long a student, however, for on the death of his father he was sent to London where he studied law in order to administer the family estates. There he met Elizabeth Bouchier, whom he married, and they settled in Huntingdon at the family home.

Oliver's marriage was to provide a steadying influence on his life, and Elizabeth wrote to him when he was away: 'Truly my life is but half a life in your absence.' He succeeded his father as a gentleman farmer and took part in local politics, becoming the town's MP in 1628. Two buildings he would still recognise are the George Inn, once owned by his grandfather, where even now plays are occasionally performed in the balconied courtyard, and the Falcon Inn, where he made his headquarters at one stage in the Civil Wars. The bridge over the Ouse linking Huntingdon with the pretty town of Godmanchester is also very old; it dates from 1332 and is interesting because its builders worked from both banks at once and only just met in the middle! In 1631 Cromwell sold up and left Huntingdon,

The bridge over the Great Ouse linking Huntingdon to Godmanchester

perhaps because of an argument, or just to raise money to pay off his debts of £1800.

The Cromwell family settled at Slepe Hall in St Ives, and by all accounts were no more successful as farmers, for they are thought to have contemplated emigration to America. 'He farmed here until he was very poor', was one wry comment.

St Ives Bridge and Chapel

The town of Slepe was owned by the monks of Ramsey Abbey, who levied a toll on travellers crossing their bridge over the river. In 1000 a ploughman found a stone coffin containing a skeleton, and the shrewd monks announced that these were the remains of St Ivo, a Persian bishop! A priory was built, pilgrims arrived and the town changed its name to St Ives. In 1426 they built a new bridge with a toll house half-way across which doubled as a tiny chapel, still in use today. During the Civil War the Roundheads demolished part of the bridge and put in a drawbridge. Only in 1716 was the drawbridge removed and the arch rebuilt, but not in the original style. The cobbled quayside is very attractive today, and the countryside comes right up to the town. In earlier centuries ice-skating on the river was a popular winter sport; nowadays you can roller-skate in the brand-new St Ivo Recreation Centre!

The Market Hill has a fine statue (1901) of Oliver Cromwell, with a Bible under his arm. In medieval times the fair held here was one of the four most important in England. A great fire in 1689 destroyed 122 houses, but the magnificent Elizabethan manor house by the bridge gives a hint of St Ives' appearance at the time. The town has two fine church spires. All Saints dates from the late 15th century, and when the local philanthropist, Potto Brown – a mill owner from nearby Houghton – provided funds to build a Free Church, the builders ensured that its spire was five feet higher!

Oliver Cromwell's fortunes changed in 1636 when a legacy enabled him to move to Ely. The Earl of Bedford was draining the Fens, deaf to the protests of those whose livelihoods were affected. Soon Oliver was championing their cause, earning himself the mock title 'Lord of the Fens'. His house in Ely was later a pub called The Cromwell Arms.

In Parliament he watched the country slide towards civil war, and when it came in 1642 he moved fast. Furious that Cambridge University was about to send its silver plate

to the King, he intercepted it and so entered the conflict. The battle of Edgehill was a muddled draw, but Cromwell was quick to see that the Royalists had the advantage of recruiting from families to whom horsemanship was a daily exercise. So in December he founded the Eastern Association as a training organisation, and this was to form the backbone of the New Model Army three years later.

This middle-aged farmer was to become a military genius, winning battles throughout Great Britain. His psalm-singing, Bible-quoting soldiers were like none before or since. He strides across the years, commanding vast armies, dealing with challenges to his leadership and even organising the trial and execution of his King. The English Revolution which he played a leading role in became the prototype for political revolutions throughout the world, and was the first and most important step towards the democracy we enjoy today. There is an endearing quality about a great man who can say 'I beseech you in the bowels of Christ, think it possible you may be wrong'.

Cromwell's statue outside the Free Church, St Ives

Hinchingbrooke House
Open: May to Aug: Sun 1400–1700
Price guide: B

Cromwell Museum, Huntingdon
Open: April to Oct: Tues to Fri 1100–1700, Sat & Sun 1100–1600,
Nov to Mar: Tues to Fri 1300–1600, Sat 1100–1600, Sun 1400–1600
Price guide: Free

Bridge Chapel, St Ives
Open: All year, key details displayed
Price guide: Free

HOUGHTON MILL

Houghton is a pretty village with an exceptionally large and well-preserved water-mill. The River Ouse near St Ives is wide and quite fast-flowing, which explains the location of such an important mill from the earliest times.

There has been a mill on this site since AD 974. It was owned by the Benedictine monks at Ramsey Abbey, ten miles away, and farmers bringing their grain to be ground at the mill paid the abbey for this service. This was normal practice; what was by no means usual, however, was that the abbey had the power to insist that the tenants use Houghton Mill, and levied fines if they declined to do so. At the time of the Domesday Book (1086) the mill was profitable and busy, but it was not popular. In medieval times millers were assumed to be swindlers – the miller in Chaucer's *Canterbury Tales* conforms to this stereotype, fooling both his masters and customers.

The animosity which existed between the monks and the farmers was forced into sharp relief in 1500 when Ramsey Abbey arbitrarily sought to dam the waters to secure a better flow through the mill race. The surrounding fields were flooded, with disastrous consequences to the crops, and the local people, whose complaints to the abbot were ignored, eventually took matters into their own hands. The abbot complained that they had 'assembled themselves in a riotous manner and notoriously, with force of arms (and) with great violence and might, took and carried away the floodgates of the mills at Houghton'. The short-term solution to their problem came in 1515 when Henry VIII sided with the villagers, but the complete victory only came in 1539 when the abbey was shut down.

Houghton Mill became the property of the Crown for almost one hundred years until Charles I sold it in 1625. Then it was owned by a succession of different families, all of whom carried out improvements or alterations. The earliest mill would have used only one water-wheel, driving a single pair of grinding stones, but by the 19th century there were three wheels and a total of ten pairs of grinding stones.

The power of a water-mill is best appreciated when the wheels are turning, for the building shudders as the enormous machinery is spun round as though it were weightless. The interior of Houghton Mill is full of interest; there are five floors, and the visitor can follow the business of milling both from displays and practical demonstrations.

Potto Brown, 'the village philanthropist', became part-owner of the mill in 1822. He was an able man and the mill turned in a healthy profit. Brown used some of this money to finance his good works in the neighbourhood. A bust of this energetic and pious benefactor stands on what is called the Market Green, although there is not much grass there today. The cast-iron water pump is said to be unique, but the casing cleverly preserves its secret. The market cross, thatched and with brick pillar supports, provides a pleasant focal point. The village has a number of pretty houses, many of them old and of timber construction.

The Church of St Mary is very small and dates from the 14th century. There is a framed outline of its architectural history on the south wall. Outside the south porch is a tombstone to Thomas Garner, who died in 1826. He was a blacksmith, and the unpretentious verse of the inscription makes amusing reading today: 'My sledge and hammers lie declined,/ My bellows too have lost their wind . . .'

Cottage in Houghton Village

Houghton Mill
National Trust
Open: Mar to Oct: Sun 1400–1730, June to Sept: Sun, Mon to Wed 1400–1730
Price guide: A

GRAFHAM WATER & BUCKDEN PALACE

Grafham Water boasts some of the finest inland sailing in the country. Set in a shallow valley just west of the A1 and some six miles from Huntingdon, this is one of the largest man-made lakes in Britain, covering some 2½ square miles, and is an important reservoir supplying 1½ million people daily in towns within a 20-mile radius. Its waters are pumped from the Great Ouse, three miles away. The approach road from the A1 sweeps up to meet the low embankment which serves as a dam.

Walkers can follow the nine-mile perimeter path. A good starting point is Plummer's Park, just south of the dam, where there is a children's playground and a picnic area on a slight incline between young trees at the water's edge. The path takes in three such parks as well as woodland, a nature reserve and a wildfowl sanctuary.

At East Perry is the headquarters of the Grafham Water Sailing Club. The clubhouse was built in the 1960s to serve the newly-created reservoir, and it has refreshment facilities on the ground floor to enable sailors to eat and drink without changing out of their wet clothes! Grafham Water's situation in such low-lying country is ideal, since the waters are almost always ruffled by a good sailing breeze, and its surface area of almost 1600 acres allows plenty of space for both experienced and novice sailors. National Championships and Olympic Trials are held here, and the lake is increasingly used for cruising and sailboarding. There is an excellent rescue service in case sailors run into difficulties. Those wanting to improve their skills may attend the nearby Residential Centre which offers weekend courses at all levels, and day or half-day tuition is also available. Permits are required for trout fishing in May and September, and the Residential Centre runs summer courses in a variety of artistic pursuits.

Grafham Water

On the eastern side of the A1, and unhappily close to this busy road lies the village of Buckden. The High Street and Church Street have some lovely brick houses and two fine old coaching inns: the timber-framed Lion Hotel which dates back to 1500, and the 18th-century George Hotel. At

Buckden Palace

the heart of the village is Buckden Palace, the residence of the Bishops of Lincoln from 1186 to 1842.

What we see today is only a fraction of the 15th-century building, but it is still impressive, with its high walls and gateway leading to a courtyard and a three-storeyed, battlemented inner gatehouse. The Great Tower is of red brick, decorated with patterns in dark blue. In one of its corner turrets Katharine of Aragon was imprisoned for a year after the dissolution of her marriage to Henry VIII. The King feared that this popular Queen might act as a focus for rebellion, and sent the Duke of Suffolk and a band of his men to remove her to a more secure place. But she refused, and local people armed with scythes and billhooks waited angrily outside the Palace for the Duke's next move. He saw sense and withdrew, but not before relieving Katharine of her furniture and most of her servants. Eventually the Queen was taken to nearby Kimbolton Castle where she died in 1536. Her ghost is said to haunt the little room behind the chapel at Buckden.

Nowadays the Palace is owned by the Claretian missionaries, a Spanish monastic order, but visitors may enter the courtyard and look round the fine church which abuts the Palace.

Buckden Palace
Open: Any reasonable time
Price guide: Donation welcome

Kimbolton Castle
Open: Selected dates
Price guide: A

THE CITY OF ELY

Hereward the Wake is as much a part of English history as King Arthur and Robin Hood, and his story is as romantic. He was outlawed from England at the time of the Norman Conquest but returned in 1069 with a force of Danes and sacked Peterborough Abbey. Pursued, he took refuge in the Fens, and from his base at Ely tormented the Normans sent to deal with him. His relationship with the monks at Ely must have been strained, for it was they who finally betrayed him to William, by showing the King a track through the swampy fenland to their inaccessible island. The village of Aldreth has a causeway which is supposed to be the very one used. It is probable that William had promised to take his enemy captive without desecrating the abbey, since it escaped destruction. In the event Hereward evaded capture and ultimately passed into legend as a symbol of English defiance.

An elegant house facing Palace Green

Ely Cathedral with its massive west tower dominates the city in many ways. Scores of buildings are associated with the monastery it once served. The west front overlooks Palace Green, where there is a cannon captured during the Crimean War and presented to the city by Queen Victoria. Close by is the Bishop's Palace, begun in the 15th century, but greatly altered since. It is now a school in the Sue Ryder Foundation.

Oliver Cromwell was MP for Ely and collector of tithes. His half-timbered house, covered with creepers, is now the Vicarage and stands next to St Mary's Church. A tablet on the church wall recalls the execution of five men in 1816 for taking part in the Littleport riots sparked off by the increased price of bread.

Southwards runs The Gallery, a road with an unusual name, running between tall, warm-coloured brick walls. Many of the gateways offer tantalising glimpses beyond. At the end of the road is the Porta, the main gate to the Benedictine monastery. The long stone building inside and to the right of the gateway is the old abbey tithe barn, now the dining hall of the King's School. Close by is Prior Crauden's Chapel, another gem by the tireless Alan of Walsingham, who also built Goldsmith's Tower and Sacristy Gate (now the museum) in High Street.

The Porta

From the Porta it is possible to follow the path to the side entrance of the cathedral, or the visitor may wish to walk across the park down towards the river. This is a delightful route to take, as it affords wonderful views of the lantern tower of the cathedral seen across fields of grazing cattle. The park is an ideal spot to enjoy a picnic, or just to prepare for the afternoon's exploration.

Suitably rested, continue down to the river. It is a walk of about a quarter of an hour and leads down Ship Lane. The large building on the right is the former maltings, now a public hall. In recent years a riverside walk has been opened which extends for some distance and takes in the most attractive stretch of water.

The River Ouse at Ely has something to offer everyone. The cabin cruisers and small boats satisfy those who love to mess about on the river; the quaysides are ideal for the rows of fishermen who cast their lines with well-practised skill, constantly refuelling their hooks from tins of live bait; and the rest of us can eat ice-creams and sit outside lovely pubs like the Cutter Inn (named after the workmen who cut the new channel from Ely to Littleport), which occupies a gentle bend in the river.

The Cutter Inn beside the River Ouse

Ely Museum
Open: Jan to Mar: Tues to Fri 1130–1530, Sat & Sun 1130–1600, April to Nov: Tues to Sun 1030–1700, Nov to Dec: Tues to Fri 1130–1530, Sat & Sun 1130–1600
Price guide: A

ELY CATHEDRAL

East Anglia has few more stirring sights than that of Ely Cathedral rising from the mists of the surrounding Fens, and seeming to glide like a stone galleon into the realms of legend and beyond. It dominates the horizon from every line of approach, and visitors cannot fail to appreciate the engineering feat it represents.

The Lantern Tower

The saintly Etheldreda founded Ely Abbey in the year 673. She died on October 17th 679 as a result of a throat tumour, attributed to her having been vain enough to wear necklaces in her youth! Her Feast Day is still celebrated by a fair held in her honour.

Ely's isolation was not sufficient to ward off the marauding Danes and the abbey was destroyed by them in 870. King Edgar refounded it a century later, and included the King's School which survives to this day. Edward the Confessor was one of the Old Boys! The Norman Conquest and Ely's subsequent defiance under Hereward the Wake caused William to appoint the loyal 87-year-old Simeon as abbot. Despite his age, he plunged into a building programme which transformed the site. He died in 1093, by which time the foundations were in place and the barges were bringing the stone which would achieve his dream. By 1106 it was possible to inter the bones of St Etheldreda in the presbytery, beside the High Altar – thus ensuring an income from pilgrims. Three years later the Pope created the diocese of Ely, and the abbot became the first bishop. Work

was completed in 1189. Although the cloisters have not survived, the magnificent Prior's Door which led to them still remains. It dates from 1140 and the carved tympanum above it depicts a beardless Christ in Majesty, with angels either side.

In 1321 work began on the Lady chapel, but ceased almost immediately because the central tower collapsed into the cathedral, causing tremendous destruction. The sacrist, Alan of Walsingham, supervised its rebuilding as well as resuming work on the Lady chapel, and both projects are the glory of Ely. The Lady chapel is an essay in stone and glass: once its walls were lined with statues showing scenes from Mary's life, and the windows glowed with stained glass. All were destroyed at the Reformation, but its beauty remains, and the clear windows allow us to appreciate the fan-vaulted roof and the intricacy of the carvings. It is sad to think that John of Wisbech, one of the builders of this magnificent chapel, died of the Black Death in 1349, the same year as work was completed.

The octagon lantern is Ely's trademark. It defies belief how 400 tons of wood, glass and lead can not only stay 94 feet above our heads, but also look so slender and light. It comprises eight oak trees, each 63 feet long, standing on stone pillars. But ignore the statistics: just stand beneath it, look up and marvel at the craftsmanship.

The nave of Ely is 208 feet long, and is particularly impressive because on many occasions it is clear of seats. The roof was repainted in the 19th century and is still vivid with bright colours.

You may be surprised to discover that on weekdays the cathedral makes a charge for entry. The work of preservation is costly, and the money is desperately needed. There is a bookstall, a tea room, and a stained glass museum, all of which raise valuable sums. Alan of Walsingham, whose features gaze down at us from the lantern tower, would no doubt approve of our efforts to preserve his glorious work.

View of the Cathedral from the south east

Ely Cathedral
Open: Mar to Oct: daily 0700–1900, Nov to Mar: Mon to Sat 0730–1800, Sun 0730–1700
Price guide: B

Stained Glass Museum
Open: Mar to Oct: Mon to Fri 1030–1600, all year: Sun 1200–1500, Sat 1030–1630
Price guide: A

THE CHURCH OF ST WENDREDA AT MARCH

For most people the name March probably conjures up an image of a very long railway platform, with a biting wind blasting across miles of rich black soil. But this is an unduly harsh way to make the acquaintance of this town, for on its southern edge stands a church of such magnificence that it is worth the trip on its own.

Cast iron fountain at March

The town gives the impression that it was founded in the middle of the 19th century. The railway reached here in the 1840s and much of the architecture derives from the prosperity which followed. March is dominated by the spire of the Town Hall, which dates from 1900. At the far end of the main street stands an ornate cast-iron fountain which recalls the coronation of George V. But the town is much older than it looks.

The name is Anglo-Saxon, for 'march' means a frontier or border. There was once not only East Anglia, but Middle Anglia, and on the line between the kingdoms (often at war in the 6th century) stood March. Most of the inhabitants would have lived by fishing or trading, centred on the fens and rivers. By medieval times March was a boom town, with flourishing guilds which supervised all the commercial activities of the area. The wide main street served as the market place.

One of these guilds was that of St Wendreda, named after a local saint. She was the daughter of a king of East Anglia called Anna. He had two daughters: one was Etheldreda, and the other was Wendreda. They both were Christians and did good works. Etheldreda founded Ely Cathedral, while Wendreda came to the area around March and cared for the poor. When she died her body was embalmed, and soon pilgrims were paying their respects. So great was their veneration for her that when the English king Edmund Ironside was at war with the Danish king Canute in 1016 he exhumed the body and had it carried before his army, confident of victory. Much good it did him, because he lost. But despite this the saint's power was proven beyond question when the great Canute was converted to Christianity upon learning her story, and he had Wendreda's bones moved to Canterbury. Not until the mid-14th century did March secure their return, and it was this event that inspired the gem of a church that stands today.

The glory of St Wendreda's is a roof of such breathtaking splendour that any description of it must fail. It is of hammer-beam construction, which allows for a wide central aisle without the use of pillars. This was the summit of the carpenter's art, and was only employed in the finest buildings, so it tells us a lot about the status of March at this time. There are 120 carved angels on the hammer-beam ends, playing musical instruments, and they are so numerous that you almost expect to feel the breeze from their wings as they ascend. This is a roof which *must* be seen. In addition to the angels there are carvings of the twelve apostles, and even the devil, mischievously hidden from view!

The graceful tower has a processional way passing through it, which may indicate that a public right of way existed there already, and the builders had to maintain it. During the Reformation St Wendreda's tomb was plundered and destroyed on the orders of Henry VIII, but local tradition says the roof survived because the townspeople treated the Commissioners to a slap-up feast and so diverted their zeal!

St Wendreda's Church

WISBECH

Man's ability to transform his surroundings is well shown at Wisbech, for whereas it was once only four miles from the sea it is now almost 11 miles, thanks to the drainage engineers of the past who have reclaimed and diverted the waterways. The town has always been a port, and its prosperity has led to a number of fine buildings, particularly from the 18th century. The River Nene was diverted centuries ago, probably by the Dutch, and the streets created either side of it, known as North and South Brinks, are a joy to the eye. The jewel of Wisbech remains Peckover House, along the cobbled serenity of North Brink, 200 yards from the modern river bridge.

Peckover House garden

Peckover House was built in 1722 by the Southwell family, and it has retained the elegance it must have displayed then. Built of yellow brick with red-brick dressings, it is perfectly proportioned. Stone steps lead to a door framed between Tuscan columns, while the windows subtly reduce in size with each new storey. Greenery seems to be everywhere, from the curved lawn to the bushes which gently brush the walls.

The Peckover family who bought the house at the end of the 18th century were Quaker bankers, and even today the house has a quiet simplicity. The furniture and wall hangings are often of the highest quality, but the overall impression is not one of ostentation, but of modest gentility. The Dining Room has a lovely carved mantelpiece, and plain but perfectly executed panelling and plasterwork. One after another the rooms impress with their perfect sense of scale. This is a town house, among others, but quietly determined to be just that little bit better!

Only in 1943 did the house come into the possession of the National Trust, which also owns the properties either side, although these are not open to the public. One of the co-founders of the Trust, Octavia Hill, was born in a house on South Brink in 1838, and Peckover House has an exhibition in her memory.

The gardens behind the house are beyond all praise. Within a relatively small space has been created the Englishman's perfect retreat. Steps lead down to a rich green lawn surrounded by hedges and flower beds. Beyond, a path wanders between trees to the conservatory, rose arches and yet more flower beds. The statues distributed throughout the walks seem to hear our envious remarks, for they smile all the time!

Wisbech is more than just Peckover House, or even the Brinks. From the bridge the visitor soon comes to Castle Street. Nothing remains of the castle built in 1072, but several well-proportioned buildings continue to use the name. Close by is the museum, built as such in 1847, which houses a collection of items of local interest. Union and Ely Place, with The Crescent, form a Regency circus around a lovely flower garden. The intimacy of the scene is captivating, and yet we are only yards from the centre of a bustling market town.

The landscape around Wisbech may seem flat and boring, but do not be deceived. From this area come fruits and flowers which are sold throughout the land. The soil is good, and in summer the corn can look like pure gold, stretching to the wide horizon. If time permits go north-east a few miles and discover the church at Walpole St Peter – you may agree with those who say it is the finest parish church in Britain.

Peckover House
National Trust
Open: House & Garden: Mar to Oct: Sun & Wed 1400–1730, Garden also Sat, Mon & Tues
Price guide: B

Wisbech Museum
Open: All year: Jan to Mar: Tues to Sat 1000–1600, April to Sept: Tues to Sat 1100–1700, Oct to Dec: Tues to Sat 1000–1600

PETERBOROUGH

Peterborough is one of Europe's fastest-growing cities, and you do not need to be long within it to understand why. It is a beneficiary of the era of New Towns, when regional centres were encouraged to develop their industries and to expand. With its excellent road and rail communications Peterborough was ideally placed to exploit the policy, and its transformation over the years has been truly astonishing. It is the home of the prestigious East of England agricultural show, has a rowing and canoeing centre of Olympic standard, and its ice rink, opened in 1981, is the largest in England.

The River Nene at Peterborough

Although it has attracted scores of new employers to the district, it continues to be famous as the producer of most of the bricks used in the building trade, and the manufacturer of a diesel engine which sells throughout the world. Perhaps the finest achievement is the least noticed: Peterborough has retained its traditional city ambience. The streets are lined with trees and flowers, and it remains a place where individuals live, rather than merely work.

The West Gate leading into the Cathedral Yard dates from Norman times, and clearly there were occasions when the church felt threatened: there is evidence of the grooves which held a portcullis, and below the present road surface there was once a moat. Royal visitors stayed at the

West Gate, and were doubtless better fed than the prisoners who languished in the same building! Across the square towards Cowgate is the 16th-century Guildhall, with its open ground floor and upper floor of warm stone. Like an Italian piazza, the market place is somewhere to linger and watch the busy world pass by. Bridge Street has been paved and brightened with flowers, so shopping is a pleasure. The Town Hall is also the city information centre.

From the River Nene bridge the view is of motor cruisers, swans and willow-lined walks. The old Custom House and Key Theatre are here, too. The river has not always been so tame. Constant flooding caused the church of St John the Baptist to be moved in 1407 from the east side of the cathedral to the west! The bells are said to have guided the charmingly named Matthew Wildbore to safety, thus saving him from the perils of mist and fen. Suitably grateful, he made a bequest that the bells be rung each year on March 15th to recall his deliverance on that day. Wildbore Day is still on the local calendar.

The Museum and Maxwell Art Gallery in the Regency House in Priestgate contain an interesting collection of ship models carved by Napoleonic war prisoners.

The futuristic Queensgate shopping centre, built of glass and steel, epitomises Peterborough's adventurous attitude to modern life. More than 80 stores are gathered together under one roof, all linked by malls, arcades and escalators. The designers retained the best aspects of the past, and some old buildings have been incorporated.

Two miles west of the city centre on the A47 is the remarkable Longthorpe Tower. It dates from 1300 and is famous for its vivid 14th-century wall-paintings which cover subjects biblical, moral, historical and seasonal.

Longthorpe Tower

City Museum and Art Gallery
Open: All year: Tues to Sat 1000–1700
Price guide: Free

Longthorpe Tower
English Heritage
Open: July & Aug weekends only 1000–1800
Price guide: A

The Guildhall

PETERBOROUGH CATHEDRAL

Nearly all great buildings, however vast or complex in design, are recognised by one particular feature. For Peterborough Cathedral it is the west front. Three Early English arches soar over 80 feet high, dominating the view across the lawns of the Minster Yard. Above their rose windows are the statues of St Peter, St Paul and St Andrew to whom the cathedral is dedicated. The central arch is infilled by a porch inserted during the 14th century, possibly to reinforce the structure, above which is the Trinity chapel and the cathedral library. There are towers and statues in plenty but the eye always returns to the magnificent entirety of the concept.

Burial Place of Mary Queen of Scots

The West Front

The long Norman nave has a fine painted ceiling, and the sheer scale of the work is breathtaking. It dates from about 1220 and depicts in diamond-shaped wooden panels both saints and monsters. The effect is of a gold tapestry, embroidered with lozenges of bright colour.

A monastery was founded on this site in 655 by Peada, King of Mercia but it was destroyed by the Danes 200 years later. Another was built, and survived until its destruction by fire in 1116. Abbot Jean de Seez began the rebuilding work only two years later, and the present cathedral began to take shape. The abbey owned the great quarries at Barnack so the supply of stone was never a problem. In 1496 work began on the New Building behind the High Altar, with its glorious fan-vaulted Perpendicular roof. Nothing can rival this style for its captivating simplicity: it is possible to follow each vein of stone upwards to the great central carved boss, but how it manages to support itself remains a perfect mystery!

The 16th century brought crisis to Peterborough. When Henry VIII grew tired of Katharine of Aragon he expected her to permit him a divorce, but she refused. His former affection turned to hate and he consigned her as a virtual prisoner to Kimbolton Castle. There she died in January 1536. The Spanish ambassador wrote of her: 'More beloved by the islanders than any Queen that has ever reigned'. Her funeral took place at Peterborough on January 29th, and by a curious irony her successor, Anne Boleyn, was delivered of a still-born child the same day. We shall never know why Henry spared the abbey from total destruction when it was dissolved in 1541, but perhaps he thought that the body of his once-beloved first wife should be left in peace. At all events, Henry raised the status of the church to that of a cathedral. Katharine's simple tomb is in the north choir aisle and over it hang the standards of both England and Spain.

Mary, Queen of Scots was executed at Fotheringhay Castle in 1587, and her body was brought to nearby Peterborough for burial, probably because Elizabeth feared to allow her rival into London, even in death. Her tomb was in the south choir aisle, and there her body remained until 1612 when her son James I had it moved to Westminster Abbey.

Just inside the great west door is a tomb marked 'R.S.', and above it a portrait of Robert Scarlett, gravedigger here until his death in 1594. He interred both Queens and claimed to have buried twice as many people as the entire population of Peterborough!

FLAG FEN

The visitors' centre at Flag Fen

In autumn 1982 archaeologists inspecting the side of an ancient dyke found a number of protruding timbers. The fact that the timbers were oak alerted them to the importance of their find, as oak trees have never grown in this marshy region; the timber must have been brought there. The question was – by whom? Work on the very wet and cold site revealed that this was evidence of a complete man-made island village covering as much as three acres, comprising possibly 50 round houses with a population of several hundred and dating from the Bronze Age. So the timbers were cut, about three thousand years ago, at a time when man was learning to combine copper and tin to make more effective tools to replace the flint of the Stone Ages. No-one really knows why the builders of this island went to the trouble of laying down perhaps as many as a million timbers to create the platform on which their houses stood; it may have been to give themselves a secure base in troubled times, but more likely it was a mark of the tribe's status. It would have been an impressive achievement. There was also a roadway exactly one kilometre long, built on 60,000 wooden posts, which may have had a ceremonial function.

The visitor approaches the site along a half mile private road which is well sign-posted. The new Visitor Centre building tells the story of the site up to the present time through photographs, finds and an audio-visual presentation. The forty-five minute guided tour starts with an overall view of the area, including the foundations of the Roman road which crosses the dyke at this point and which led to the discovery of the Flag Fen settlement. Several large round houses have been reconstructed and one is sensibly available for rainy-day picnics!

If a house was built on stilts of thick timber, with flooring and walls of slightly less substantial planks, then when it collapsed the result would resemble the game of Chinese sticks where each stick has to be removed without disturbing the others. That is what you see here, for the waterlogged soil has preserved the jumble of collapsed timbers. It requires the practised eye of the expert to reconstruct the original building, but the evidence is there in great quantities. In the first three weeks of excavation five hundred planks were identified. Even the carpenter's axe marks can be detected. At the time of building it seems likely bronze spearheads and suchlike were placed in the foundations. Over 300 such items have been found to date.

In large water tanks certain of the more substantial timbers are being preserved, because as the wood dries out it crumbles like a well known chocolate flake. The archaeologists are involved in a race against time to save this and other ancient sites because as the fens are drained the water level falls and the timber decays and is lost for ever.

Flag Fen Bronze Age Museum
Open: All year: daily 1100–1600
Price guide: A

Bronze Age oak timbers, part of the remains of a complete island village built over 3,000 years ago

THE NENE VALLEY RAILWAY

Hundreds of thousands of visitors have travelled on the Nene Valley International Steam Railway since its beginning in 1974, so great is the attraction of this bygone age. Here a willing band of volunteers has skilfully recreated the heyday of steam travel, and with an ever-increasing collection, this railway looks set to thrive.

The first trains ran along the Nene valley in 1845. This mode of transport was then regarded with apprehension, and there were fears that the vibration would undermine the foundations of nearby Peterborough Cathedral and that the noise would interrupt the services! But the building went ahead, and the city of Peterborough soon became the focal point for the Midland, Eastern Counties and Great Northern Railways. The network flourished for a hundred years. In the middle of this century, however, road traffic increased and the railways declined; steam was last used in 1964, then diesel took over, and towards the end the Nene Valley Railway was used only to transport freight and spoil from the quarries, with the occasional schoolboys' special to Oundle School.

The line was closed in 1972, but not for long; a group of enthusiasts set about restoring the neglected track and buildings (the signal box at Wansford, dating from 1910 and one of the largest in Britain, had been used as a chicken shed), and new stations were constructed to serve the recreated line.

The railway now has a unique collection of engines and rolling stock. It is the only steam railway in the country capable of running Continental locomotives, which are higher and wider than their British counterparts. To accommodate them, a low road bridge was demolished and the track was widened; British coaches, too, had to be adapted. The result of all this hard work is a fascinating collection which realistically evokes past times; indeed, the railway has been used many times as a film set. Notable among the collection are the 1927 Wagons-Lits Dining Car which has travelled throughout Europe and still sees use as a restaurant on Sundays, and *Thomas*, named in 1973 by the Reverend

Awdrey after his famous tank engine. There are also locomotives from the Scandinavian countries, France and Germany.

The headquarters of the Nene Valley Railway are at Wansford, several miles to the west of Peterborough city centre. Here you will find many enthusiasts inspecting the 67-foot diameter turntable and the locomotive yard. There is also an education centre. The railway caters particularly for children – it runs special services for schools in June and July, as well as Teddy Bears' Picnic Weekends, and Santa Specials in December when Father Christmas himself travels on the trains and gives out presents to the youngsters! The buffet car on Platform 1 was a GWR parcels brake, and you will find a small museum in another 1880 brake van. The waiting room has a model railway. The whole station is decorated with old posters and advertisements, so that the atmosphere of nostalgia and excitement is preserved.

Most important of all is the 15 mile round trip on the railway through the picturesque Nene valley. The train passes through the landscaped grounds of the Ferry Meadows Country Park and continues to its terminus in Peterborough. Here the Railway is approached down a steep flight of steps from Bridge Street, and you must pass under the arches of the present main line railway. At this junction of steam, diesel and electric trains, an ambitious new project has been realised: Railworld. It has become a mecca for all rail enthusiasts.

Nene Valley Railway
Open: All year Sun, Sept & Oct: Sat & Sun, May to Aug: some weekdays
Train timetable phone 01780 782854
Price guide: A (+ fare)

FERRY MEADOWS COUNTRY PARK

It is nothing short of the truth to say that the new town of Peterborough grew out of the Ferry Meadows Country Park. When gravel was needed for the construction of the concrete buildings put up as a result of the expansion of the city in the 1960s, a ready source was available in the nearby Nene valley, where the river had left ample deposits of shingle. At the same time it was recognised that the now-populous city would need wide open spaces for recreation. So the Country Park was created by the judicious removal of the necessary gravel and the landscaping of the grounds. Here are 500 acres of varied scenery: woodland, grassland, and at its heart a series of interesting lakes and islands set in a crescent and linked to the Nene river as it loops and winds through this pleasant valley.

Overton Lake

The Country Park was opened in 1978 and in a short time became a magnet for city dwellers and visitors alike with its wide range of facilities catering for all ages. It is part of the much larger Nene Park, which stretches from the city centre eastwards to Wansford, a distance of some eight miles, and access is from the A605 Oundle Road.

Miniature Railway

The focal point for all activities is the Visitor Centre, with its modern display covering the natural history of the valley, and its information office. From here you overlook the wide Overton Lake where you can take a cruise on the *Nene Star*, hire a rowing boat or a pedalo, or simply feed the ducks and geese. Paths from here lead to Gunwade Lake, the largest of the lakes. This lake has facilities for coarse fishing (including stands for the disabled at its south end), and day tickets can be obtained from the bailiffs on the bank. There is also dinghy sailing and boardsailing here, and the Watersports Centre offers hire of equipment as well as tuition in sailing. Between the two larger lakes is Lynch lake, with its pebbly beach and children's adventure playground.

Gunwade Lake

Other attractions include pony and trap rides which leave from outside the Visitor Centre, and for those better acquainted with horses there is even a riding school, on the south-western edge of the park. A miniature steam railway runs from the Visitor Centre across Coney Meadow (where indeed you may still spot rabbits) and alongside the lakes. For the energetic walker there are footpaths all around the park, and at several points these join with the much longer Nene Way which runs from the city centre to the A1 at Wansford. The sporting will enjoy golf courses, pitch-and-putt facilities and the rowing course. There is also an excellent camp site.

For the naturalist, there is a small bird reserve with hides, and to the north is Thorpe Wood Nature Reserve, an area of ancient woodland with hundreds of species of woodland plants, butterflies and birds.

Special events at the Country Park include showjumping, sheepdog trials and firework displays. There is also a full range of walks and talks, concentrating on local and natural history, since the valley is rich in interest. There are guided walks on the first Sunday of every month throughout the year, including one to hear the dawn chorus which starts at four in the morning! In summer you may choose to study pond life, bats or sites of archaeological importance. Children may attend activity sessions in their school holidays, and some events are held in the evenings. Whatever the season, there is something to interest the whole family.

Open: All year
Price guide: Parking fee at weekends

ELTON HALL

The attractive village of Elton is only just in East Anglia, as it is situated within a mile of the Cambridgeshire border on the A605 south-east of Peterborough.

There is thought to have been a moated hall on the site in the medieval period, but this was replaced in the 15th century by a house and tower built by the Sapcote family. The tower was subsequently incorporated into the present house and the Sapcote family crest still adorns it.

For the last 300 years the residents have been the Proby family, whose ancestor Sir Peter Proby was Lord Mayor of London during the reign of Queen Elizabeth. His grandson, Sir Thomas, made a good marriage and so had the money to rebuild the Hall. Later members of the family acquired lands in Ireland and with them the title of the Earls of Carysfort. This title lapsed in 1909; indeed the family itself seemed set to follow it into oblivion when the third Earl's two sons both died without issue, but a nephew, Douglas Hamilton, assumed the surname Proby and so continued the line. Sir Richard Proby was created a baronet in 1952.

A guided tour round Elton Hall is most enjoyable because you are looking at rooms which are lived in by the family today. The guide may well be the owner, which enlivens the descriptions of the scores of portraits on display.

The Hall has many fine and memorable paintings. Perhaps the best of these is *Eastward Ho!* by Henry O'Neil. It shows a troop transport leaving for India at the time of the Indian Mutiny, and the anguish at separation on the faces of soldiers and loved ones is very affecting. Other artists represented in the rooms and stairways of Elton Hall include Millais, Turner, Constable, Gainsborough, Reynolds and Poussin.

There are many fine pieces of furniture. The large Drawing Room retains the style of an 18th-century French château and may be described as luxurious. Two rare cabinets made from a Japanese lacquer box dating from the 17th century were worth £3000 when made! This was because it was a capital offence to export lacquer work from Japan in those days. In the same room is an unfinished painting by Reynolds of Kitty Fisher, a lady of doubtful reputation. The portrait gives nothing away.

The Ante-dining Room, a much more intimate affair, contains a display cabinet of 18th-century porcelain, much of it bearing the Proby heraldic device. The house also has examples of china salvaged recently from the wreck of the Dutch East Indiaman *Nanking*.

The main Library houses many of the Hall's 12,000 books, and of special interest is a prayer book which belonged to Henry VIII, inscribed by that irascible monarch and two of his royal children. From the windows of the Inner Library it is said the ghost of the Hall may be seen. Legend claims it to be Robert Sapcote who lost his fortune in gambling with his guests, and regained it later the same night as a highwayman!

The gardens of Elton Hall on a summer afternoon are as perfect as anyone has a right to expect – and there is only one full-time gardener. A walled rose garden has been replanted and miniature hedges weave complex patterns around exquisite flower beds. It is all lovely.

Open: July: Wed, Sun 1400–1700, Aug: Wed, Thur, Sun 1400–1700
Price guide: B

BURGHLEY HOUSE

On November 17th, 1558 a mud-stained messenger rode into the park at Hatfield, dismounted and ran towards a young lady standing beneath a tree. He knelt, and informed Princess Elizabeth that she was Queen. One of her very first acts was to appoint William Cecil to be her Principal Secretary of State, and he was to serve her until his death in 1598. The Cecil family owned land outside Stamford, in Lincolnshire, and on the site of a former monastery he built a residence which epitomised the honour, power and wealth of this remarkable public servant.

The first glimpse of the house, through the trees which line the main avenue, gives an impression of size and complexity. The roofline is a delightful jumble of linked chimneys, graceful cupolas, glittering weather vanes and ornate balustrading. Closer inspection reveals a great block of Barnack stone, pierced by hundreds of delicate windows, and of rose gardens surrounded by wonderfully intricate ironwork gates and fencing. The exterior remains much as William Cecil intended, but the interior has been greatly altered by successive generations. The house has 240 rooms, and the guided tours for visitors take in all 18 state apartments.

The Gateway

During the 17th century Burghley was home to John, fifth Earl of Exeter. He travelled widely throughout Europe, bringing back paintings by the great masters or their pupils. There are 700 canvases in the house, and the guidebook lists them all. While the Great Hall with its double hammer-beam roof retains its Tudor atmosphere, most of the rooms reflect the tastes of later owners. The Heaven Room is a

The West Front

The Deer Park

breathtaking extravaganza: the portico of a richly decorated temple swarms with airborne gods and goddesses, while to one side Cyclops works at his forge (helped by the artist Antonio Verrio who depicts himself sitting close by!). In the chapel there is an altarpiece by Veronese, and two Gainsboroughs hang in the billiard room.

In July 1643 Oliver Cromwell laid siege to Burghley House which was defended by 200 Royalists under the command of the Countess of Exeter. She declined the invitation to surrender, and prepared to fight. By the rules of war Cromwell was now absolved of the need to take prisoners, and a one-sided massacre seemed inevitable when he marched up three squadrons of musketeers and a troop of cavalry. Seeing the strength of the enemy, the defenders quickly surrendered, expecting the worst. But Cromwell spared them all, and instead sent them as prisoners to Cambridge – while presenting a portrait of himself to the Countess! This fine early likeness by Robert Walker now hangs in the Pagoda Room.

The vast park at Burghley was landscaped in the 18th century by the indefatigable 'Capability' Brown. Beside the house is the Orangery, now a restaurant, which overlooks a delightful ornamental garden with fish pond and fountain at its centre. The poet John Clare was briefly employed here as a gardener in 1809 but left, complaining that his room was unsatisfactory and the head gardener was always drunk! In fairness it must be added that when Clare's poems were published in 1820 the 2nd Marquis gave him a pension of £20.

The Burghley Horse Trials have an international reputation, and it is hard to think of a more splendid setting for such an event. For days Burghley is at the centre of media interest, but eventually the crowds and the horse-boxes depart, and the deer are left to graze in peace before Lord Burghley's magnificent creation, as they have done for over 400 years.

Open: April to Oct: daily 1100–1700
Price guide: C

The Orangery

SACREWELL FARMING AND COUNTRY LIFE CENTRE

All of us have dreams at some time of living in the country, and the ideal for many of us is the life of a farmer working in some beautiful valley. Those who live on the land nowadays, however, lead an existence far removed from our romanticised picture of leisurely contemplation. The use of heavy, noisy machinery, fertilisers and weedkillers may be disturbing, but it is nonetheless a necessary feature of commercial farming life today.

Sacrewell Mill and farm convey to the visitor both sides of the picture. Situated in a pleasantly wooded valley just off the A1 where it intersects the A47, it plunges us straight away into the tranquillity of a bygone age. But this is no museum; machinery is used here, hedges have been uprooted where the farmer thought fit, and fertilisers are used to enhance the crop, for this is a farm with a past and present.

On arrival the visitor sees a group of stone-built outbuildings. These house many interesting exhibits on such themes as the dairy, wheelwrighting and the smithy. The exhibits are well labelled and many of them can be closely examined. Intriguing questions are also posed: How did the farmer rid himself of pests such as rats? How did the country veterinary surgeon spend his day? What is a 'foster mum'? and how do you use the 'rule of thumb'?

The farmhouse with the mill on the left

A working watermill is always exciting. Milling, in common with many traditional crafts, has many unfamiliar terms – wallower, spur wheel, stone bill . . . Here these terms are explained. The building is on several storeys so be prepared for a steep climb up narrow stairs into long, dusty storerooms containing farming bygones.

The Well

The farmhouse stands in a flower-filled garden accompanied by the sound of running water from the millhouse. Indeed, water has always been vital to this settlement; its name means 'sacred well', and the well still exists. It produces 100 gallons of water a day, and is more picturesque, if less productive than the water pipes running underneath the farm which carry about 120 million gallons a day to Rutland Water!

You can take a walk of about half a mile through the farm guided by a leaflet obtainable at the mill. The walk encourages you to use your eyes and common sense to study the world about you. This is particularly valuable for children. The continuity of life in this valley is stressed (there have been farmers here for thousands of years, as the archaeological finds make clear). Many of the fields have vivid names: Silk Fisheries, Drummer's Lets, Bodger's Barn, Riding School, and Fish Ponds (where there were trout-rearing ponds in the 19th century).

Sacrewell is administered by the William Scott Abbott Trust which devotes itself to education in farming, and the mill and collection of bygones are in the care of David Powell who has lived at the farm for 40 years.

Farming is one of those activities which in essence has changed very little through the ages. It still requires skill, dedication and hard work. A visit to Sacrewell gives an insight into the farmer's life.

Open: All year: daily 0900–2100
Price guide: B

BRAMPTON AND HELPSTON

The village of Brampton lies just west of Huntingdon, between the A604 and the A141. On the outskirts, beside a field and behind a tall hedge, stands a pretty house, and a small plaque on the gatepost proclaims it to have been the family home of Samuel Pepys. The house was owned by his grandfather Robert, and Samuel attended the grammar school in Huntingdon. He visited Brampton regularly throughout his life. He began his famous diary in 1660, and an entry in July 1661 tells that when he heard of Robert's death he sped from London to Brampton (nine hours) only to discover that the body had begun to smell, and had been removed to the courtyard during the night! With a disarming honesty Pepys admits his real concern was to hear the will read. On one occasion he wrote of the property that 'it is very pretty and I bless God that I am like to have such a place to retire to'.

Pepys' house at Brampton

Another celebrated incident occurred in June 1667. Pepys was an Admiralty official, and a succession of English humiliations at the hands of the Dutch led him to fear arrest. He gave his wife a large sum of money and she and Pepys' father buried it in the garden at Brampton. Only in October did Pepys return to collect it, and he was furious to learn that the gold coins had been buried in broad daylight, in full view of Sunday churchgoers. Worse, when Pepys went to dig it up, his father had forgotten where it was hidden! They dug throughout the night, but they never did find all the money.

Pepys was not to inherit the house, and he was buried in London. In the village church is his sister's tomb; she died in 1689, and was the last of the family to live there. The house can be seen by appointment.

Boundary changes always annoy those affected, but were he alive today the poet John Clare would have been particularly aggrieved, for he tells us he was born on 'July 13th, 1793, at Helpston, a gloomy village in Northamptonshire'. It is now part of Cambridgeshire! The village itself has changed too: at that time enormous fields surrounded it and the people worked long hours at back-breaking tasks for pathetically meagre wages. Today Helpston is certainly not gloomy; it is exceptionally pretty. John's birthplace (which is occasionally open to the public) is a whitewashed stone cottage with a thatched roof.

John Clare received very little education, but from infancy was fascinated by the countryside. He ran away once in search of the edge of the world. 'The sky still touched the ground in the distance, and my childish wisdom was puzzled . . . when I got home I found my parents in the greatest distress and half the village about hunting me'. For a short time he worked as horse boy at the Blue Bell Inn next door. Later he tried ploughboy, shoemaker's apprentice, clerk and gardener, but he could not settle to anything, preferring to walk his beloved fields. Throughout his life he was a keen observer of nature, and his best poems equal any natural history textbook in their descriptions of wildlife behaviour and habitats. In 1820 his first collection, *Poems Descriptive of Rural Life and Scenery*, was published and it received enthusiastic reviews. Sadly, public taste changed and he never repeated this success.

In 1837 he suffered the first bout of the madness that was to afflict him for the remainder of his life. He was obliged to live in mental asylums, although kind friends saw to it that he was not ill-treated. He died in St Andrew's County Lunatic Asylum, Northampton, on May 20th, 1864.

Memorial to John Clare

John Clare's Birthplace
Open: Consult Huntingdon Tourist Office

PEAKIRK WILDFOWL TRUST

In 1946 the naturalist and artist Sir Peter Scott set up the Wildfowl Trust at Slimbridge in Gloucestershire. The idea of allowing the public to see birds in their natural habitat, free of cages and concrete, was such a success that others followed. Peakirk was established in 1957, on a 14-acre site which had been an osier bed crossed by the Roman Car Dyke. Now it has 17 acres of water and woodland, providing homes for about 700 wildfowl, of perhaps 112 species. Welney, near Wisbech, is another Wildfowl Trust site.

The approach to the village of Peakirk is along arrow-straight roads, slicing across the rich farmland and alongside alarmingly deep and unfenced ditches. Even in the 9th century, when people first came to live here, the area was known for its wildfowl and fish. In those days Peakirk was an island rising up out of the surrounding fenland; today it is easier to reach. Follow the A15 north from Peterborough for five miles and turn off on to the B1443 one mile from Peakirk. The Wildfowl Trust centre is well signposted and there is a large car park.

The visitor centre is modern and attractively set out. A plaque commemorates the Williams family who were wildfowlers on this very site for a century and whose wish it was to see a bird sanctuary established. Although the shop and observation lounge might perhaps intimidate the non-ornithologically inclined, they need not worry, for the guide-book contains photographs of all the species likely to be encountered. The children can have the fun of completing well-presented work sheets. It is quite possible to wander around the site without any prior knowledge and have an enjoyable time, as the place is so tranquil and unspoilt.

Chilean Flamingos

On leaving the visitor centre you are immediately in a world apart. A large pond teeming with bird life confronts you, and should panic set in at ignorance of the birds on show then the first of a succession of display boards will rescue you. These inform you of the name, description, origin and feeding habits of all the birds you are likely to see.

South African Crowned Cranes

Paths lead alongside a number of different pools, each of which attracts different species. The visitor who wants a closer view only has only to throw a handful of seed (available from the shop) and the only problem is one of choice. Not all the wildfowl are so keen to be on show, though, and you are encouraged to scan the trees, bushes and grassy banks for shy and breeding species. Within minutes of setting off you should see tiny ducks like the hottentot duck from Africa and the ringed teal from South America. Geese like the Hawaiian goose should also catch the attention, and while the black-necked swans need to be treated with respect they are beautiful to look at, especially if their cygnets are riding on their backs. At other times the vivid Chilean flamingos provide an added burst of colour to enhance the beautiful rose gardens.

Hides are provided for those who prefer to spend more time in one area studying one particular pool. Many of these hides are decorated with paintings by children who have visited – a nice touch. There is so much to see and enjoy that the only problem is how to identify the birds, throw the seed and focus the camera all at once! The café gives you time to compare notes with others while the coffee cools.

Wildfowl Trust
Open: All year: daily 0930 to dusk, except Mar to Oct: 0930–1830
Price guide: B

INDEX